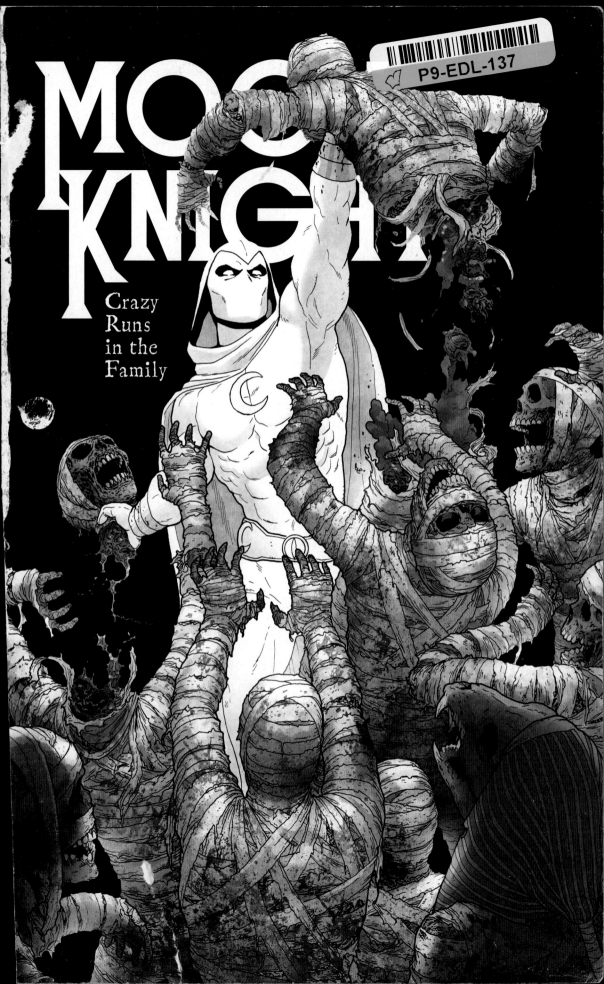

MOON KNIGHT

Crazy Runs in the Family

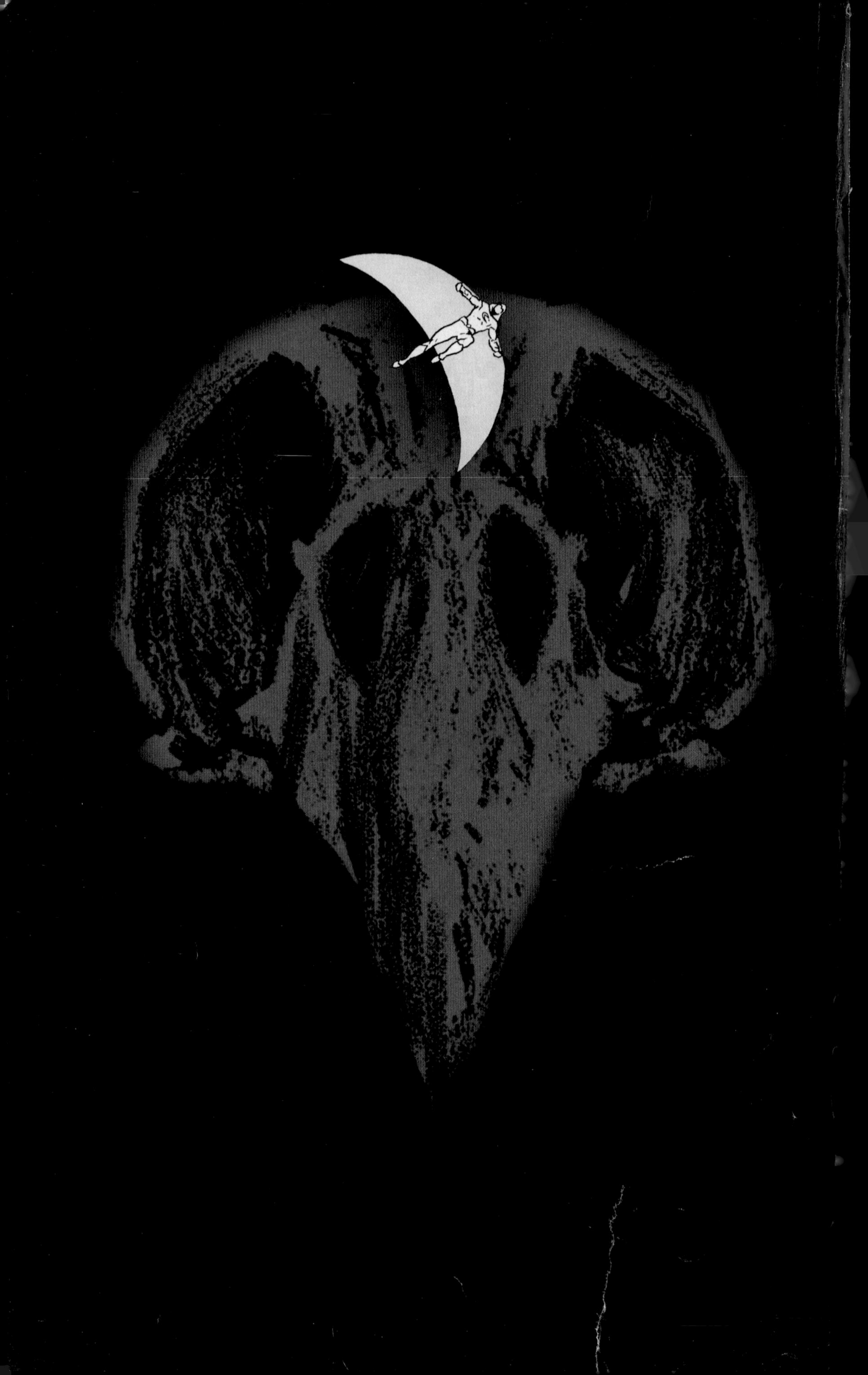

MOON KNIGHT

Crazy Runs in the Family

Max Bemis
WRITER

Jacen Burrows
PENCILER

Jacen Burrows (#188-189) & **Guillermo Ortego** (#189-193)
INKERS

Mat Lopes
COLOR ARTIST

VC's Cory Petit
LETTERER

Kathleen Wisneski
ASSISTANT EDITOR

Mark Basso
ASSOCIATE EDITOR

Jake Thomas
EDITOR

COLLECTION EDITOR: JENNIFER GRÜNWALD
ASSISTANT EDITOR: CAITLIN O'CONNELL
ASSOCIATE MANAGING EDITOR: KATERI WOODY
EDITOR, SPECIAL PROJECTS: MARK D. BEAZLEY

VP PRODUCTION & SPECIAL PROJECTS: JEFF YOUNGQUIST
SVP PRINT, SALES & MARKETING: DAVID GABRIEL
BOOK DESIGNER: ADAM DEL RE

EDITOR IN CHIEF: C.B. CEBULSKI
CHIEF CREATIVE OFFICER: JOE QUESADA
PRESIDENT: DAN BUCKLEY
EXECUTIVE PRODUCER: ALAN FINE

MOON KNIGHT: LEGACY VOL. 1 — CRAZY RUNS IN THE FAMILY. Contains material originally published in magazine form as MOON KNIGHT #188-193. First printing 2018. ISBN 978-1-302-90937-6. Published by MARVEL WORLDWIDE, INC., a subsidiary of MARVEL ENTERTAINMENT, LLC. OFFICE OF PUBLICATION: 135 West 50th Street, New York, NY 10020. Copyright © 2018 MARVEL No similarity between any of the names, characters, persons, and/or institutions in this magazine with those of any living or dead person or institution is intended, and any such similarity which may exist is purely coincidental. **Printed in the U.S.A.** DAN BUCKLEY, President, Marvel Entertainment; JOHN NEE, Publisher; JOE QUESADA, Chief Creative Officer; TOM BREVOORT, SVP of Publishing; DAVID BOGART, SVP of Business Affairs & Operations, Publishing & Partnership; DAVID GABRIEL, SVP of Sales & Marketing, Publishing; JEFF YOUNGQUIST, VP of Production & Special Projects; DAN CARR, Executive Director of Publishing Technology; ALEX MORALES, Director of Publishing Operations; SUSAN CRESPI, Production Manager; STAN LEE, Chairman Emeritus. For information regarding advertising in Marvel Comics or on Marvel.com, please contact Vit DeBellis, Custom Solutions & Integrated Advertising Manager, at vdebellis@marvel.com. For Marvel subscription inquiries, please call 888-511-5480. **Manufactured between 3/23/2018 and 4/24/2018 by LSC COMMUNICATIONS INC., KENDALLVILLE, IN, USA.**

10 9 8 7 6 5 4 3 2 1

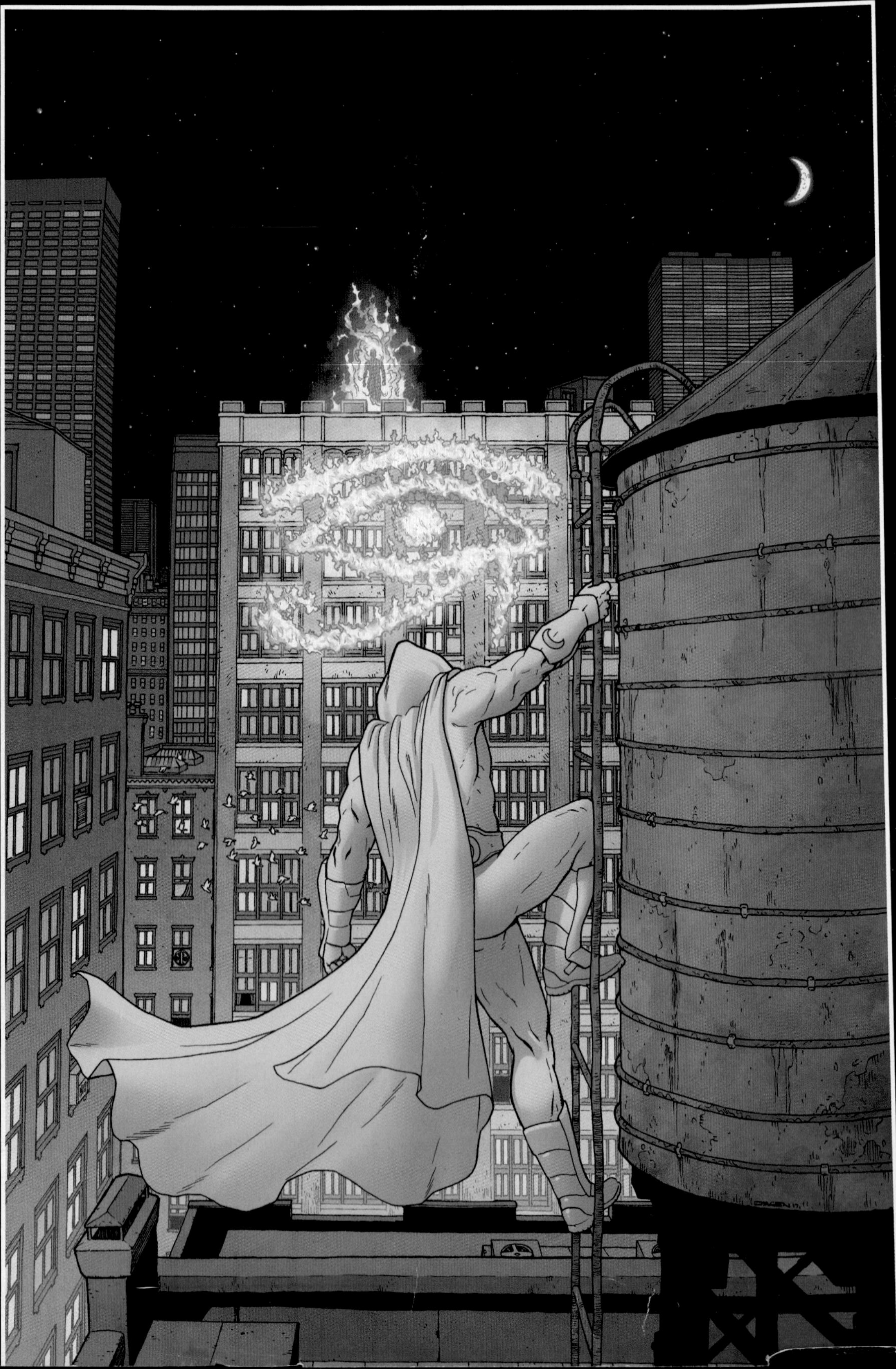

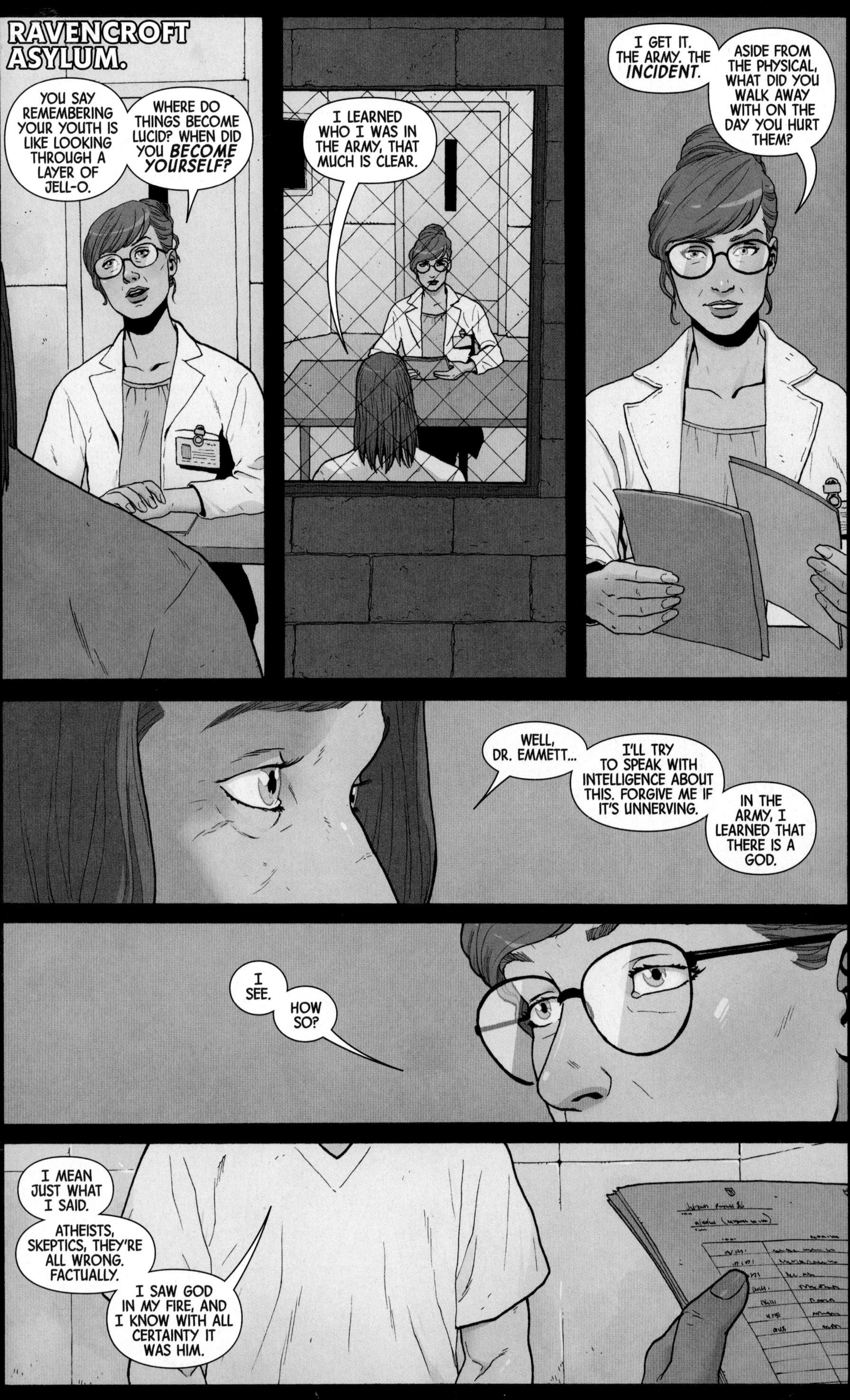
RAVENCROFT ASYLUM.
YOU SAY REMEMBERING YOUR YOUTH IS LIKE LOOKING THROUGH A LAYER OF JELL-O.
WHERE DO THINGS BECOME LUCID? WHEN DID YOU BECOME YOURSELF?
I LEARNED WHO I WAS IN THE ARMY, THAT MUCH IS CLEAR.
I GET IT. THE ARMY. THE INCIDENT.
ASIDE FROM THE PHYSICAL, WHAT DID YOU WALK AWAY WITH ON THE DAY YOU HURT THEM?
WELL, DR. EMMETT...
I'LL TRY TO SPEAK WITH INTELLIGENCE ABOUT THIS. FORGIVE ME IF IT'S UNNERVING.
IN THE ARMY, I LEARNED THAT THERE IS A GOD.
I SEE.
HOW SO?
I MEAN JUST WHAT I SAID.
ATHEISTS, SKEPTICS, THEY'RE ALL WRONG. FACTUALLY.
I SAW GOD IN MY FIRE, AND I KNOW WITH ALL CERTAINTY IT WAS HIM.

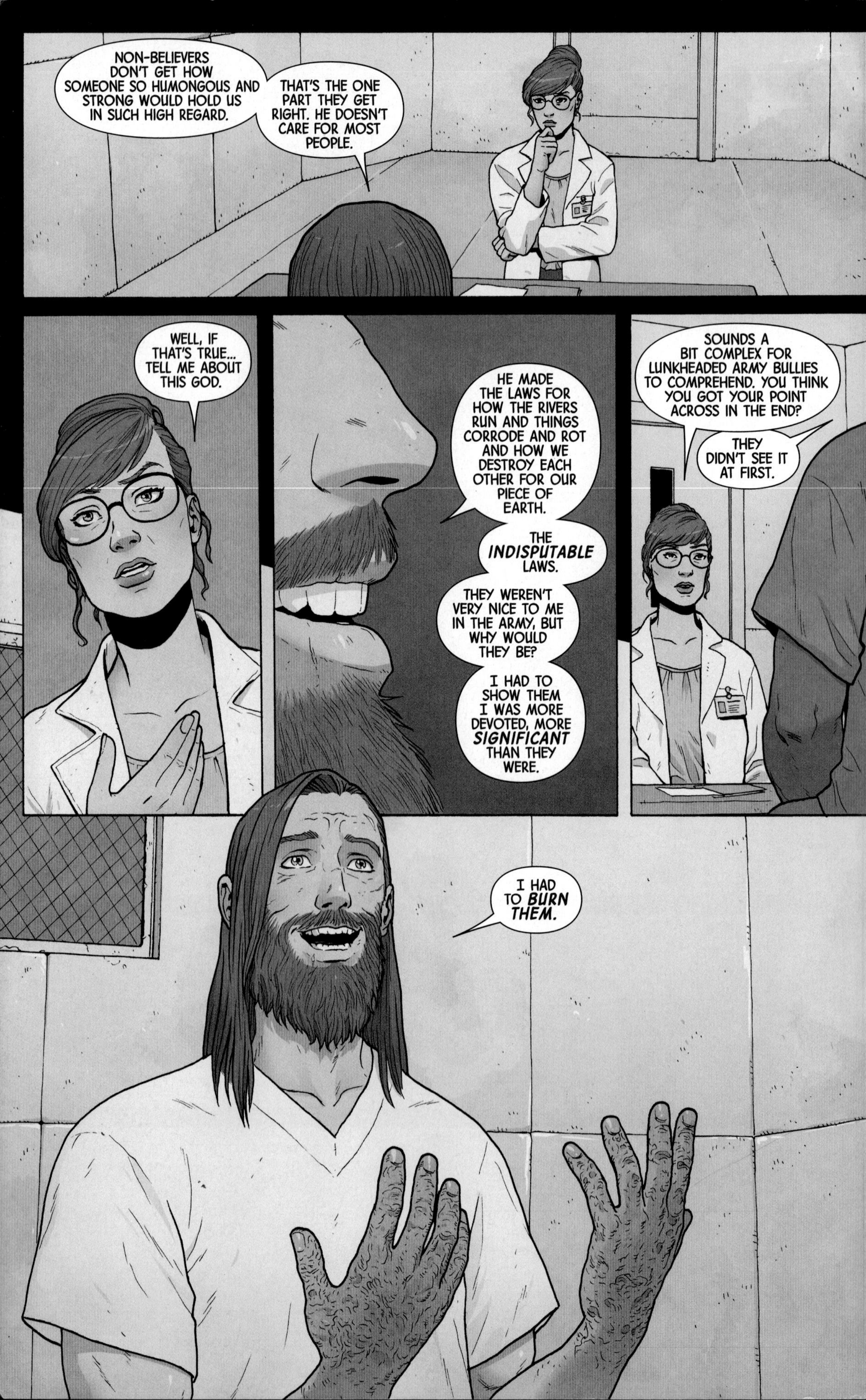
NON-BELIEVERS DON'T GET HOW SOMEONE SO HUMONGOUS AND STRONG WOULD HOLD US IN SUCH HIGH REGARD.
THAT'S THE ONE PART THEY GET RIGHT. HE DOESN'T CARE FOR MOST PEOPLE.
WELL, IF THAT'S TRUE... TELL ME ABOUT THIS GOD.
HE MADE THE LAWS FOR HOW THE RIVERS RUN AND THINGS CORRODE AND ROT AND HOW WE DESTROY EACH OTHER FOR OUR PIECE OF EARTH.
THE *INDISPUTABLE* LAWS.
THEY WEREN'T VERY NICE TO ME IN THE ARMY, BUT WHY WOULD THEY BE?
I HAD TO SHOW THEM I WAS MORE DEVOTED, MORE *SIGNIFICANT* THAN THEY WERE.
SOUNDS A BIT COMPLEX FOR LUNKHEADED ARMY BULLIES TO COMPREHEND. YOU THINK YOU GOT YOUR POINT ACROSS IN THE END?
THEY DIDN'T SEE IT AT FIRST.
I HAD TO *BURN THEM.*

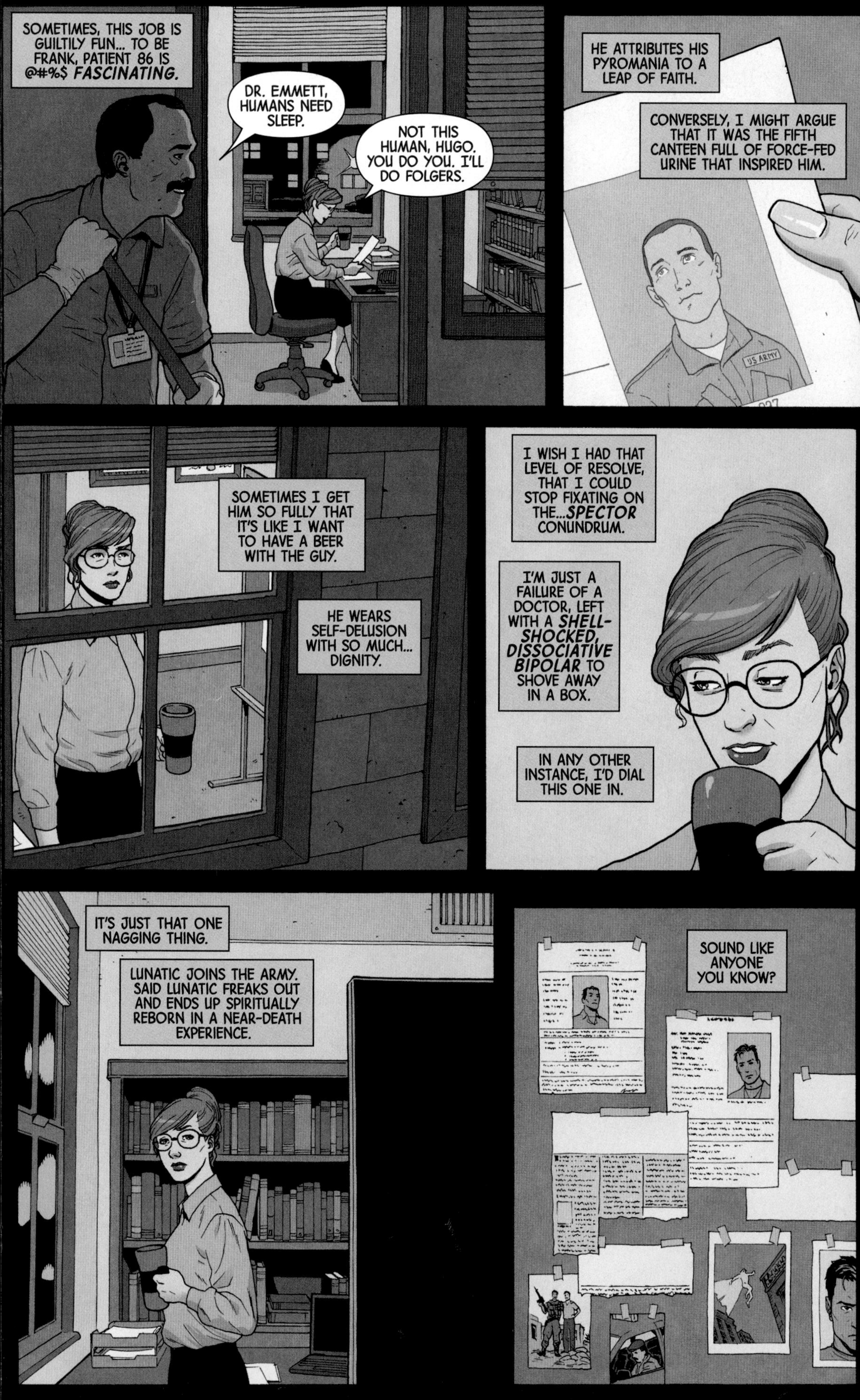
SOMETIMES, THIS JOB IS GUILTILY FUN... TO BE FRANK, PATIENT 86 IS @#%$ FASCINATING.
DR. EMMETT, HUMANS NEED SLEEP.
NOT THIS HUMAN, HUGO. YOU DO YOU. I'LL DO FOLGERS.
HE ATTRIBUTES HIS PYROMANIA TO A LEAP OF FAITH.
CONVERSELY, I MIGHT ARGUE THAT IT WAS THE FIFTH CANTEEN FULL OF FORCE-FED URINE THAT INSPIRED HIM.
US ARMY
SOMETIMES I GET HIM SO FULLY THAT IT'S LIKE I WANT TO HAVE A BEER WITH THE GUY.
HE WEARS SELF-DELUSION WITH SO MUCH... DIGNITY.
I WISH I HAD THAT LEVEL OF RESOLVE, THAT I COULD STOP FIXATING ON THE...SPECTOR CONUNDRUM.
I'M JUST A FAILURE OF A DOCTOR, LEFT WITH A SHELL-SHOCKED, DISSOCIATIVE BIPOLAR TO SHOVE AWAY IN A BOX.
IN ANY OTHER INSTANCE, I'D DIAL THIS ONE IN.
IT'S JUST THAT ONE NAGGING THING.
LUNATIC JOINS THE ARMY. SAID LUNATIC FREAKS OUT AND ENDS UP SPIRITUALLY REBORN IN A NEAR-DEATH EXPERIENCE.
SOUND LIKE ANYONE YOU KNOW?

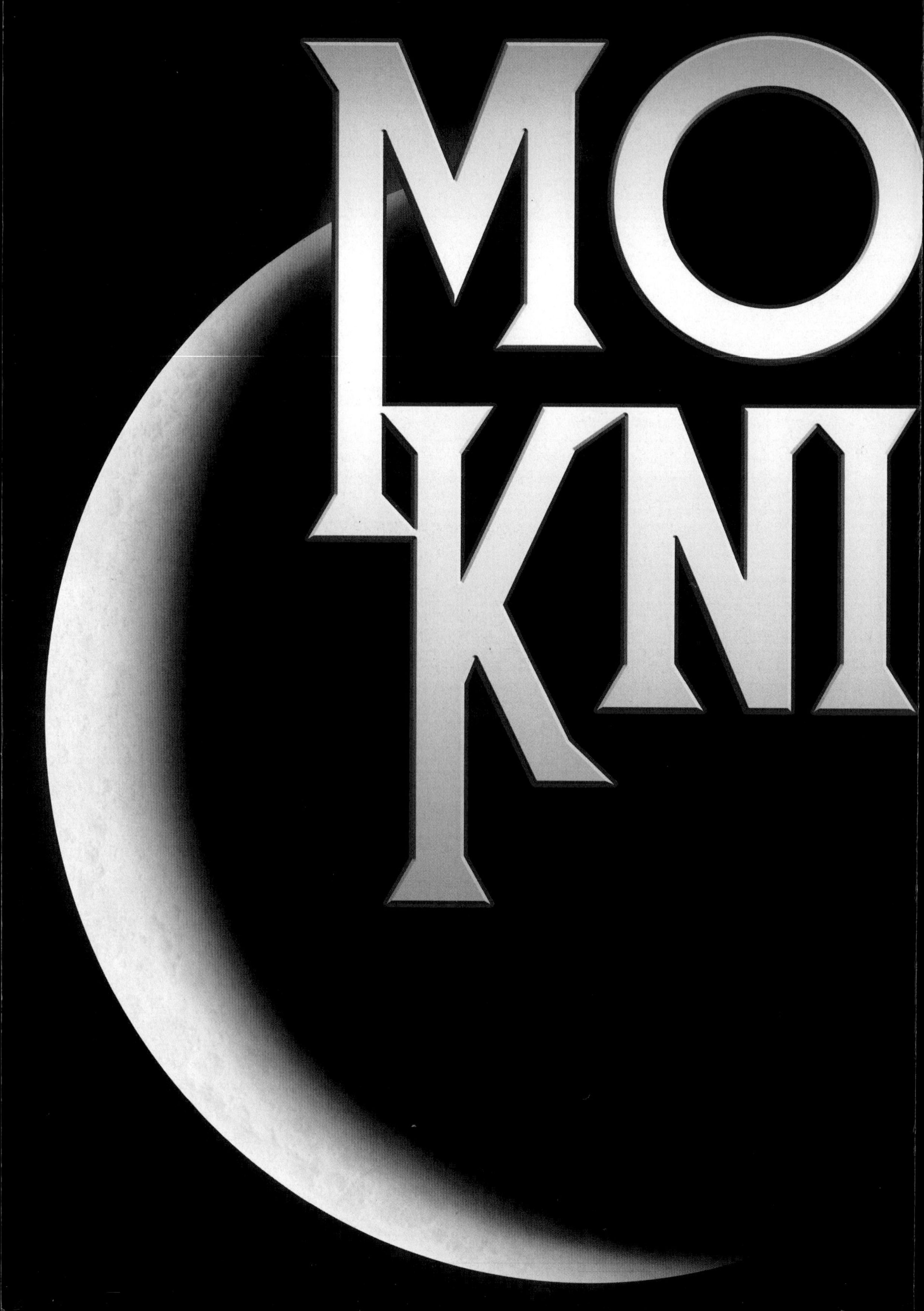

ON
GHT

Marc Spector. Steven Grant. Jake Lockley. Each a distinct personality of one man vying for control. Spector, the original personality, has asserted his dominance and fights to retain that control.

But years ago, as a mercenary, Spector died in Egypt under a statue of the Moon God **Khonshu.** In the shadow of the ancient deity, Marc returned

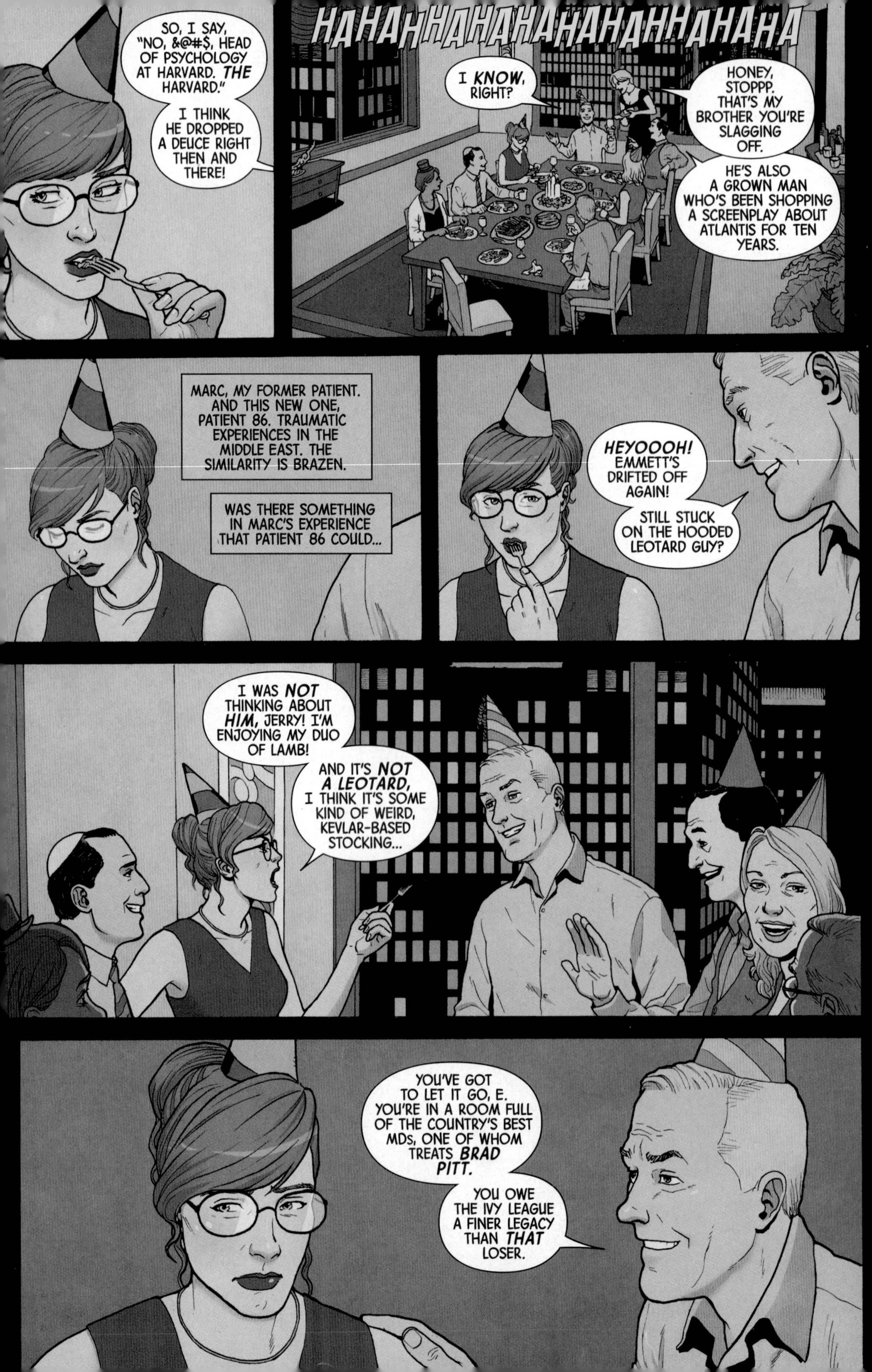

SO, I SAY, "NO, &@#$, HEAD OF PSYCHOLOGY AT HARVARD. *THE* HARVARD."
I THINK HE DROPPED A DEUCE RIGHT THEN AND THERE!
HAHAHHAHAHAHAHAHHAHAHA
I *KNOW*, RIGHT?
HONEY, STOPPP. THAT'S MY BROTHER YOU'RE SLAGGING OFF.
HE'S ALSO A GROWN MAN WHO'S BEEN SHOPPING A SCREENPLAY ABOUT ATLANTIS FOR TEN YEARS.
MARC, MY FORMER PATIENT. AND THIS NEW ONE, PATIENT 86. TRAUMATIC EXPERIENCES IN THE MIDDLE EAST. THE SIMILARITY IS BRAZEN.
WAS THERE SOMETHING IN MARC'S EXPERIENCE THAT PATIENT 86 COULD...
HEYOOOH! EMMETT'S DRIFTED OFF AGAIN!
STILL STUCK ON THE HOODED LEOTARD GUY?
I WAS *NOT* THINKING ABOUT *HIM*, JERRY! I'M ENJOYING MY DUO OF LAMB!
AND IT'S *NOT A LEOTARD*, I THINK IT'S SOME KIND OF WEIRD, KEVLAR-BASED STOCKING...
YOU'VE GOT TO LET IT GO, E. YOU'RE IN A ROOM FULL OF THE COUNTRY'S BEST MDs, ONE OF WHOM TREATS *BRAD PITT*.
YOU OWE THE IVY LEAGUE A FINER LEGACY THAN *THAT* LOSER.

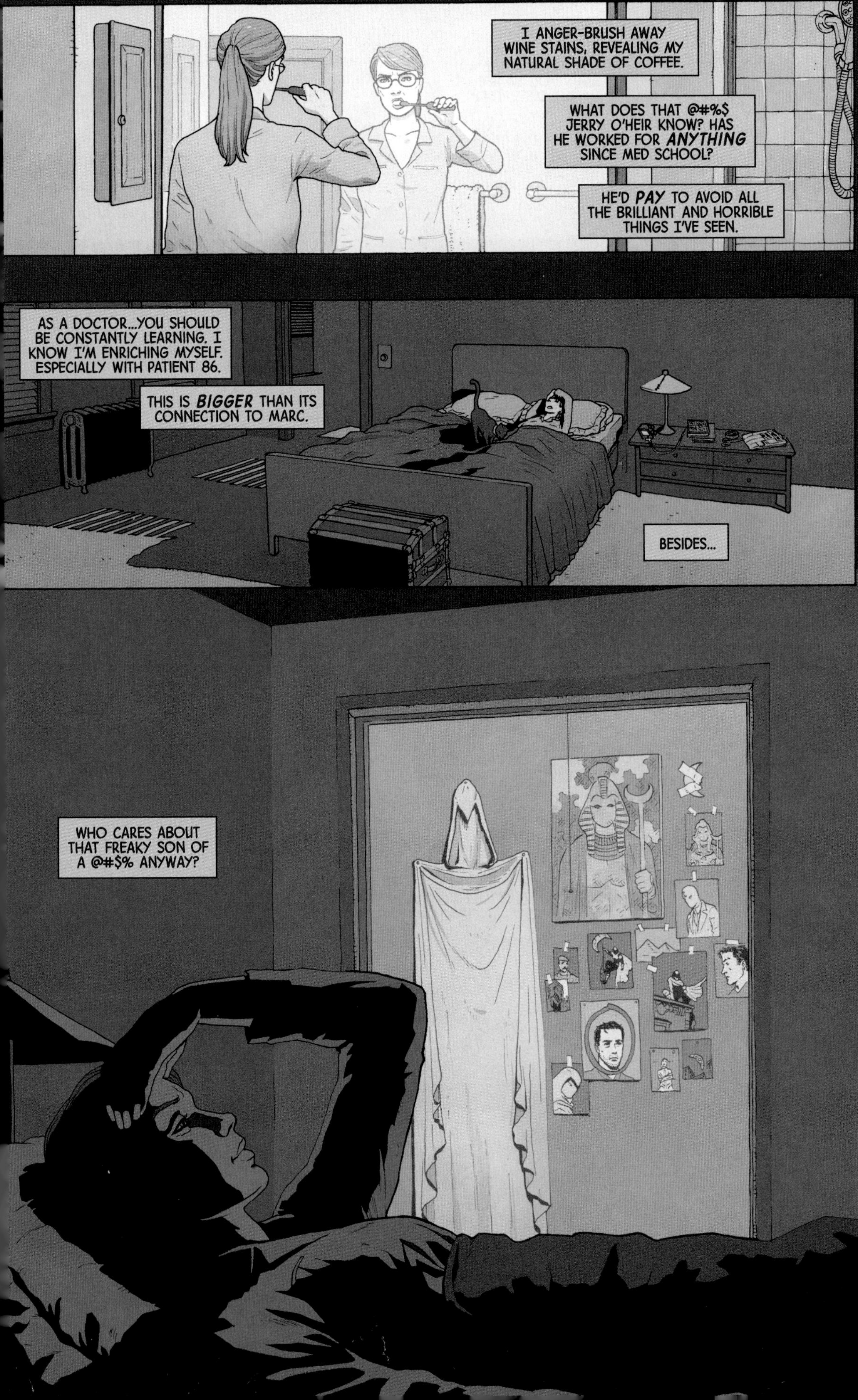
I ANGER-BRUSH AWAY WINE STAINS, REVEALING MY NATURAL SHADE OF COFFEE.
WHAT DOES THAT @#%$ JERRY O'HEIR KNOW? HAS HE WORKED FOR ANYTHING SINCE MED SCHOOL?
HE'D PAY TO AVOID ALL THE BRILLIANT AND HORRIBLE THINGS I'VE SEEN.
AS A DOCTOR...YOU SHOULD BE CONSTANTLY LEARNING. I KNOW I'M ENRICHING MYSELF. ESPECIALLY WITH PATIENT 86.
THIS IS BIGGER THAN ITS CONNECTION TO MARC.
BESIDES...
WHO CARES ABOUT THAT FREAKY SON OF A @#$% ANYWAY?

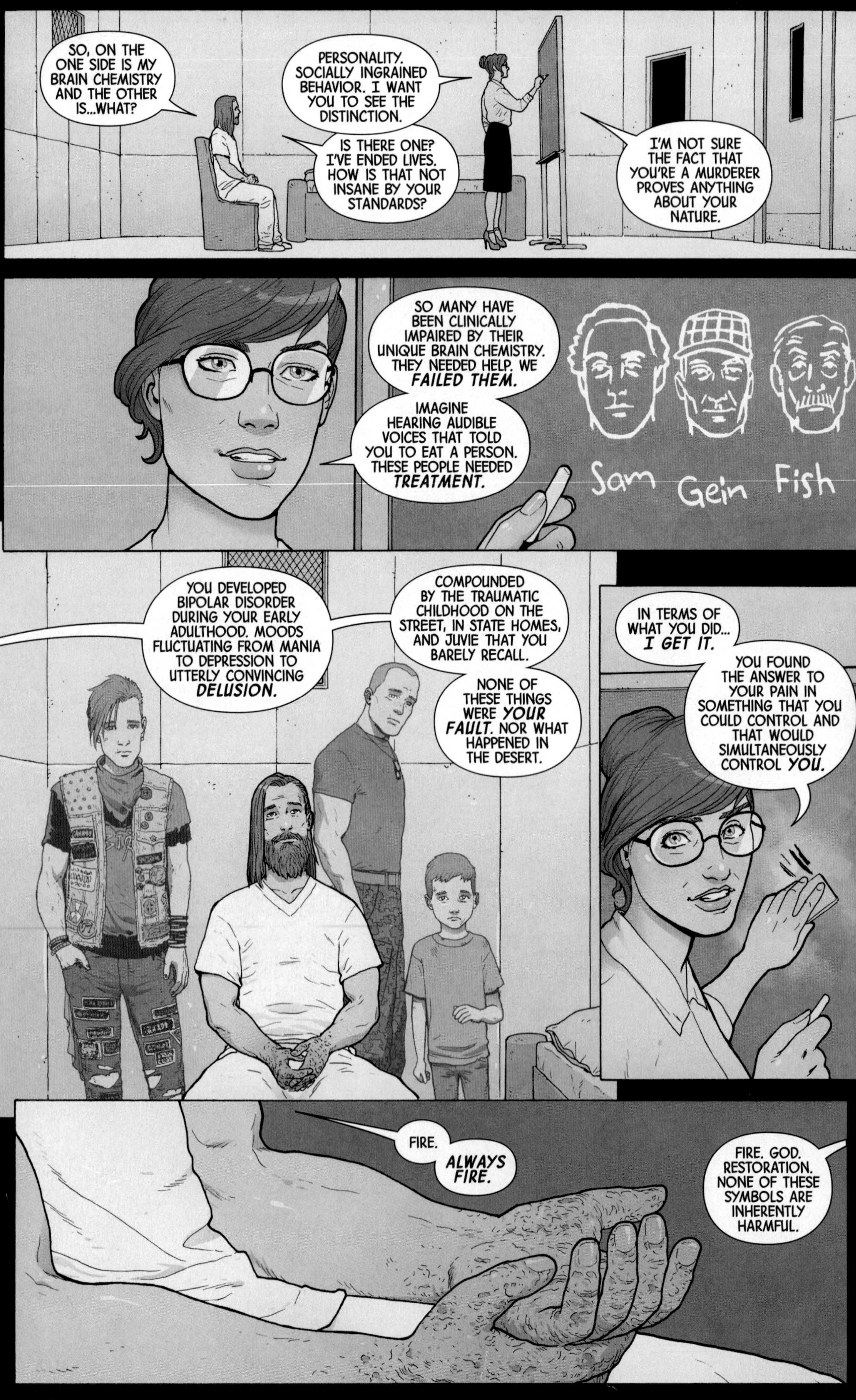
SO, ON THE ONE SIDE IS MY BRAIN CHEMISTRY AND THE OTHER IS...WHAT?
PERSONALITY. SOCIALLY INGRAINED BEHAVIOR. I WANT YOU TO SEE THE DISTINCTION.
IS THERE ONE? I'VE ENDED LIVES. HOW IS THAT NOT INSANE BY YOUR STANDARDS?
I'M NOT SURE THE FACT THAT YOU'RE A MURDERER PROVES ANYTHING ABOUT YOUR NATURE.
SO MANY HAVE BEEN CLINICALLY IMPAIRED BY THEIR UNIQUE BRAIN CHEMISTRY. THEY NEEDED HELP. WE ***FAILED THEM.***
IMAGINE HEARING AUDIBLE VOICES THAT TOLD YOU TO EAT A PERSON. THESE PEOPLE NEEDED ***TREATMENT.***
Sam
Gein
Fish
YOU DEVELOPED BIPOLAR DISORDER DURING YOUR EARLY ADULTHOOD. MOODS FLUCTUATING FROM MANIA TO DEPRESSION TO UTTERLY CONVINCING ***DELUSION.***
COMPOUNDED BY THE TRAUMATIC CHILDHOOD ON THE STREET, IN STATE HOMES, AND JUVIE THAT YOU BARELY RECALL.
NONE OF THESE THINGS WERE ***YOUR FAULT.*** NOR WHAT HAPPENED IN THE DESERT.
IN TERMS OF WHAT YOU DID... ***I GET IT.***
YOU FOUND THE ANSWER TO YOUR PAIN IN SOMETHING THAT YOU COULD CONTROL AND THAT WOULD SIMULTANEOUSLY CONTROL ***YOU.***
FIRE. ***ALWAYS FIRE.***
FIRE. GOD. RESTORATION. NONE OF THESE SYMBOLS ARE INHERENTLY HARMFUL.

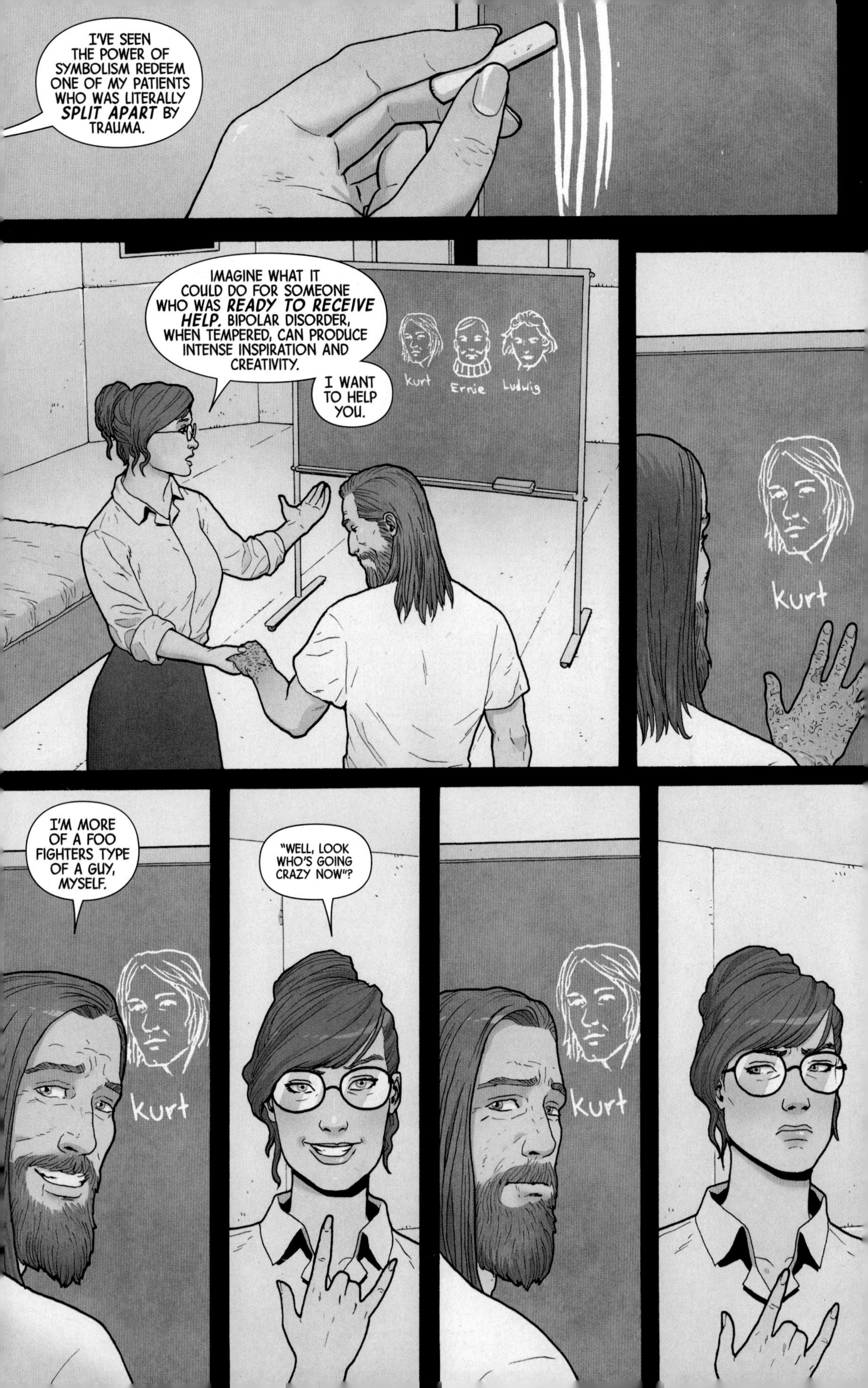

I'VE SEEN THE POWER OF SYMBOLISM REDEEM ONE OF MY PATIENTS WHO WAS LITERALLY *SPLIT APART* BY TRAUMA.
IMAGINE WHAT IT COULD DO FOR SOMEONE WHO WAS *READY TO RECEIVE HELP.* BIPOLAR DISORDER, WHEN TEMPERED, CAN PRODUCE INTENSE INSPIRATION AND CREATIVITY.
I WANT TO HELP YOU.
Kurt
Ernie
Ludwig
Kurt
I'M MORE OF A FOO FIGHTERS TYPE OF A GUY, MYSELF.
Kurt
"WELL, LOOK WHO'S GOING CRAZY NOW"?
Kurt

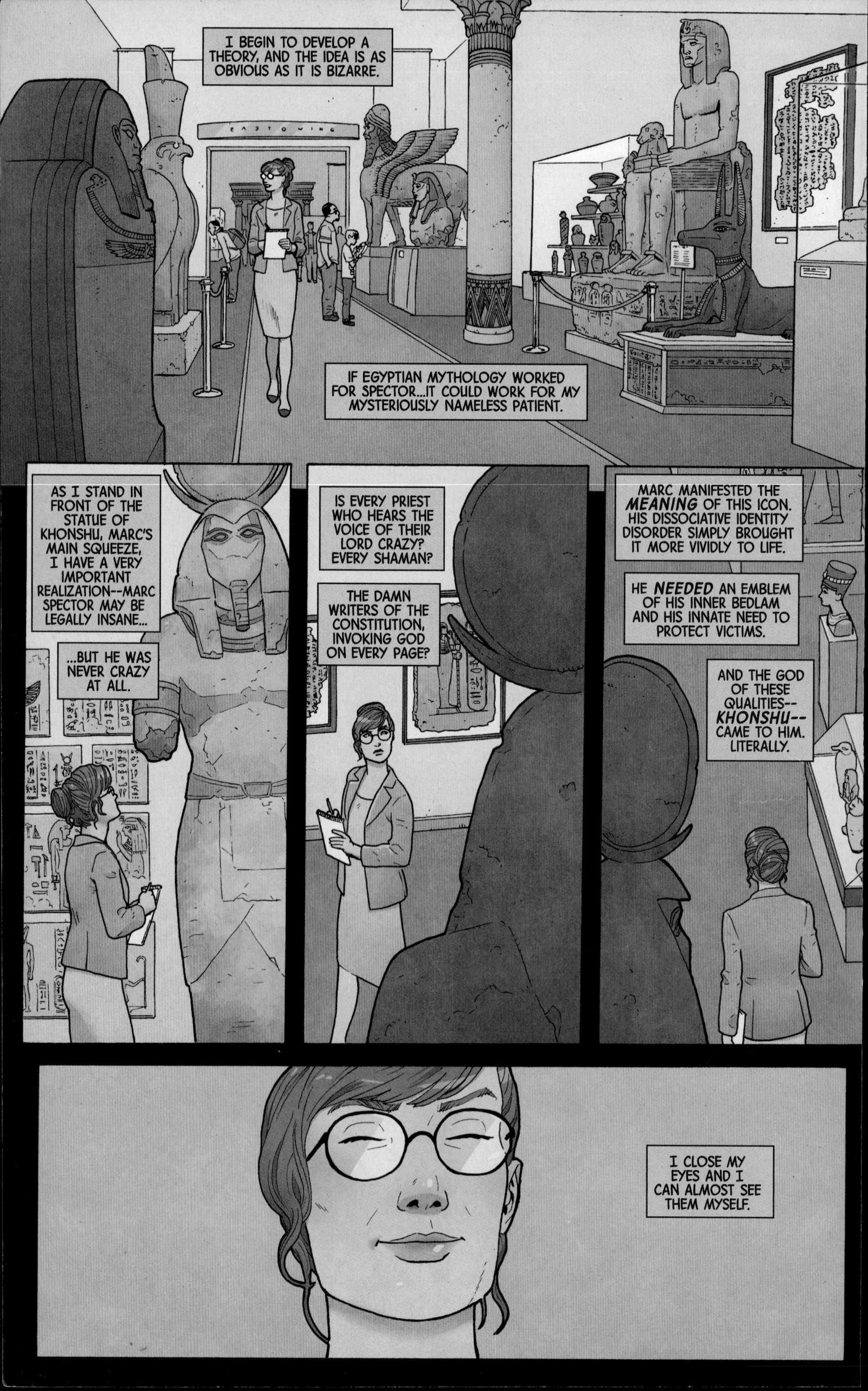
I BEGIN TO DEVELOP A THEORY, AND THE IDEA IS AS OBVIOUS AS IT IS BIZARRE.
EAST WING
IF EGYPTIAN MYTHOLOGY WORKED FOR SPECTOR...IT COULD WORK FOR MY MYSTERIOUSLY NAMELESS PATIENT.
AS I STAND IN FRONT OF THE STATUE OF KHONSHU, MARC'S MAIN SQUEEZE, I HAVE A VERY IMPORTANT REALIZATION--MARC SPECTOR MAY BE LEGALLY INSANE...
...BUT HE WAS NEVER CRAZY AT ALL.
IS EVERY PRIEST WHO HEARS THE VOICE OF THEIR LORD CRAZY? EVERY SHAMAN?
THE DAMN WRITERS OF THE CONSTITUTION, INVOKING GOD ON EVERY PAGE?
MARC MANIFESTED THE MEANING OF THIS ICON. HIS DISSOCIATIVE IDENTITY DISORDER SIMPLY BROUGHT IT MORE VIVIDLY TO LIFE.
HE NEEDED AN EMBLEM OF HIS INNER BEDLAM AND HIS INNATE NEED TO PROTECT VICTIMS.
AND THE GOD OF THESE QUALITIES--KHONSHU--CAME TO HIM. LITERALLY.
I CLOSE MY EYES AND I CAN ALMOST SEE THEM MYSELF.

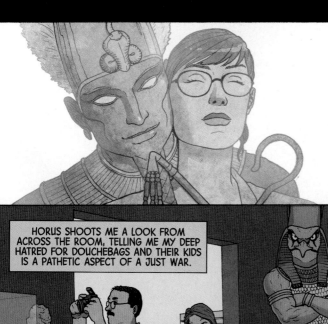

OSIRIS DRAWS A LINE FROM LOVE TO DEATH WITH AN INSPIRED BRUSHSTROKE AND AFFIRMS MY ACHING MORTALITY.

HORUS SHOOTS ME A LOOK FROM ACROSS THE ROOM, TELLING ME MY DEEP HATRED FOR DOUCHEBAGS AND THEIR KIDS IS A PATHETIC ASPECT OF A JUST WAR.

COULD IMHOTEP BE THE LIVING IDEA THAT BRINGS CLARITY AND HEALING TO 86's TORTURED MIND?

THEN, I SEE RA.

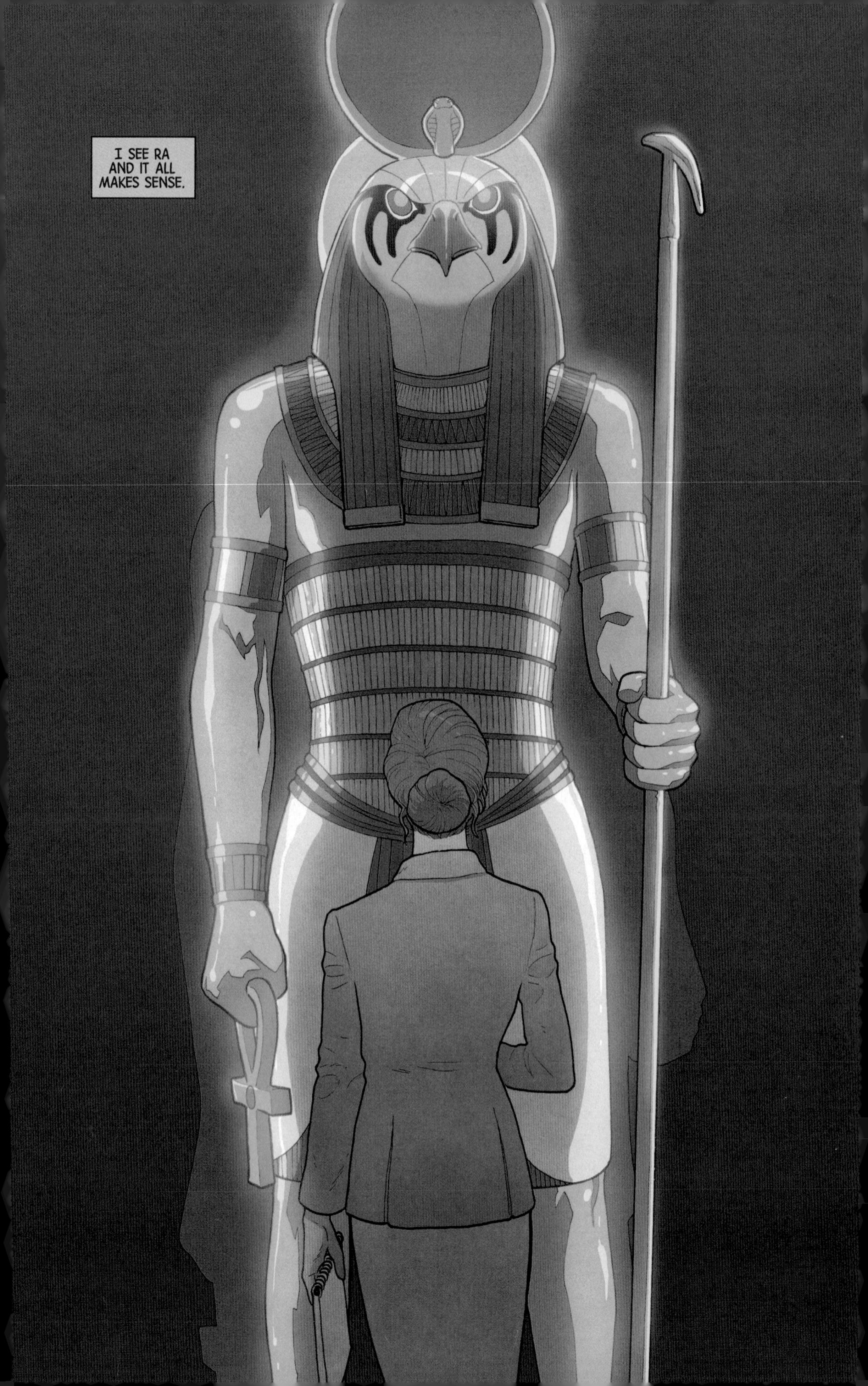
I SEE RA AND IT ALL MAKES SENSE.

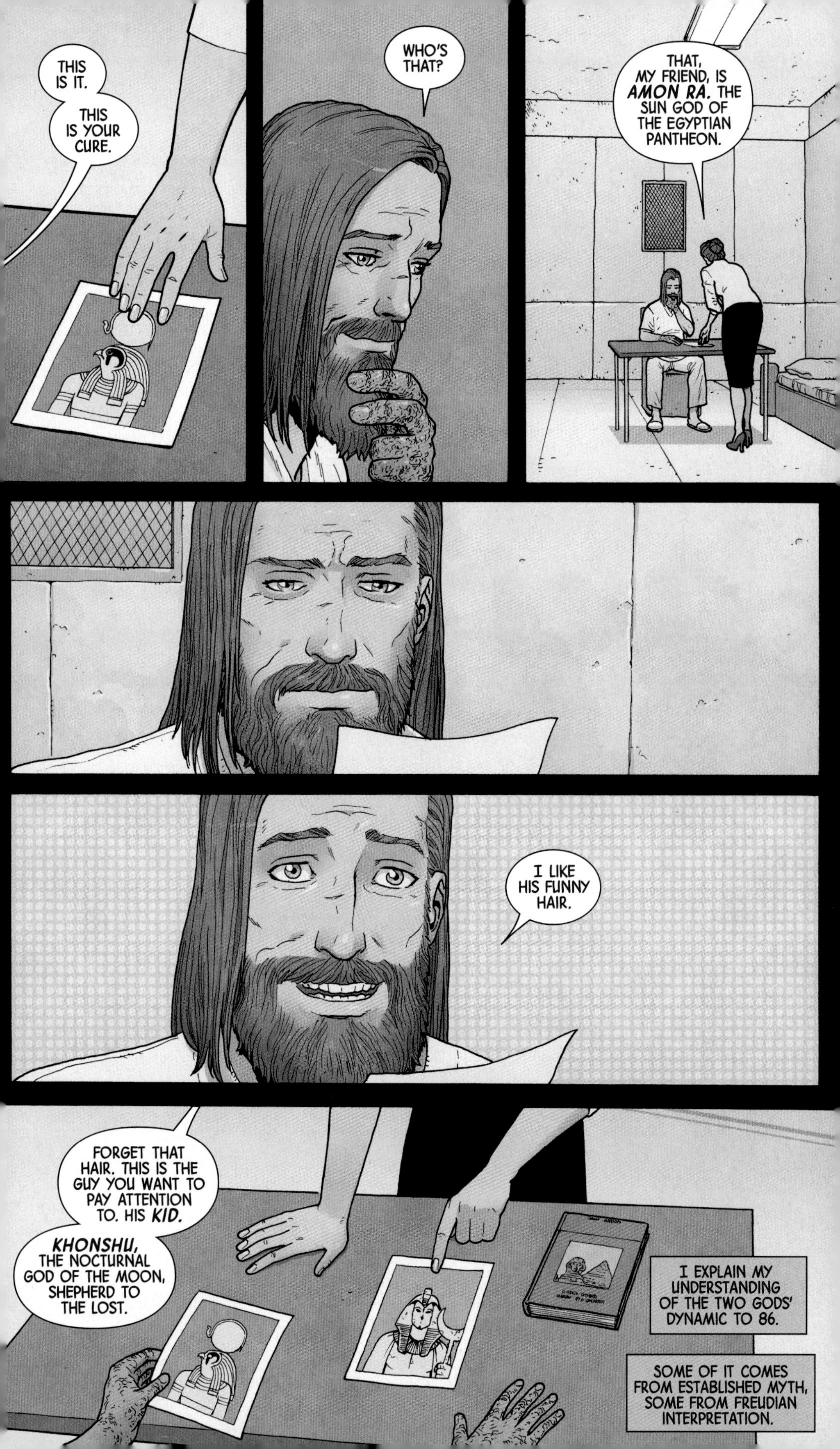

THIS IS IT.
THIS IS YOUR CURE.
WHO'S THAT?
THAT, MY FRIEND, IS **AMON RA.** THE SUN GOD OF THE EGYPTIAN PANTHEON.
I LIKE HIS FUNNY HAIR.
FORGET THAT HAIR. THIS IS THE GUY YOU WANT TO PAY ATTENTION TO. HIS ***KID.***
KHONSHU, THE NOCTURNAL GOD OF THE MOON, SHEPHERD TO THE LOST.
I EXPLAIN MY UNDERSTANDING OF THE TWO GODS' DYNAMIC TO 86.
SOME OF IT COMES FROM ESTABLISHED MYTH, SOME FROM FREUDIAN INTERPRETATION.

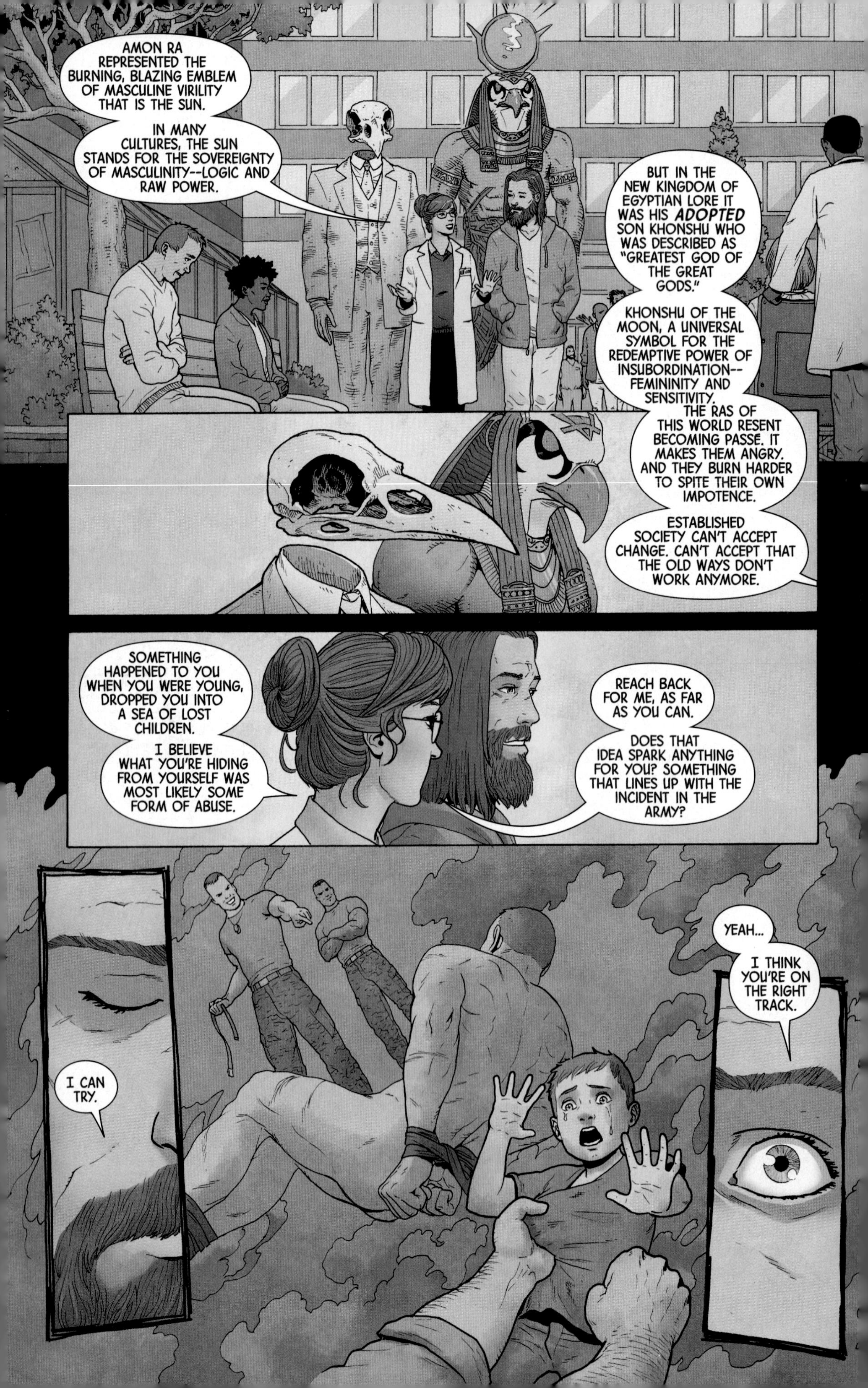

AMON RA REPRESENTED THE BURNING, BLAZING EMBLEM OF MASCULINE VIRILITY THAT IS THE SUN.
IN MANY CULTURES, THE SUN STANDS FOR THE SOVEREIGNTY OF MASCULINITY--LOGIC AND RAW POWER.
BUT IN THE NEW KINGDOM OF EGYPTIAN LORE IT WAS HIS *ADOPTED* SON KHONSHU WHO WAS DESCRIBED AS "GREATEST GOD OF THE GREAT GODS."
KHONSHU OF THE MOON, A UNIVERSAL SYMBOL FOR THE REDEMPTIVE POWER OF INSUBORDINATION--FEMININITY AND SENSITIVITY.
THE RAS OF THIS WORLD RESENT BECOMING PASSÉ. IT MAKES THEM ANGRY. AND THEY BURN HARDER TO SPITE THEIR OWN IMPOTENCE.
ESTABLISHED SOCIETY CAN'T ACCEPT CHANGE. CAN'T ACCEPT THAT THE OLD WAYS DON'T WORK ANYMORE.
SOMETHING HAPPENED TO YOU WHEN YOU WERE YOUNG, DROPPED YOU INTO A SEA OF LOST CHILDREN.
I BELIEVE WHAT YOU'RE HIDING FROM YOURSELF WAS MOST LIKELY SOME FORM OF ABUSE.
REACH BACK FOR ME, AS FAR AS YOU CAN.
DOES THAT IDEA SPARK ANYTHING FOR YOU? SOMETHING THAT LINES UP WITH THE INCIDENT IN THE ARMY?
I CAN TRY.
YEAH...
I THINK YOU'RE ON THE RIGHT TRACK.

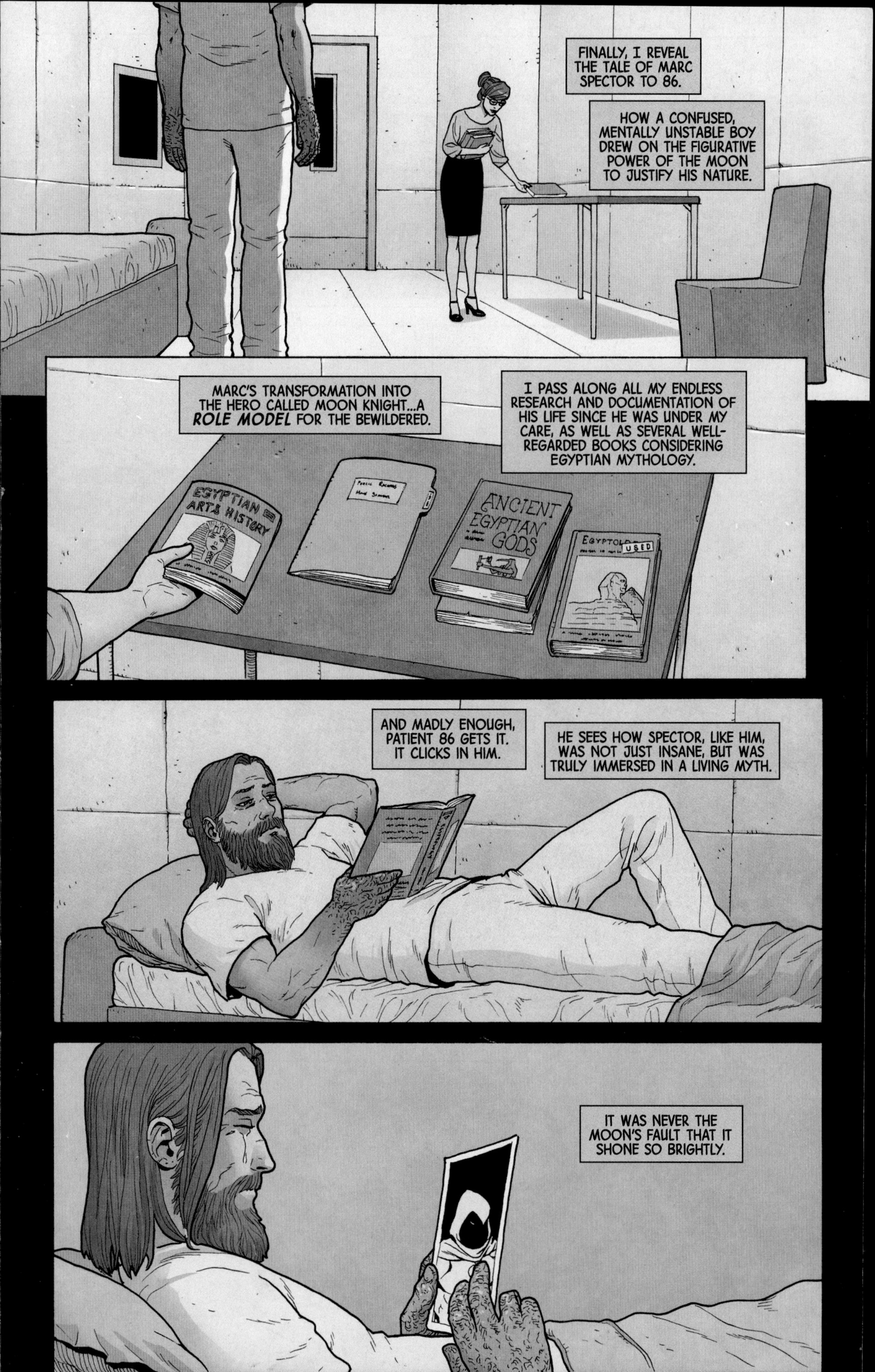

FINALLY, I REVEAL THE TALE OF MARC SPECTOR TO 86.
HOW A CONFUSED, MENTALLY UNSTABLE BOY DREW ON THE FIGURATIVE POWER OF THE MOON TO JUSTIFY HIS NATURE.
MARC'S TRANSFORMATION INTO THE HERO CALLED MOON KNIGHT...A *ROLE MODEL* FOR THE BEWILDERED.
I PASS ALONG ALL MY ENDLESS RESEARCH AND DOCUMENTATION OF HIS LIFE SINCE HE WAS UNDER MY CARE, AS WELL AS SEVERAL WELL-REGARDED BOOKS CONSIDERING EGYPTIAN MYTHOLOGY.
EGYPTIAN ARTS HISTORY
ANCIENT EGYPTIAN GODS
USED
AND MADLY ENOUGH, PATIENT 86 GETS IT. IT CLICKS IN HIM.
HE SEES HOW SPECTOR, LIKE HIM, WAS NOT JUST INSANE, BUT WAS TRULY IMMERSED IN A LIVING MYTH.
IT WAS NEVER THE MOON'S FAULT THAT IT SHONE SO BRIGHTLY.

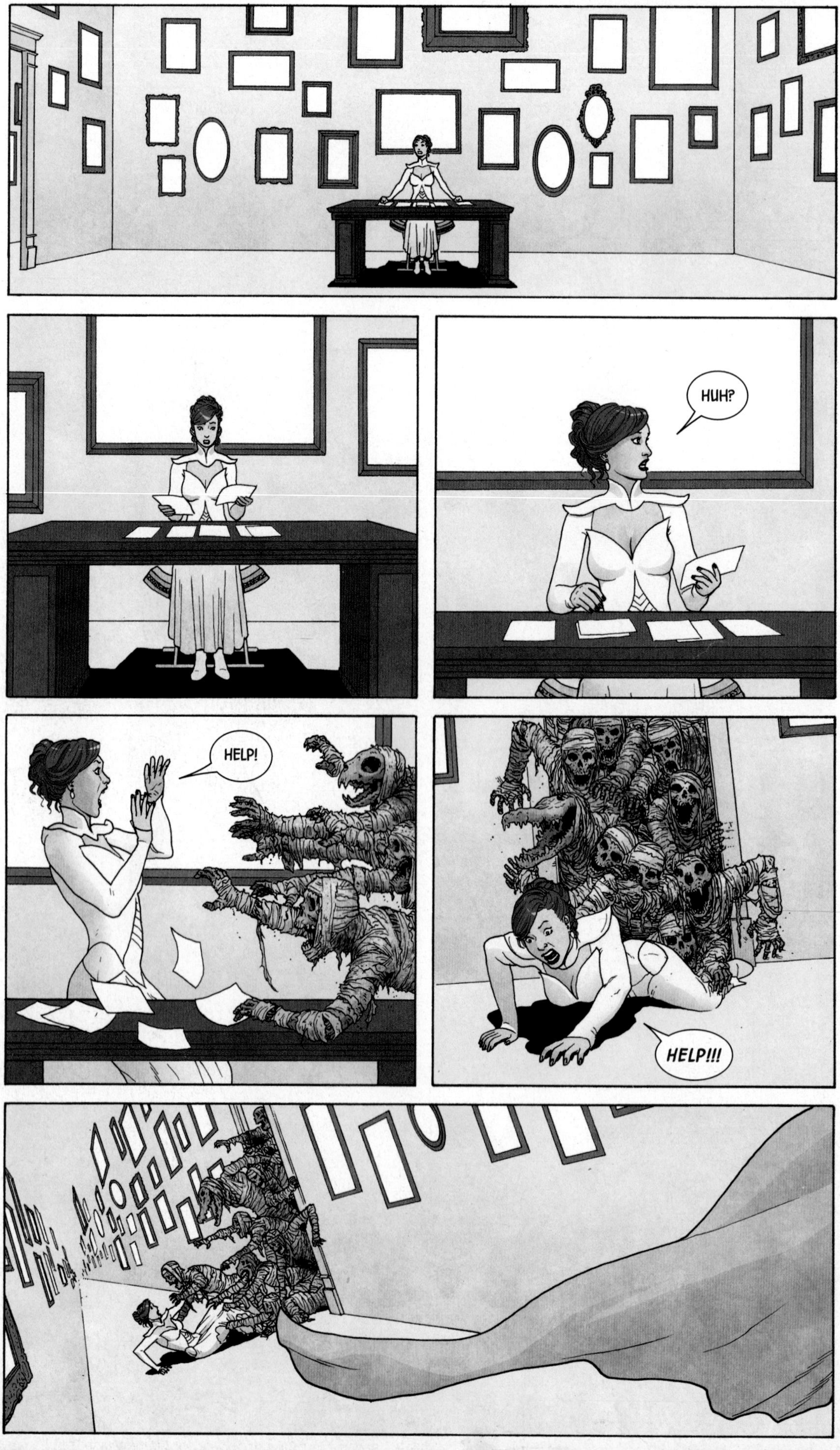
HUH?
HELP!
HELP!!!

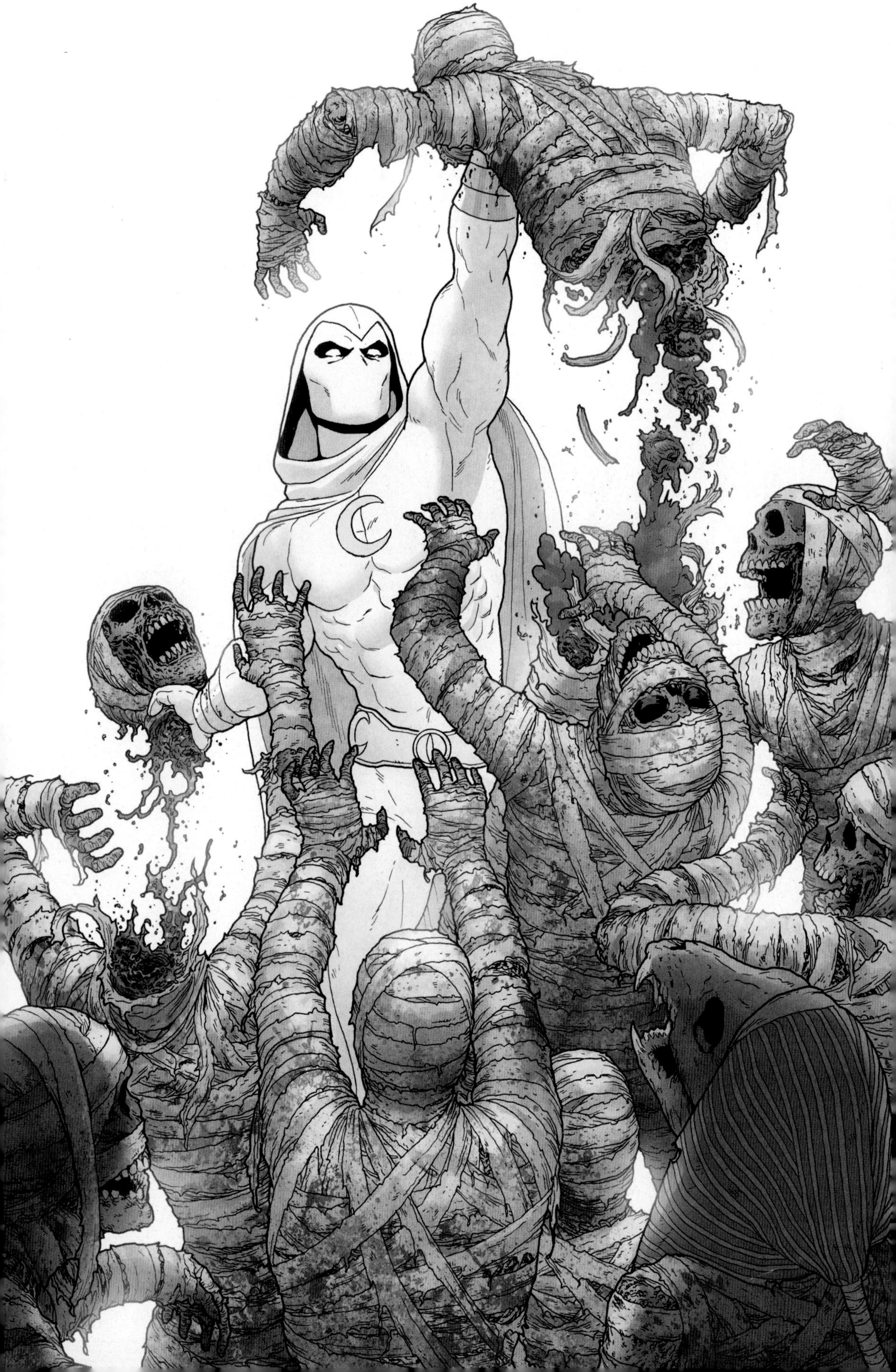

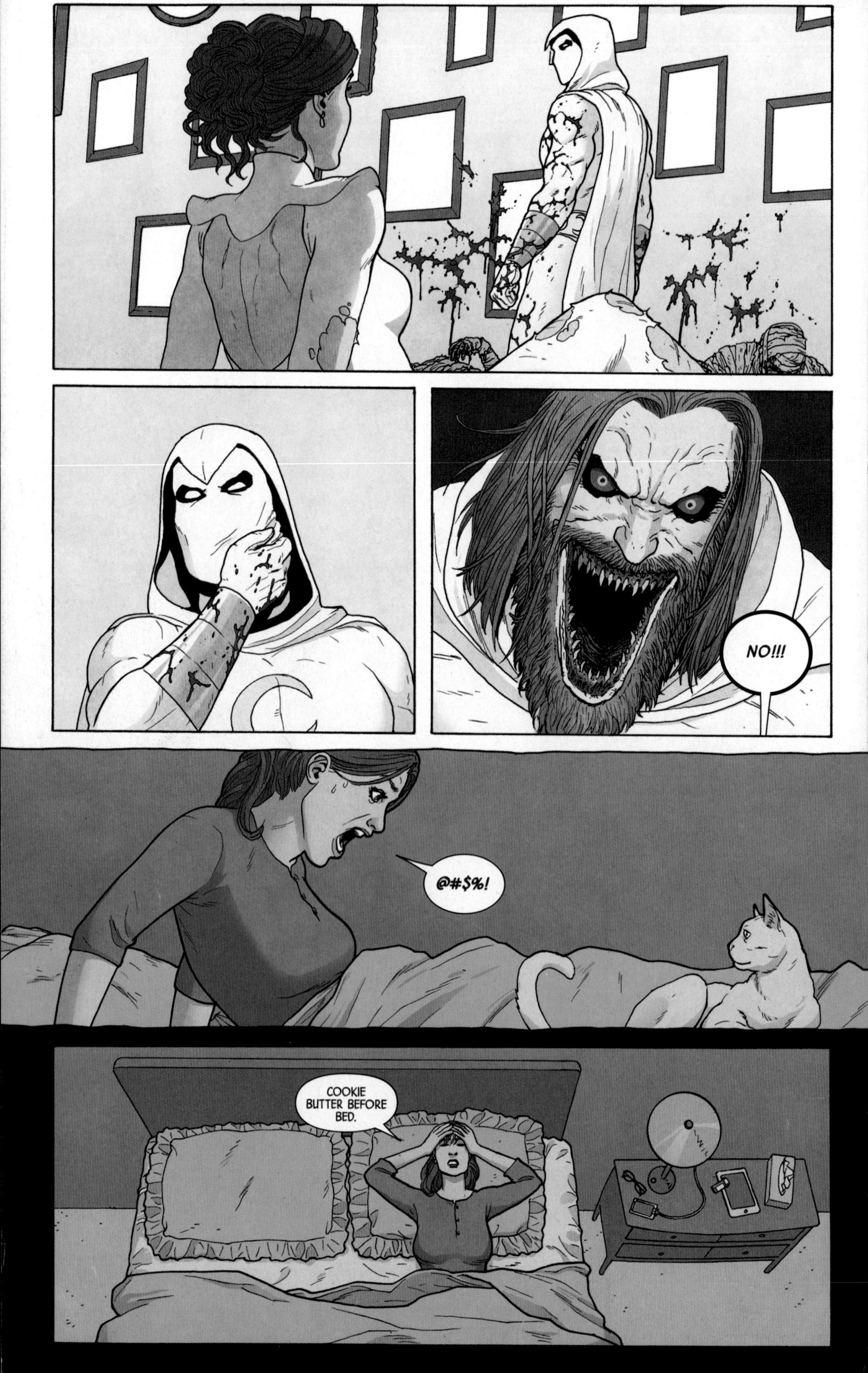
NO!!!
@#$%!
COOKIE BUTTER BEFORE BED.

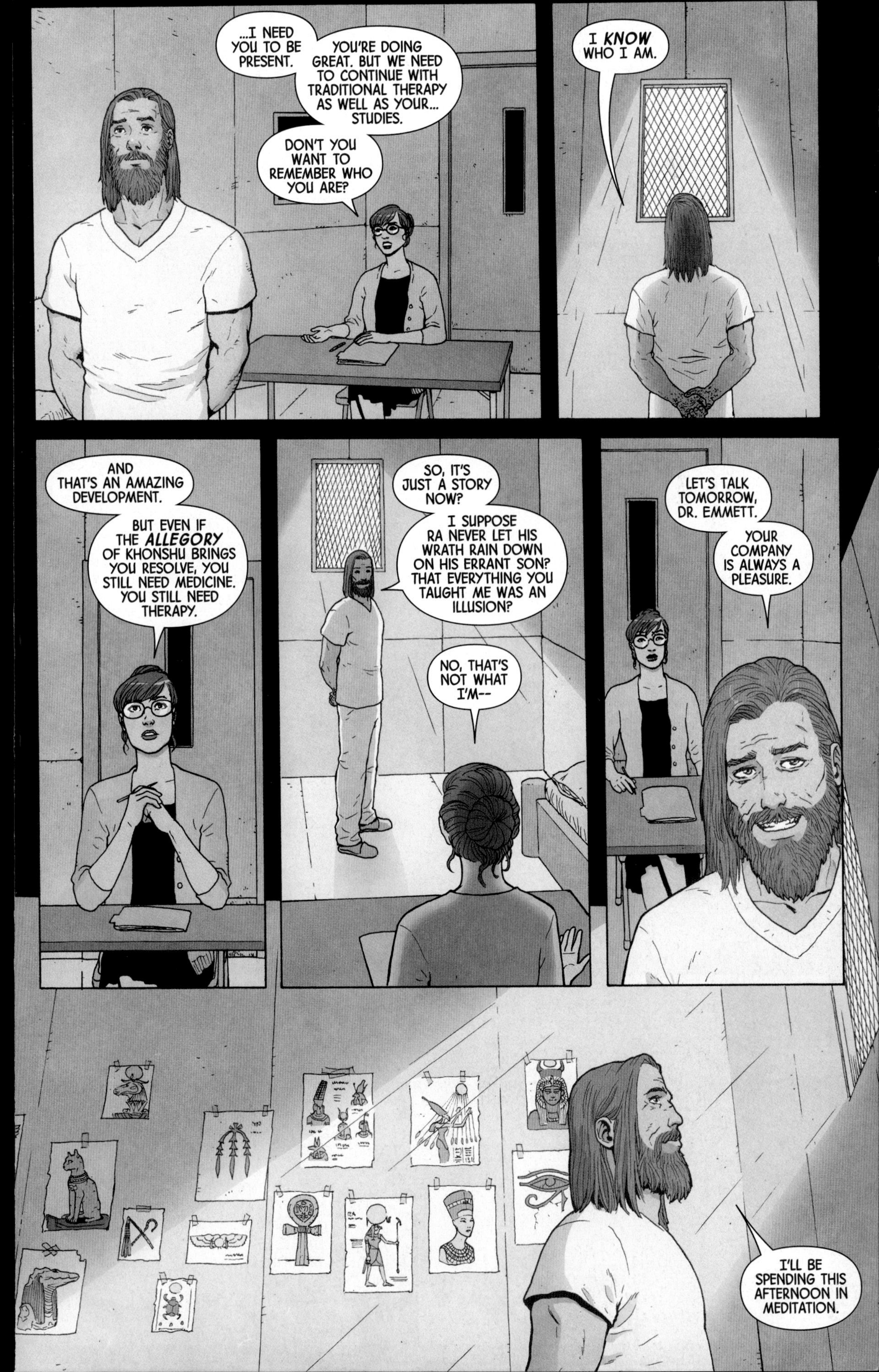
...I NEED YOU TO BE PRESENT.
YOU'RE DOING GREAT. BUT WE NEED TO CONTINUE WITH TRADITIONAL THERAPY AS WELL AS YOUR... STUDIES.
DON'T YOU WANT TO REMEMBER WHO YOU ARE?
I KNOW WHO I AM.
AND THAT'S AN AMAZING DEVELOPMENT.
BUT EVEN IF THE ALLEGORY OF KHONSHU BRINGS YOU RESOLVE, YOU STILL NEED MEDICINE. YOU STILL NEED THERAPY.
SO, IT'S JUST A STORY NOW?
I SUPPOSE RA NEVER LET HIS WRATH RAIN DOWN ON HIS ERRANT SON? THAT EVERYTHING YOU TAUGHT ME WAS AN ILLUSION?
NO, THAT'S NOT WHAT I'M--
LET'S TALK TOMORROW, DR. EMMETT.
YOUR COMPANY IS ALWAYS A PLEASURE.
I'LL BE SPENDING THIS AFTERNOON IN MEDITATION.

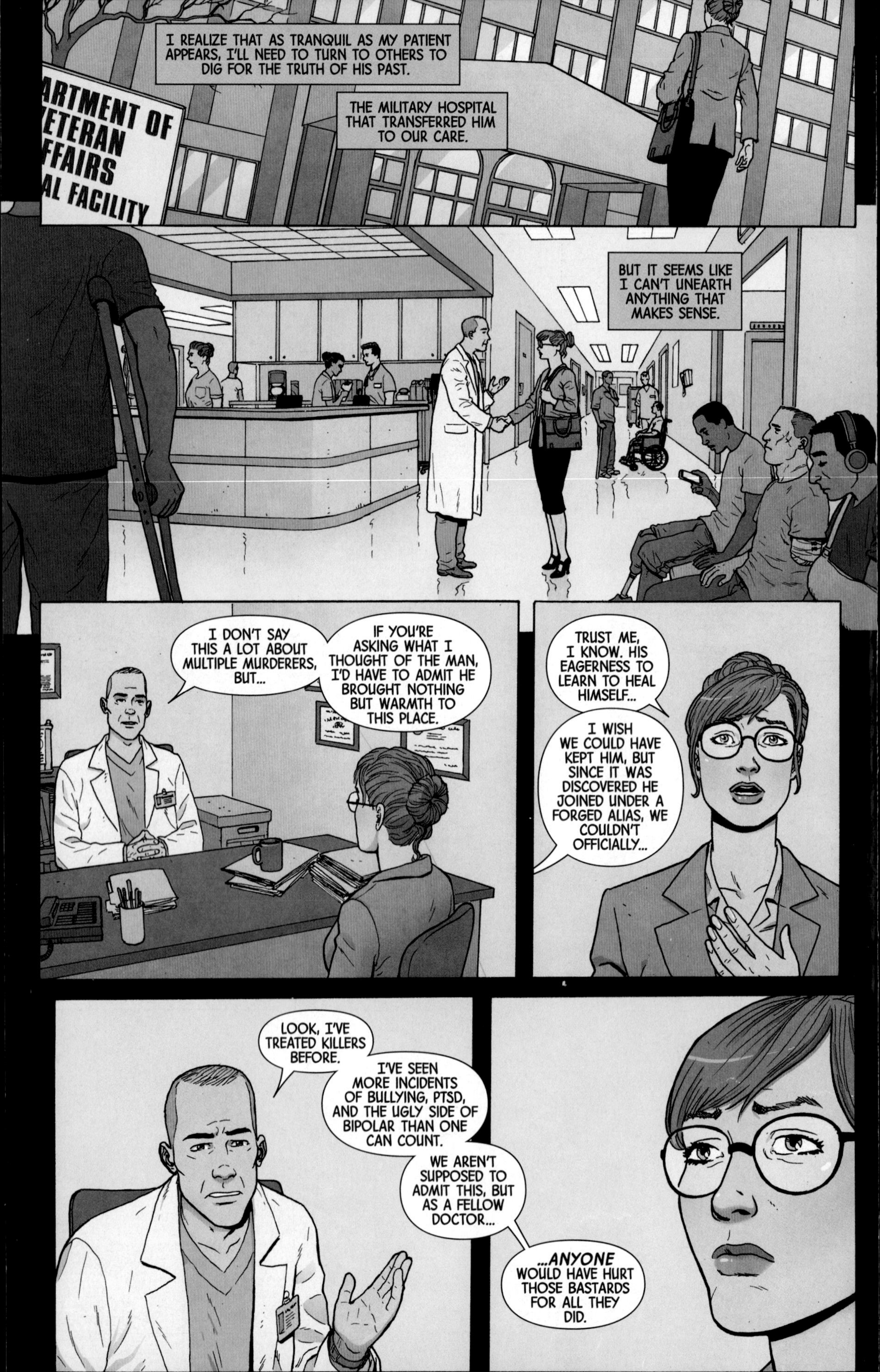
I REALIZE THAT AS TRANQUIL AS MY PATIENT APPEARS, I'LL NEED TO TURN TO OTHERS TO DIG FOR THE TRUTH OF HIS PAST.
ARTMENT OF ETERAN FFAIRS AL FACILITY
THE MILITARY HOSPITAL THAT TRANSFERRED HIM TO OUR CARE.
BUT IT SEEMS LIKE I CAN'T UNEARTH ANYTHING THAT MAKES SENSE.
I DON'T SAY THIS A LOT ABOUT MULTIPLE MURDERERS, BUT...
IF YOU'RE ASKING WHAT I THOUGHT OF THE MAN, I'D HAVE TO ADMIT HE BROUGHT NOTHING BUT WARMTH TO THIS PLACE.
TRUST ME, I KNOW. HIS EAGERNESS TO LEARN TO HEAL HIMSELF...
I WISH WE COULD HAVE KEPT HIM, BUT SINCE IT WAS DISCOVERED HE JOINED UNDER A FORGED ALIAS, WE COULDN'T OFFICIALLY...
LOOK, I'VE TREATED KILLERS BEFORE.
I'VE SEEN MORE INCIDENTS OF BULLYING, PTSD, AND THE UGLY SIDE OF BIPOLAR THAN ONE CAN COUNT.
WE AREN'T SUPPOSED TO ADMIT THIS, BUT AS A FELLOW DOCTOR...
...*ANYONE* WOULD HAVE HURT THOSE BASTARDS FOR ALL THEY DID.

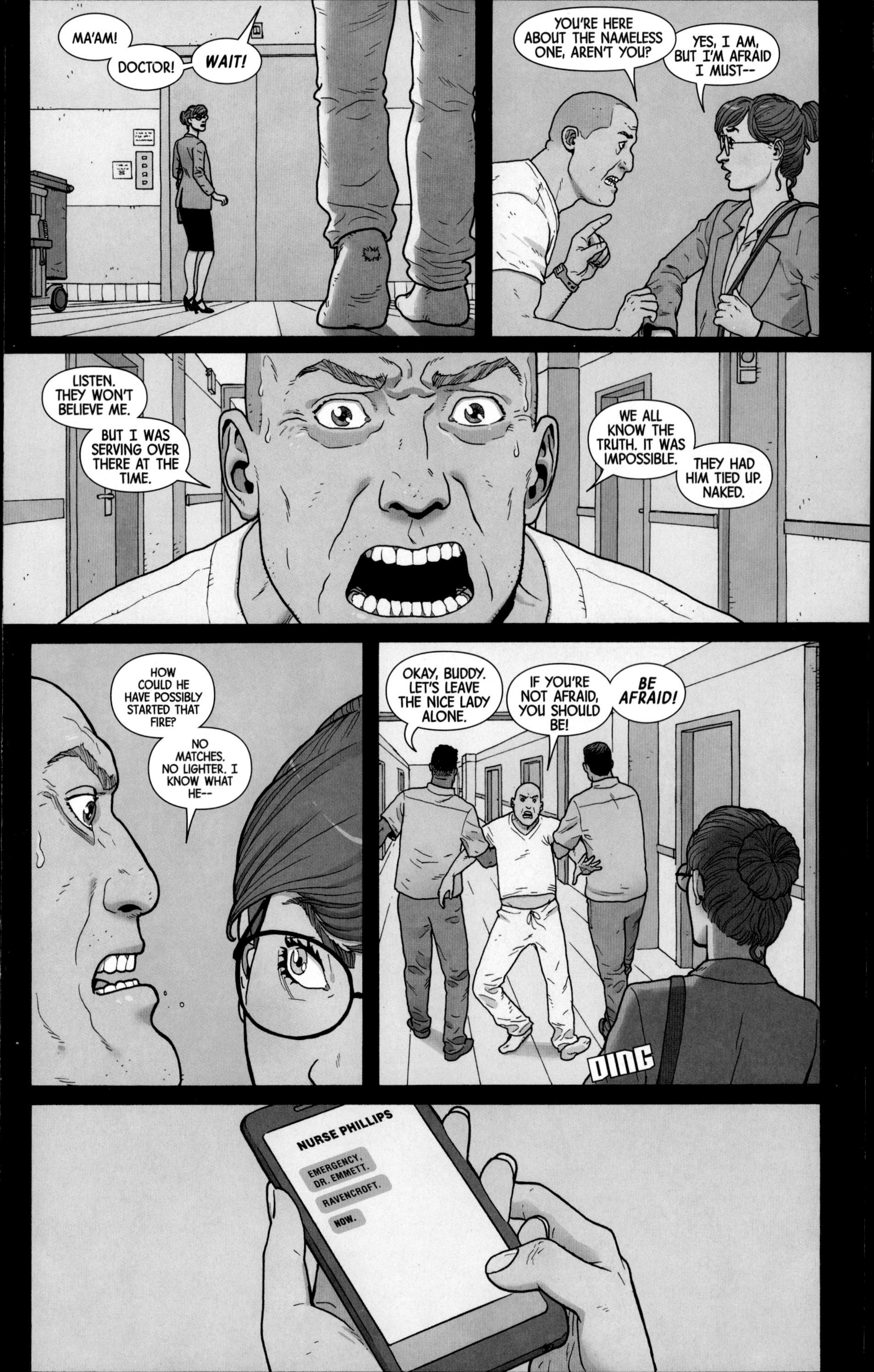
MA'AM!
DOCTOR!
WAIT!
YOU'RE HERE ABOUT THE NAMELESS ONE, AREN'T YOU?
YES, I AM, BUT I'M AFRAID I MUST--
LISTEN. THEY WON'T BELIEVE ME.
BUT I WAS SERVING OVER THERE AT THE TIME.
WE ALL KNOW THE TRUTH. IT WAS IMPOSSIBLE.
THEY HAD HIM TIED UP. NAKED.
HOW COULD HE HAVE POSSIBLY STARTED THAT FIRE?
NO MATCHES. NO LIGHTER. I KNOW WHAT HE--
OKAY, BUDDY. LET'S LEAVE THE NICE LADY ALONE.
IF YOU'RE NOT AFRAID, YOU SHOULD BE!
BE AFRAID!
DING
NURSE PHILLIPS
EMERGENCY, DR. EMMETT.
RAVENCROFT.
NOW.

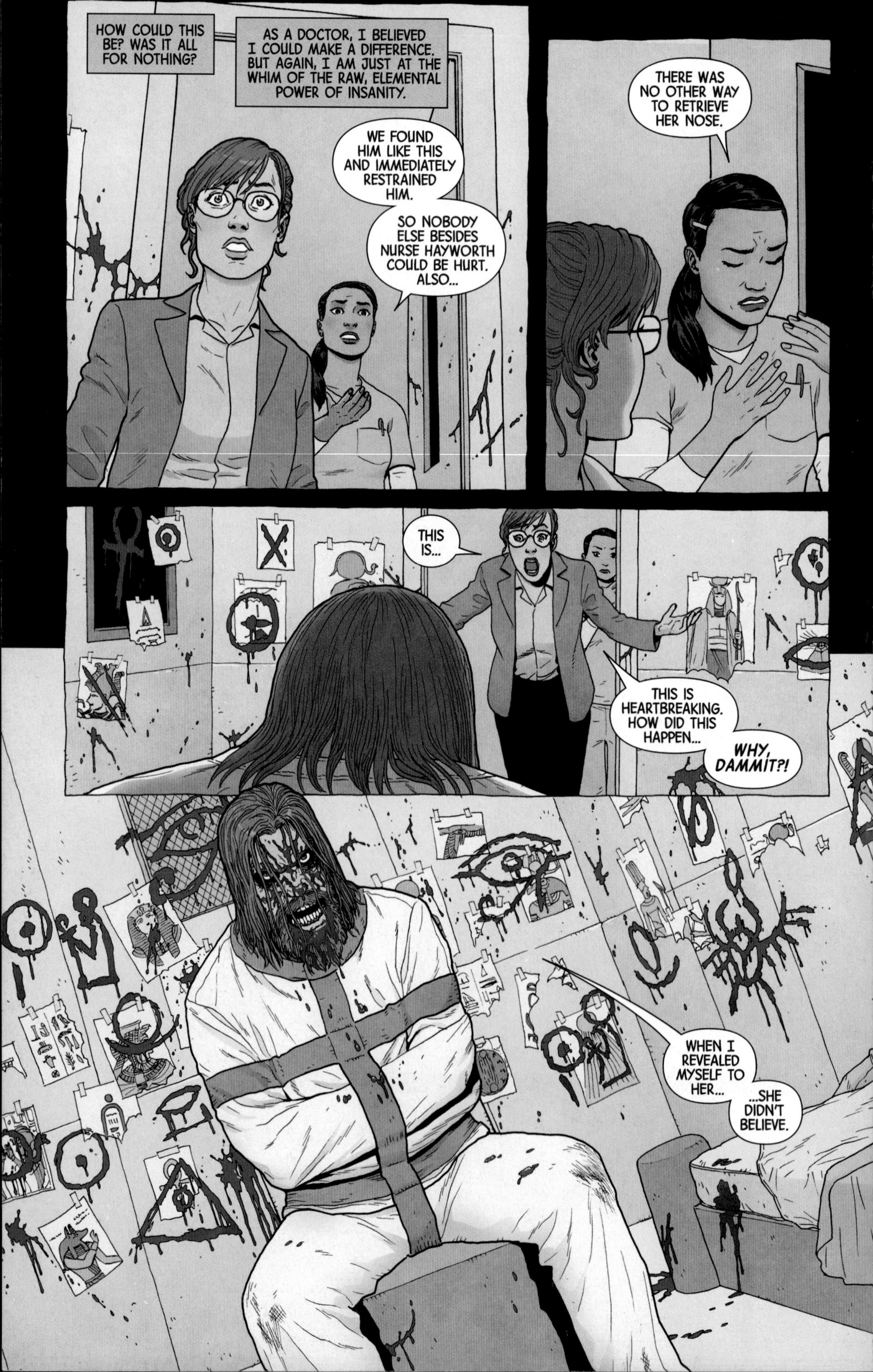
HOW COULD THIS BE? WAS IT ALL FOR NOTHING?
AS A DOCTOR, I BELIEVED I COULD MAKE A DIFFERENCE. BUT AGAIN, I AM JUST AT THE WHIM OF THE RAW, ELEMENTAL POWER OF INSANITY.
WE FOUND HIM LIKE THIS AND IMMEDIATELY RESTRAINED HIM.
SO NOBODY ELSE BESIDES NURSE HAYWORTH COULD BE HURT. ALSO...
THERE WAS NO OTHER WAY TO RETRIEVE HER NOSE.
THIS IS...
THIS IS HEARTBREAKING. HOW DID THIS HAPPEN...
WHY, DAMMIT?!
WHEN I REVEALED MYSELF TO HER...
...SHE DIDN'T BELIEVE.

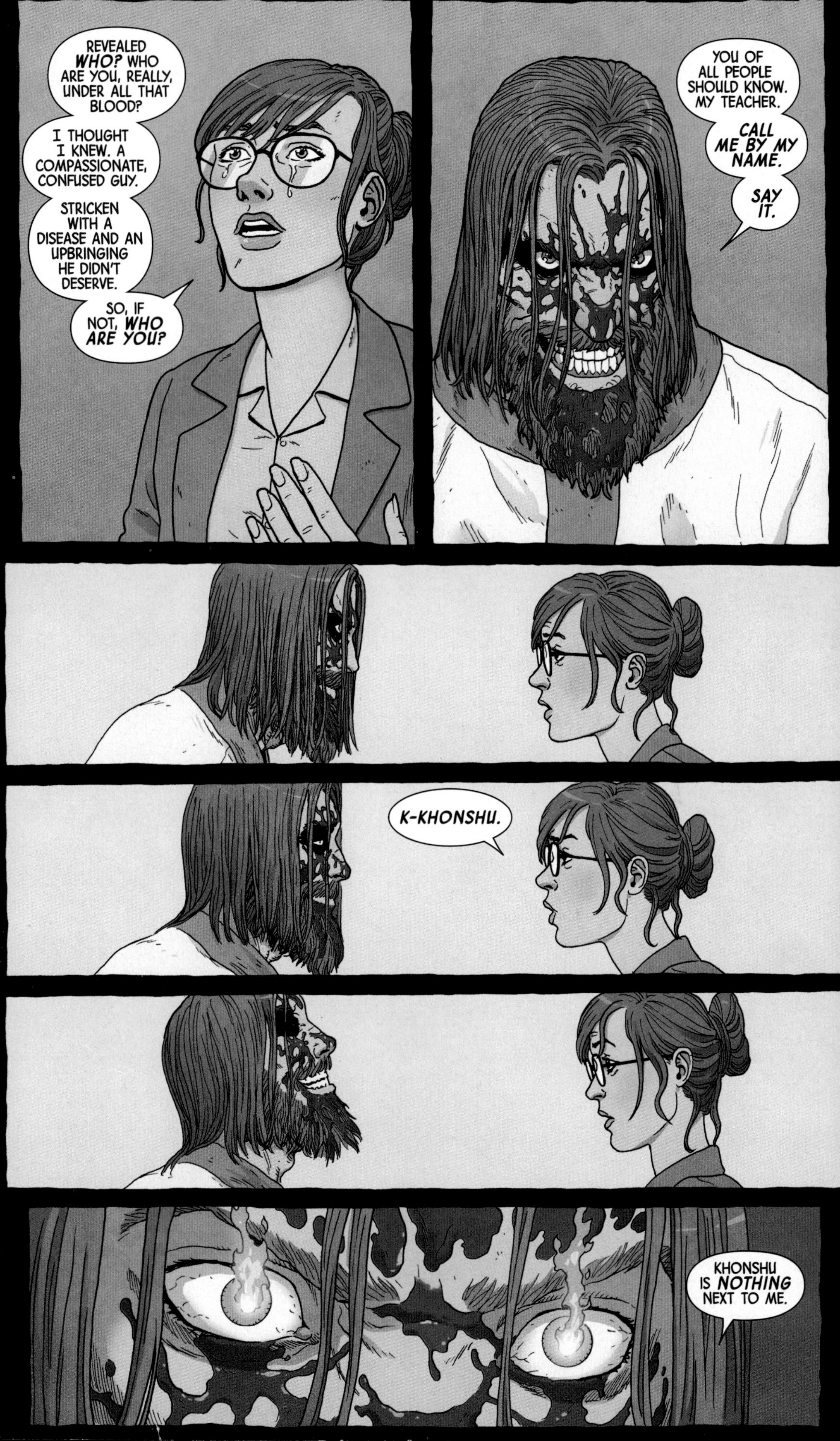
REVEALED WHO? WHO ARE YOU, REALLY, UNDER ALL THAT BLOOD?
I THOUGHT I KNEW. A COMPASSIONATE, CONFUSED GUY.
STRICKEN WITH A DISEASE AND AN UPBRINGING HE DIDN'T DESERVE.
SO, IF NOT, WHO ARE YOU?
YOU OF ALL PEOPLE SHOULD KNOW. MY TEACHER.
CALL ME BY MY NAME.
SAY IT.
K-KHONSHU.
KHONSHU IS NOTHING NEXT TO ME.

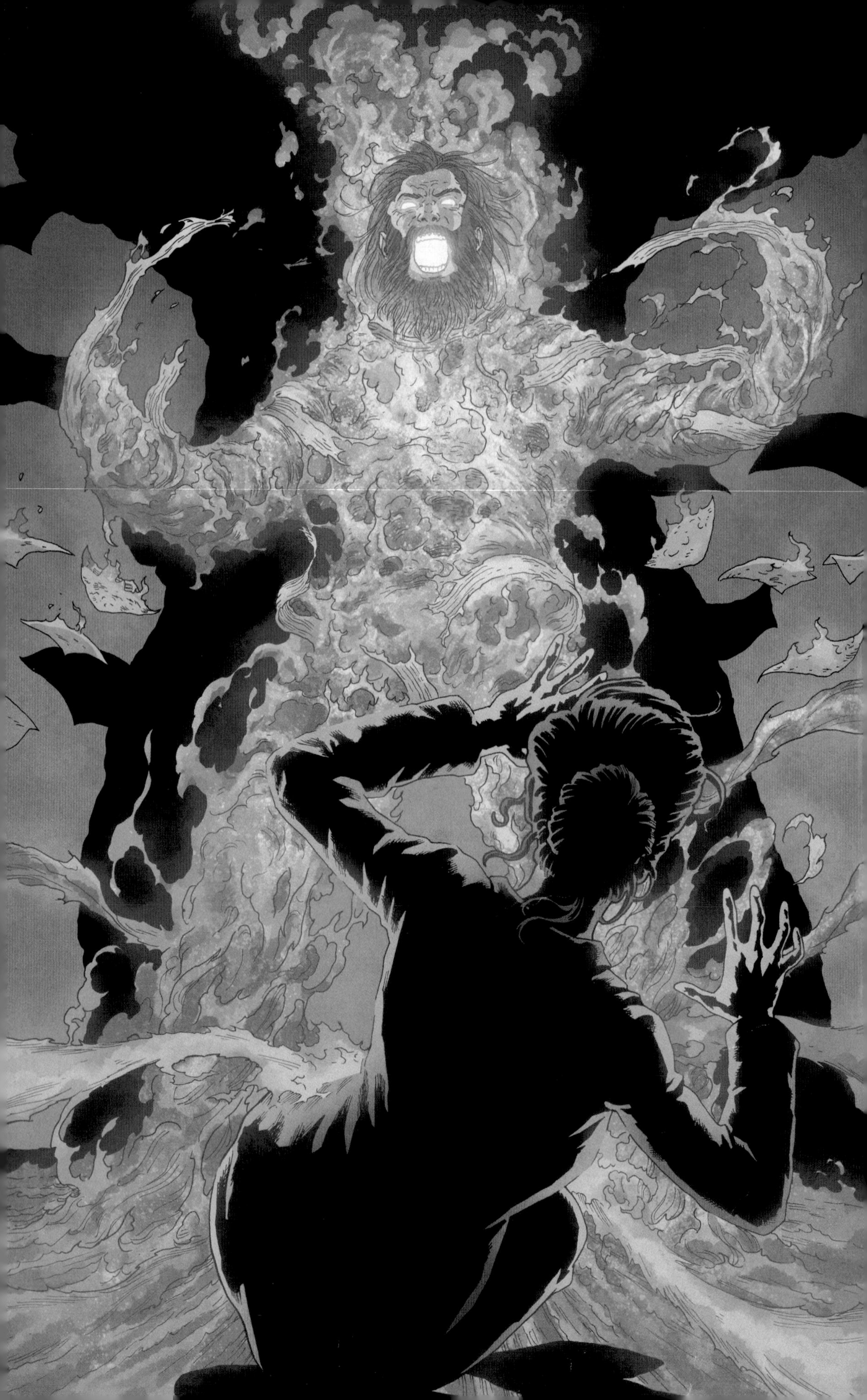

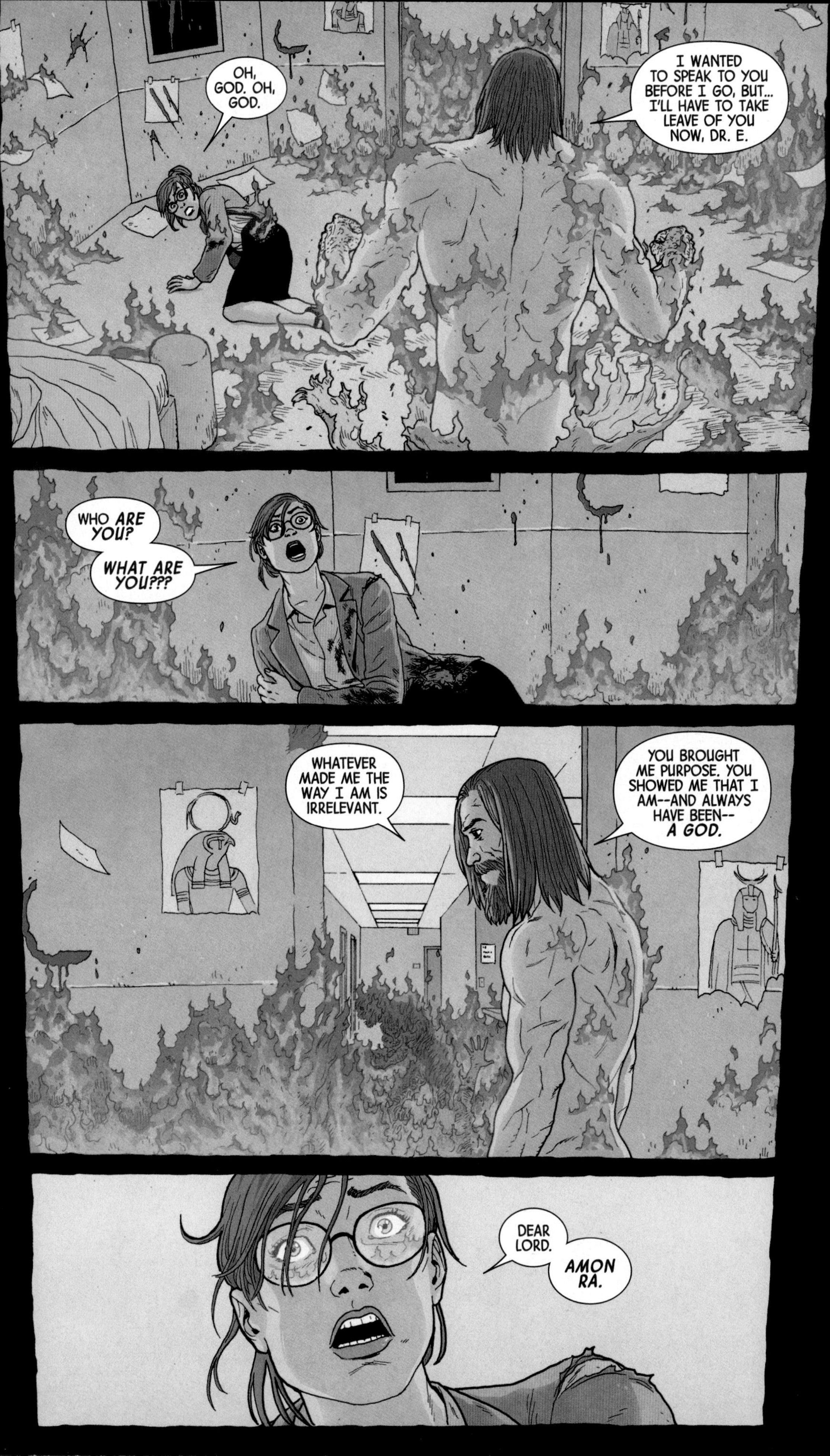

OH, GOD. OH, GOD.
I WANTED TO SPEAK TO YOU BEFORE I GO, BUT... I'LL HAVE TO TAKE LEAVE OF YOU NOW, DR. E.
WHO *ARE YOU?*
WHAT ARE YOU???
WHATEVER MADE ME THE WAY I AM IS IRRELEVANT.
YOU BROUGHT ME PURPOSE. YOU SHOWED ME THAT I AM--AND ALWAYS HAVE BEEN-- *A GOD.*
DEAR LORD.
AMON RA.

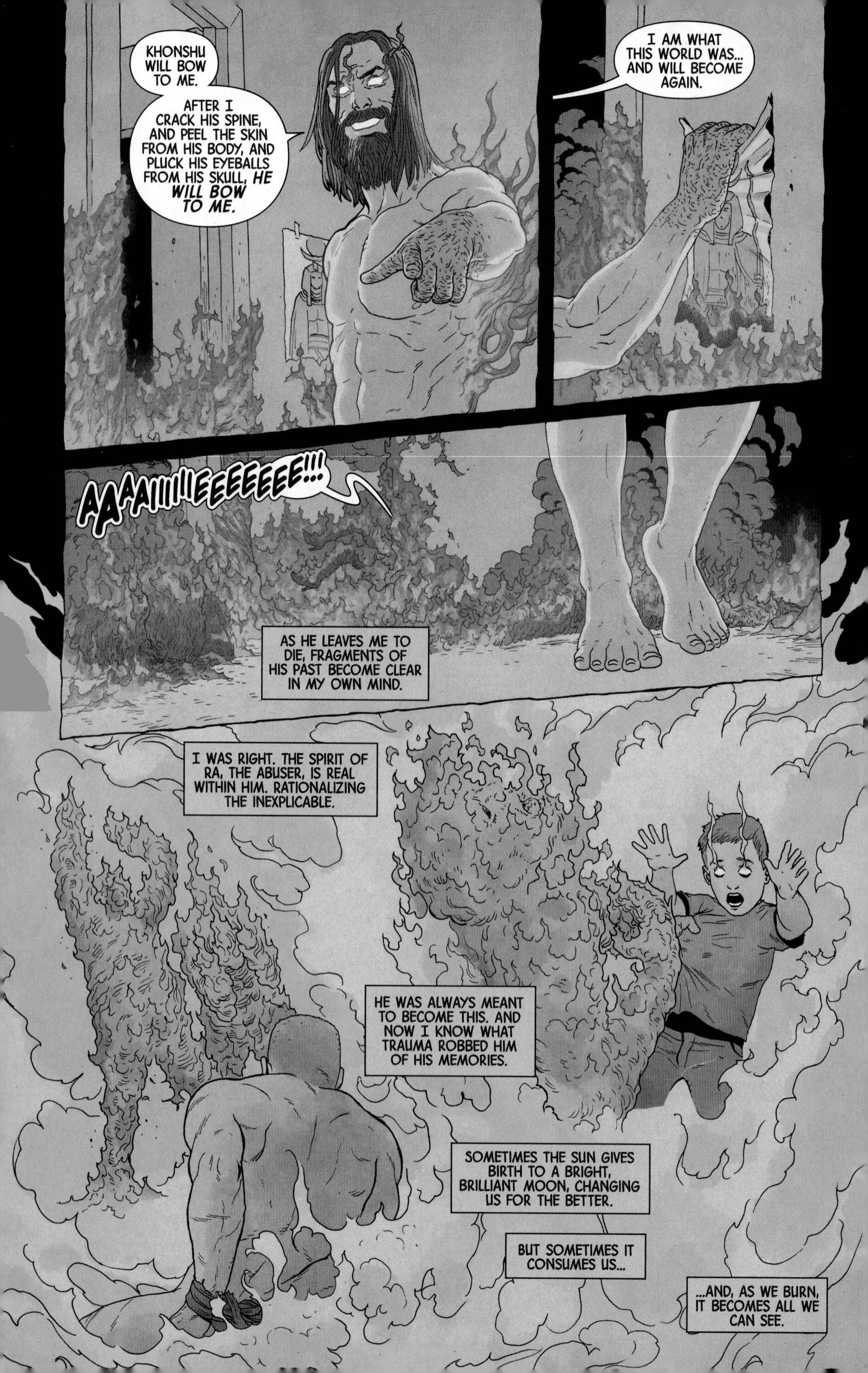
KHONSHU WILL BOW TO ME.
AFTER I CRACK HIS SPINE, AND PEEL THE SKIN FROM HIS BODY, AND PLUCK HIS EYEBALLS FROM HIS SKULL, *HE WILL BOW TO ME.*
I AM WHAT THIS WORLD WAS... AND WILL BECOME AGAIN.
AAAAIIIIIIEEEEEEE!!!
AS HE LEAVES ME TO DIE, FRAGMENTS OF HIS PAST BECOME CLEAR IN MY OWN MIND.
I WAS RIGHT. THE SPIRIT OF RA, THE ABUSER, IS REAL WITHIN HIM. RATIONALIZING THE INEXPLICABLE.
HE WAS ALWAYS MEANT TO BECOME THIS. AND NOW I KNOW WHAT TRAUMA ROBBED HIM OF HIS MEMORIES.
SOMETIMES THE SUN GIVES BIRTH TO A BRIGHT, BRILLIANT MOON, CHANGING US FOR THE BETTER.
BUT SOMETIMES IT CONSUMES US...
...AND, AS WE BURN, IT BECOMES ALL WE CAN SEE.

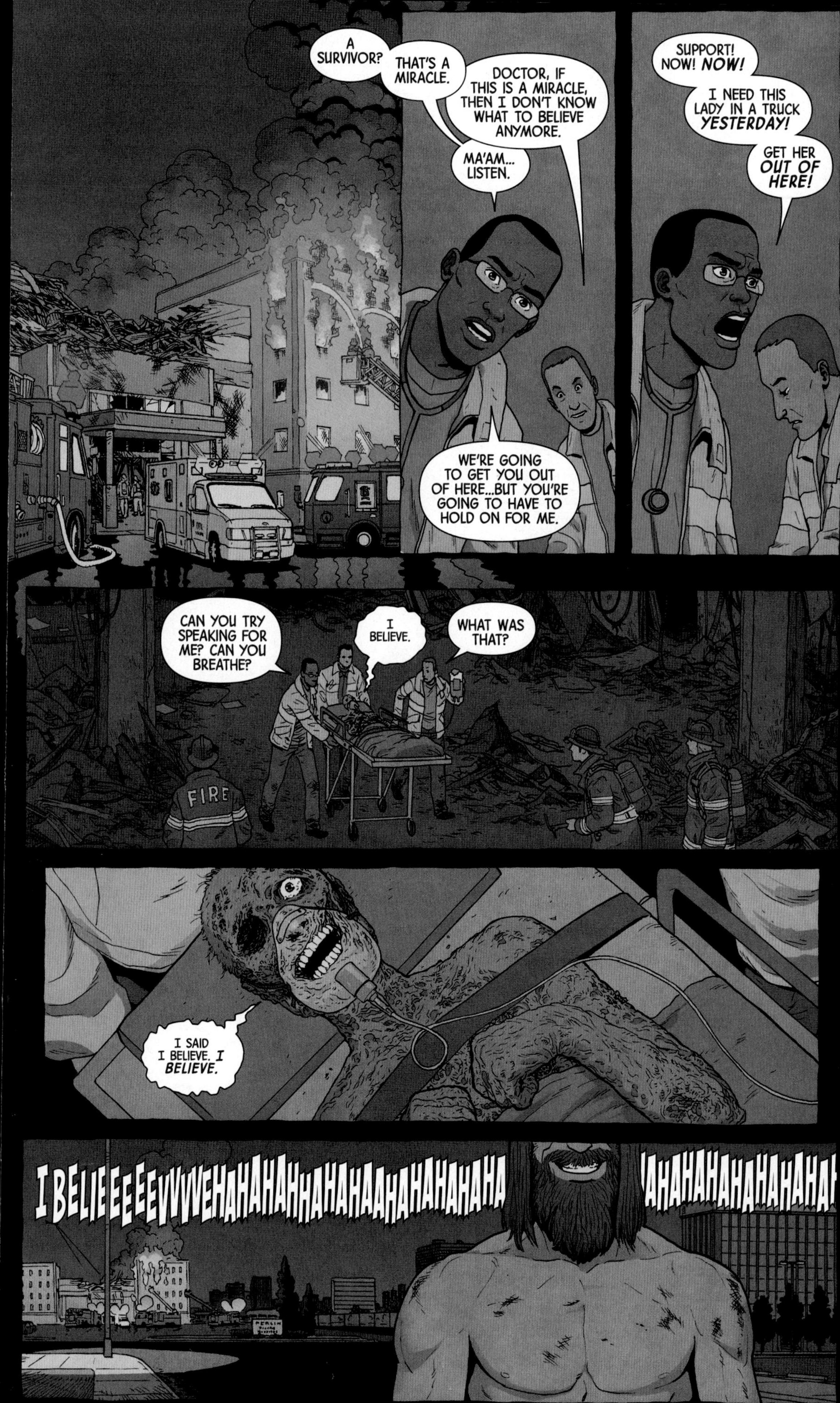

A SURVIVOR?
THAT'S A MIRACLE.
DOCTOR, IF THIS IS A MIRACLE, THEN I DON'T KNOW WHAT TO BELIEVE ANYMORE.
MA'AM... LISTEN.
WE'RE GOING TO GET YOU OUT OF HERE...BUT YOU'RE GOING TO HAVE TO HOLD ON FOR ME.
SUPPORT! NOW! *NOW!*
I NEED THIS LADY IN A TRUCK *YESTERDAY!*
GET HER *OUT OF HERE!*
CAN YOU TRY SPEAKING FOR ME? CAN YOU BREATHE?
I BELIEVE.
WHAT WAS THAT?
FIRE
I SAID I BELIEVE. *I BELIEVE.*
I BELIEEEEEVVVVEHAHAHAHHAHAHAAHAHAHAHAHA
HAHAHAHAHAHAHAHA!

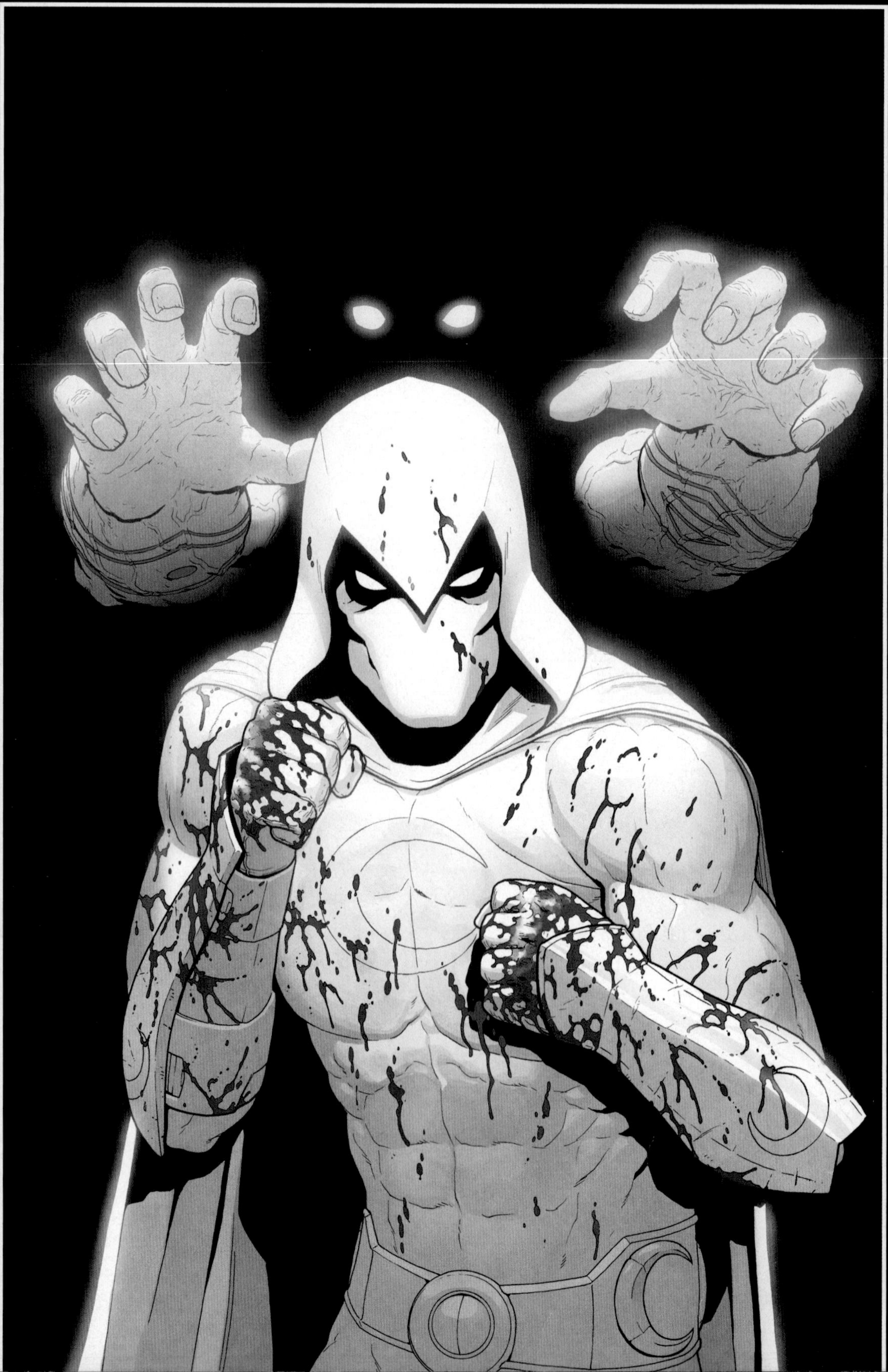

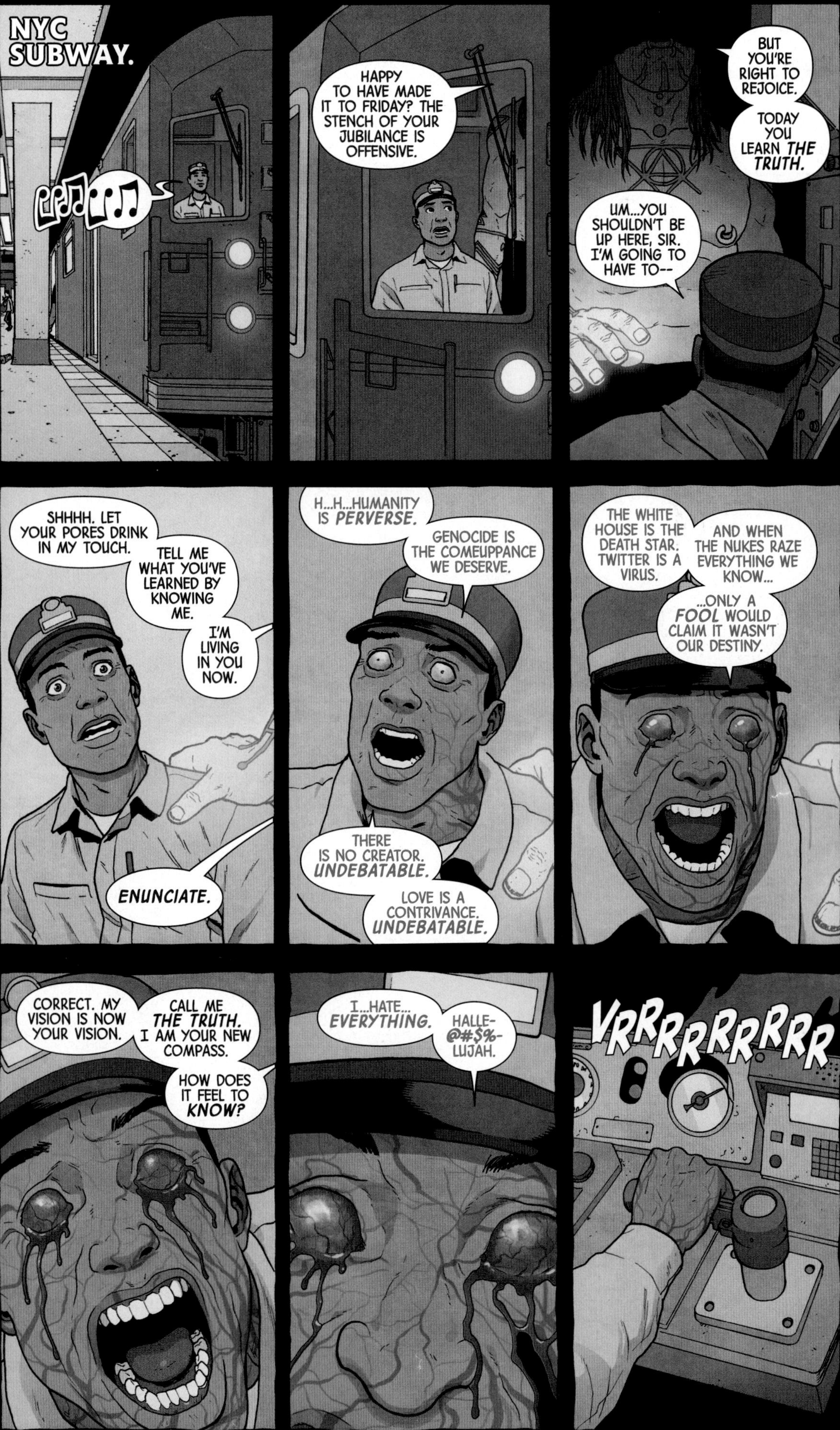

NYC SUBWAY.
HAPPY TO HAVE MADE IT TO FRIDAY? THE STENCH OF YOUR JUBILANCE IS OFFENSIVE.
BUT YOU'RE RIGHT TO REJOICE.
TODAY YOU LEARN THE TRUTH.
UM...YOU SHOULDN'T BE UP HERE, SIR. I'M GOING TO HAVE TO--
SHHHH. LET YOUR PORES DRINK IN MY TOUCH.
TELL ME WHAT YOU'VE LEARNED BY KNOWING ME.
I'M LIVING IN YOU NOW.
ENUNCIATE.
H...H...HUMANITY IS PERVERSE.
GENOCIDE IS THE COMEUPPANCE WE DESERVE.
THERE IS NO CREATOR. UNDEBATABLE.
LOVE IS A CONTRIVANCE. UNDEBATABLE.
THE WHITE HOUSE IS THE DEATH STAR. TWITTER IS A VIRUS.
AND WHEN THE NUKES RAZE EVERYTHING WE KNOW...
...ONLY A FOOL WOULD CLAIM IT WASN'T OUR DESTINY.
CORRECT. MY VISION IS NOW YOUR VISION.
CALL ME THE TRUTH. I AM YOUR NEW COMPASS.
HOW DOES IT FEEL TO KNOW?
I...HATE... EVERYTHING.
HALLE-@#$%-LUJAH.
VRRRRRRRRR

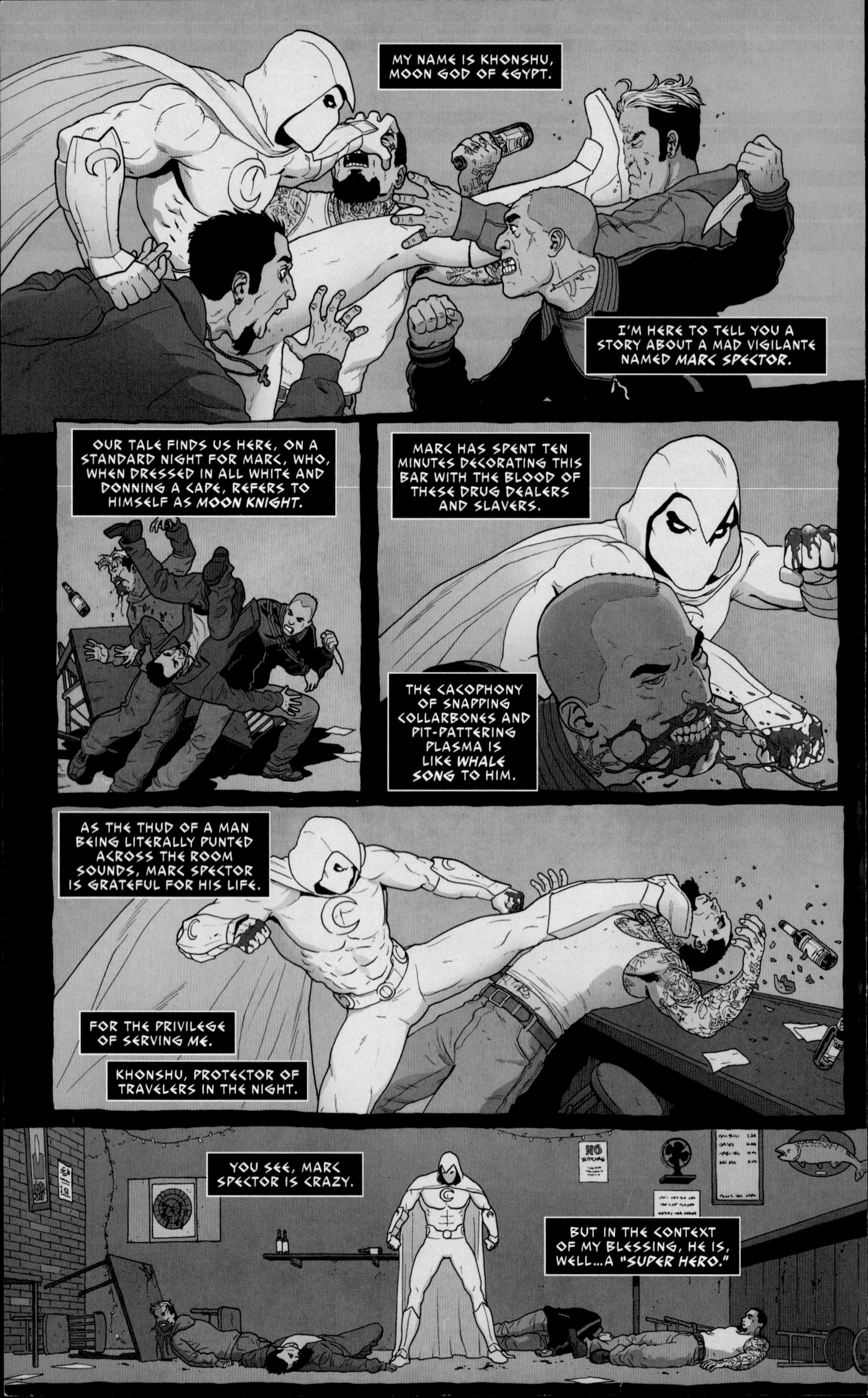
MY NAME IS KHONSHU, MOON GOD OF EGYPT.
I'M HERE TO TELL YOU A STORY ABOUT A MAD VIGILANTE NAMED MARC SPECTOR.
OUR TALE FINDS US HERE, ON A STANDARD NIGHT FOR MARC, WHO, WHEN DRESSED IN ALL WHITE AND DONNING A CAPE, REFERS TO HIMSELF AS MOON KNIGHT.
MARC HAS SPENT TEN MINUTES DECORATING THIS BAR WITH THE BLOOD OF THESE DRUG DEALERS AND SLAVERS.
THE CACOPHONY OF SNAPPING COLLARBONES AND PIT-PATTERING PLASMA IS LIKE WHALE SONG TO HIM.
AS THE THUD OF A MAN BEING LITERALLY PUNTED ACROSS THE ROOM SOUNDS, MARC SPECTOR IS GRATEFUL FOR HIS LIFE.
FOR THE PRIVILEGE OF SERVING ME.
KHONSHU, PROTECTOR OF TRAVELERS IN THE NIGHT.
YOU SEE, MARC SPECTOR IS CRAZY.
BUT IN THE CONTEXT OF MY BLESSING, HE IS, WELL...A "SUPER HERO."

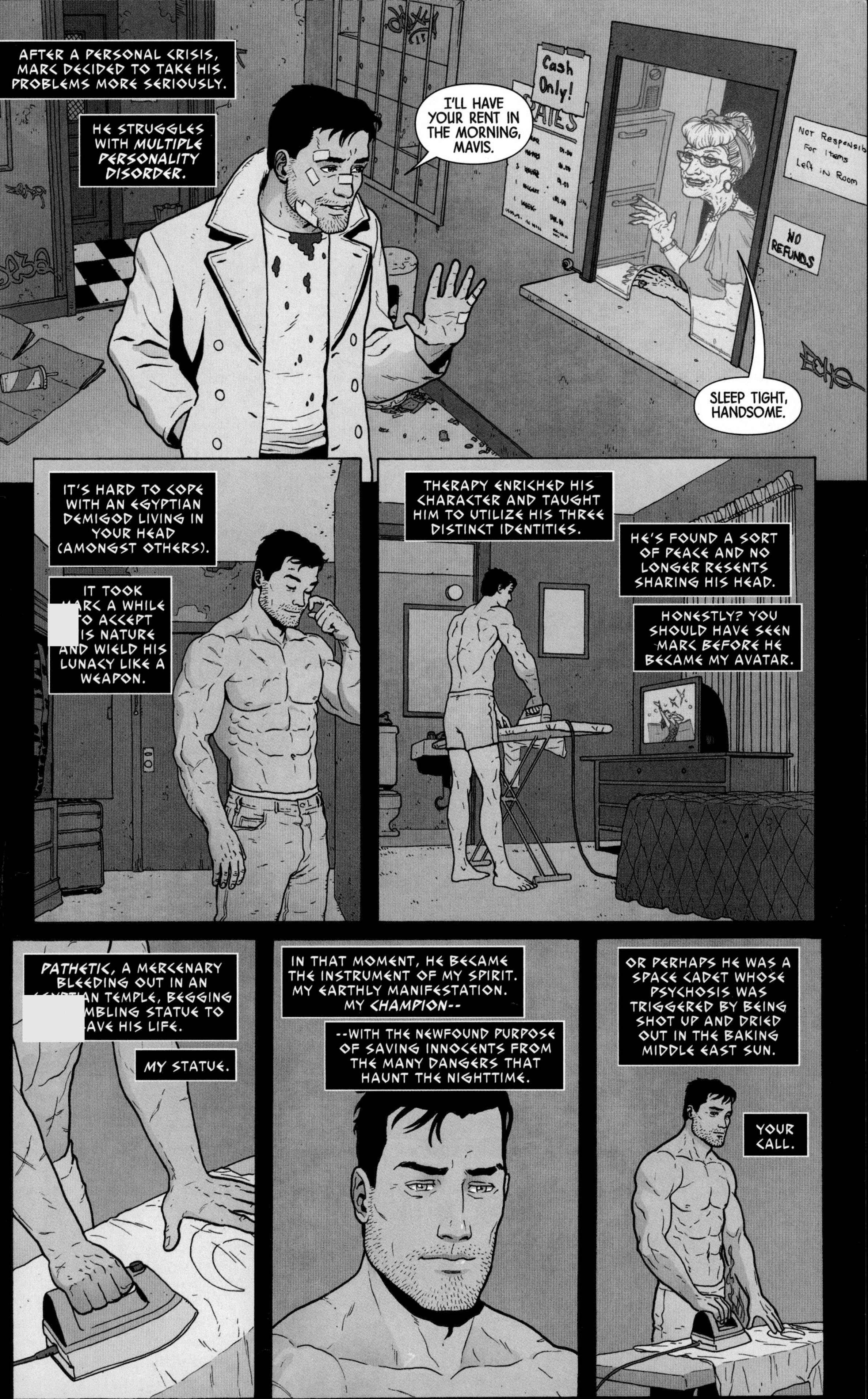
AFTER A PERSONAL CRISIS, MARC DECIDED TO TAKE HIS PROBLEMS MORE SERIOUSLY.
HE STRUGGLES WITH *MULTIPLE PERSONALITY DISORDER.*
I'LL HAVE YOUR RENT IN THE MORNING, MAVIS.
Cash Only!
RATES
Not Responsible For Items Left in Room
NO REFUNDS
SLEEP TIGHT, HANDSOME.
IT'S HARD TO COPE WITH AN EGYPTIAN DEMIGOD LIVING IN YOUR HEAD (AMONGST OTHERS).
IT TOOK
ARC A WHILE
O ACCEPT
IS NATURE
AND WIELD HIS LUNACY LIKE A WEAPON.
THERAPY ENRICHED HIS CHARACTER AND TAUGHT HIM TO UTILIZE HIS THREE DISTINCT IDENTITIES.
HE'S FOUND A SORT OF PEACE AND NO LONGER RESENTS SHARING HIS HEAD.
HONESTLY? YOU SHOULD HAVE SEEN MARC *BEFORE* HE BECAME MY AVATAR.
PATHETIC, A MERCENARY BLEEDING OUT IN AN
AN TEMPLE, BEGGING
MBLING STATUE TO
AVE HIS LIFE.
MY STATUE.
IN THAT MOMENT, HE BECAME THE INSTRUMENT OF MY SPIRIT. MY EARTHLY MANIFESTATION. MY *CHAMPION*--
--WITH THE NEWFOUND PURPOSE OF SAVING INNOCENTS FROM THE MANY DANGERS THAT HAUNT THE NIGHTTIME.
OR PERHAPS HE WAS A SPACE CADET WHOSE PSYCHOSIS WAS TRIGGERED BY BEING SHOT UP AND DRIED OUT IN THE BAKING MIDDLE EAST SUN.
YOUR CALL.

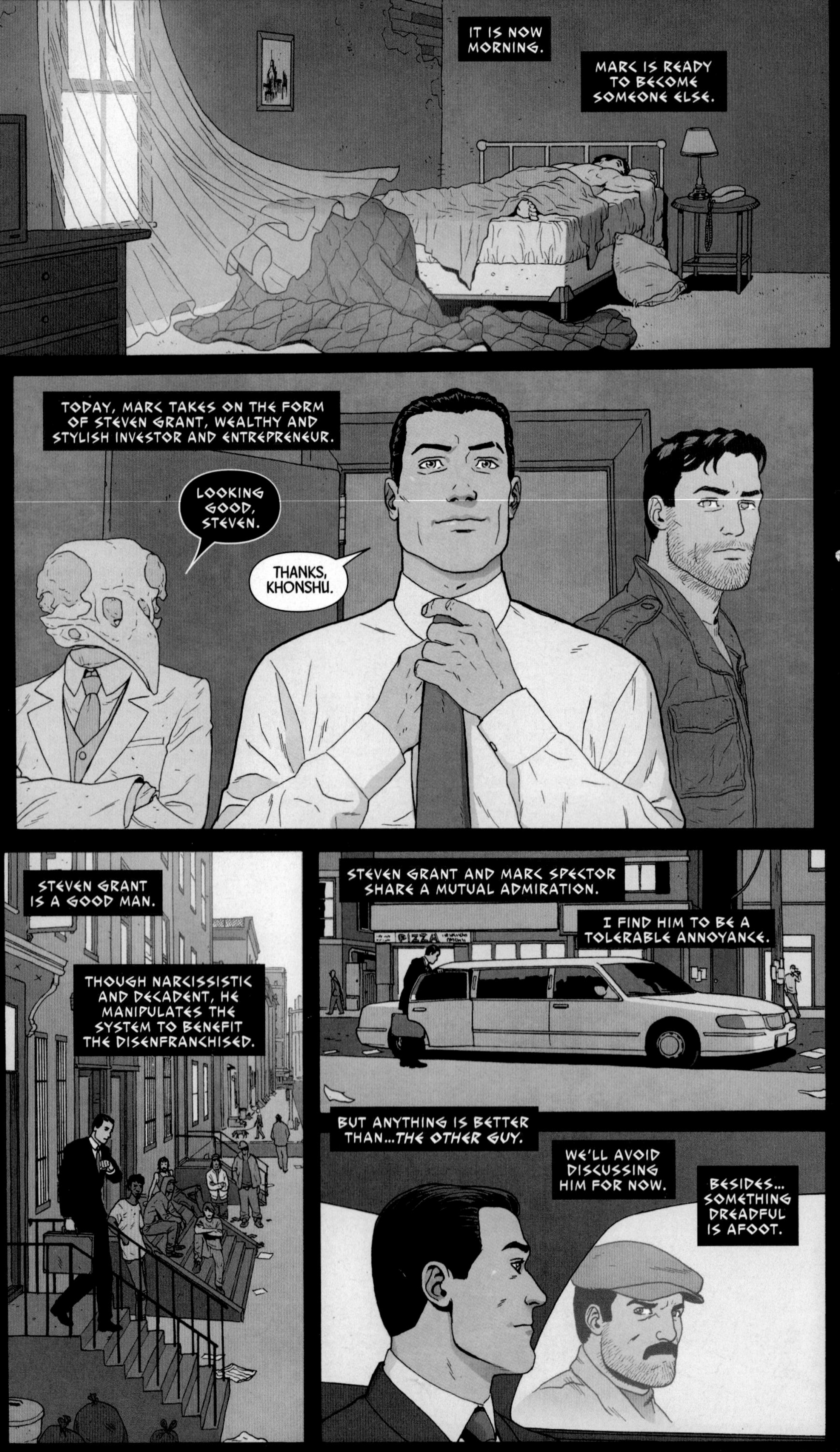
IT IS NOW MORNING.
MARC IS READY TO BECOME SOMEONE ELSE.
TODAY, MARC TAKES ON THE FORM OF STEVEN GRANT, WEALTHY AND STYLISH INVESTOR AND ENTREPRENEUR.
LOOKING GOOD, STEVEN.
THANKS, KHONSHU.
STEVEN GRANT IS A GOOD MAN.
THOUGH NARCISSISTIC AND DECADENT, HE MANIPULATES THE SYSTEM TO BENEFIT THE DISENFRANCHISED.
STEVEN GRANT AND MARC SPECTOR SHARE A MUTUAL ADMIRATION.
PIZZA
I FIND HIM TO BE A TOLERABLE ANNOYANCE.
BUT ANYTHING IS BETTER THAN...*THE OTHER GUY.*
WE'LL AVOID DISCUSSING HIM FOR NOW.
BESIDES... SOMETHING DREADFUL IS AFOOT.

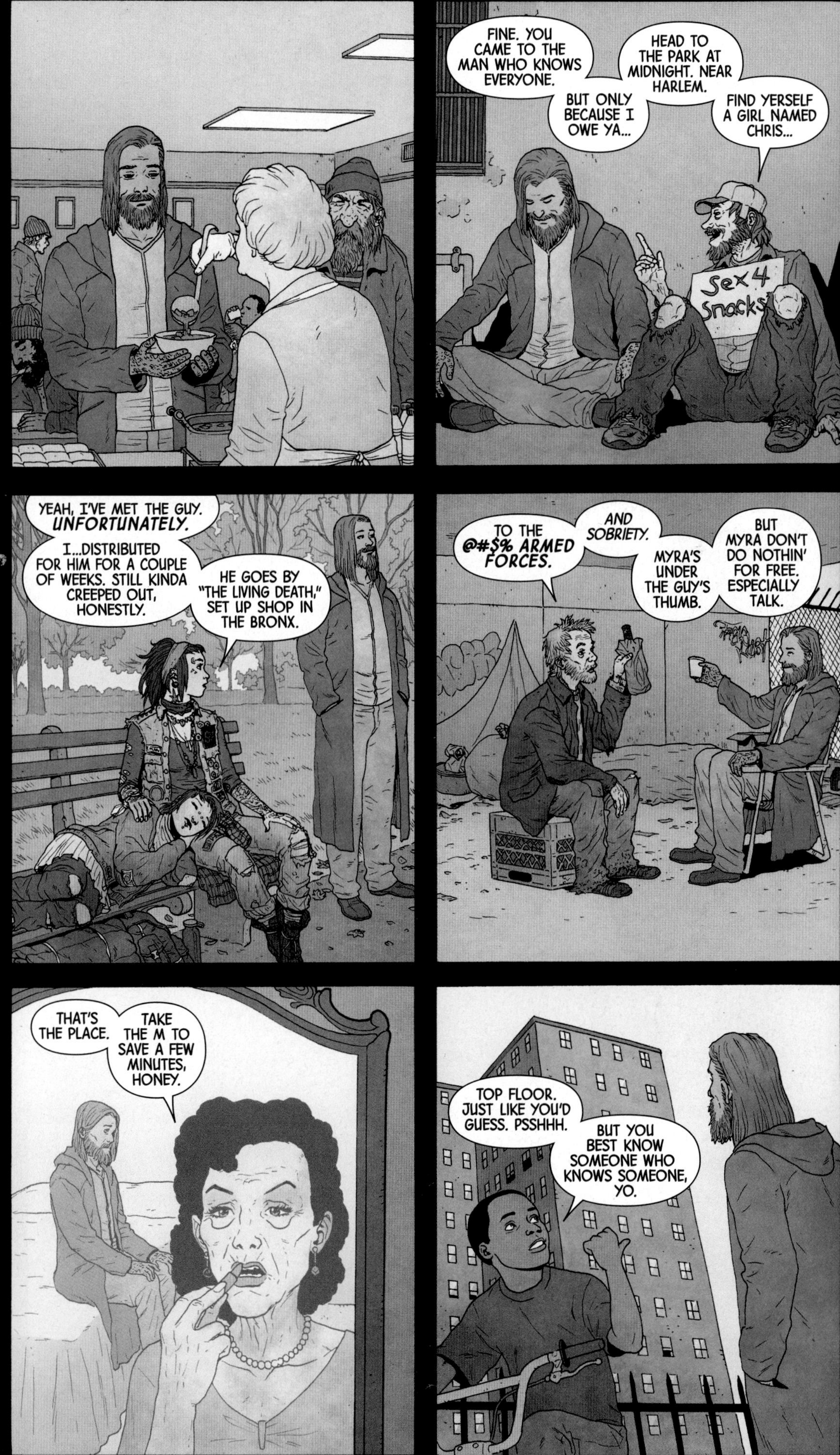

FINE. YOU CAME TO THE MAN WHO KNOWS EVERYONE.
BUT ONLY BECAUSE I OWE YA...
HEAD TO THE PARK AT MIDNIGHT. NEAR HARLEM.
FIND YERSELF A GIRL NAMED CHRIS...
Sex 4 Snacks
YEAH, I'VE MET THE GUY. UNFORTUNATELY.
I...DISTRIBUTED FOR HIM FOR A COUPLE OF WEEKS. STILL KINDA CREEPED OUT, HONESTLY.
HE GOES BY "THE LIVING DEATH," SET UP SHOP IN THE BRONX.
TO THE @#$% ARMED FORCES.
AND SOBRIETY.
MYRA'S UNDER THE GUY'S THUMB.
BUT MYRA DON'T DO NOTHIN' FOR FREE. ESPECIALLY TALK.
THAT'S THE PLACE.
TAKE THE M TO SAVE A FEW MINUTES, HONEY.
TOP FLOOR. JUST LIKE YOU'D GUESS. PSSHHH.
BUT YOU BEST KNOW SOMEONE WHO KNOWS SOMEONE, YO.

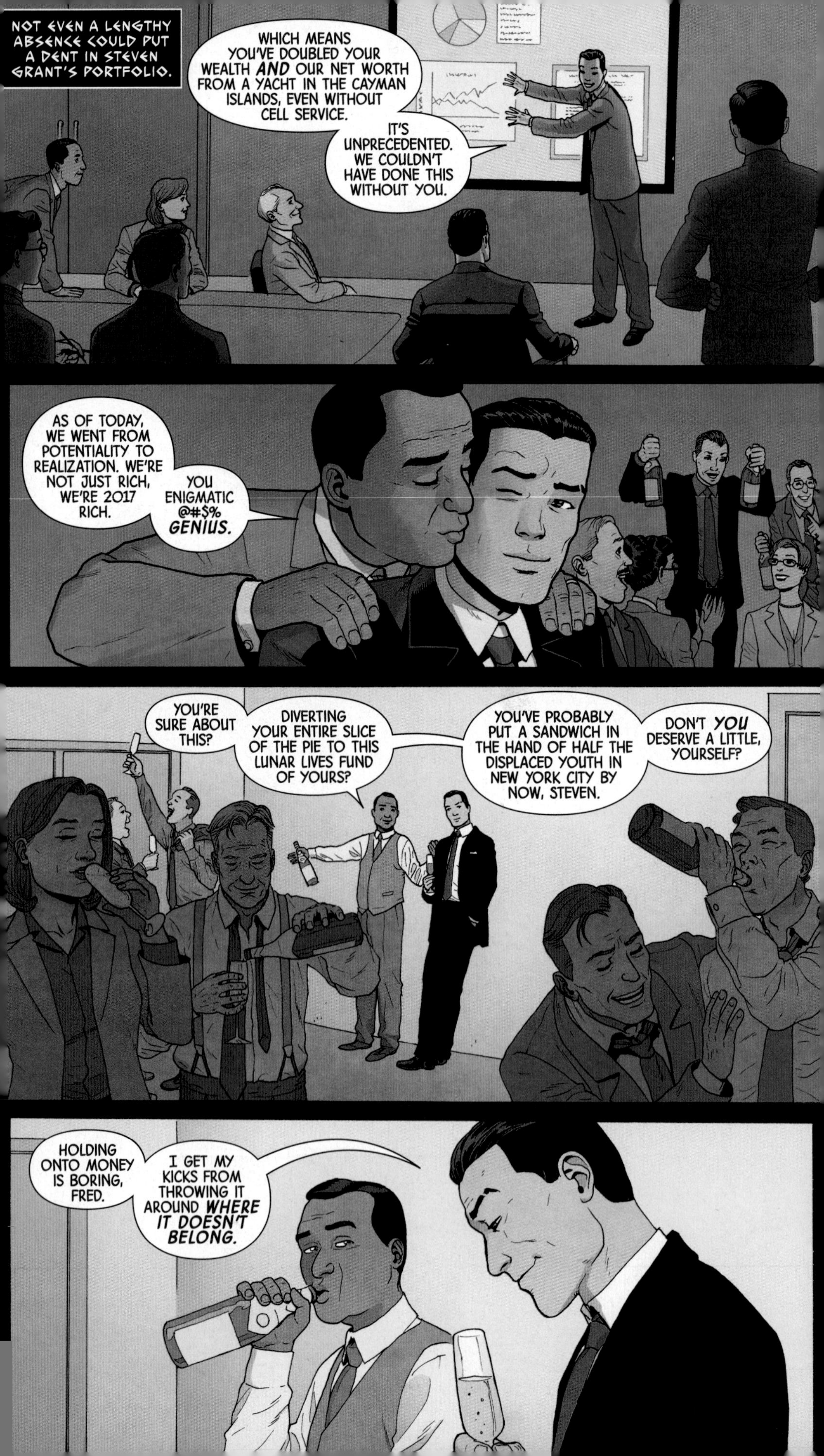
NOT EVEN A LENGTHY ABSENCE COULD PUT A DENT IN STEVEN GRANT'S PORTFOLIO.
WHICH MEANS YOU'VE DOUBLED YOUR WEALTH AND OUR NET WORTH FROM A YACHT IN THE CAYMAN ISLANDS, EVEN WITHOUT CELL SERVICE.
IT'S UNPRECEDENTED. WE COULDN'T HAVE DONE THIS WITHOUT YOU.
AS OF TODAY, WE WENT FROM POTENTIALITY TO REALIZATION. WE'RE NOT JUST RICH, WE'RE 2017 RICH.
YOU ENIGMATIC @#$% GENIUS.
YOU'RE SURE ABOUT THIS?
DIVERTING YOUR ENTIRE SLICE OF THE PIE TO THIS LUNAR LIVES FUND OF YOURS?
YOU'VE PROBABLY PUT A SANDWICH IN THE HAND OF HALF THE DISPLACED YOUTH IN NEW YORK CITY BY NOW, STEVEN.
DON'T YOU DESERVE A LITTLE, YOURSELF?
HOLDING ONTO MONEY IS BORING, FRED.
I GET MY KICKS FROM THROWING IT AROUND WHERE IT DOESN'T BELONG.

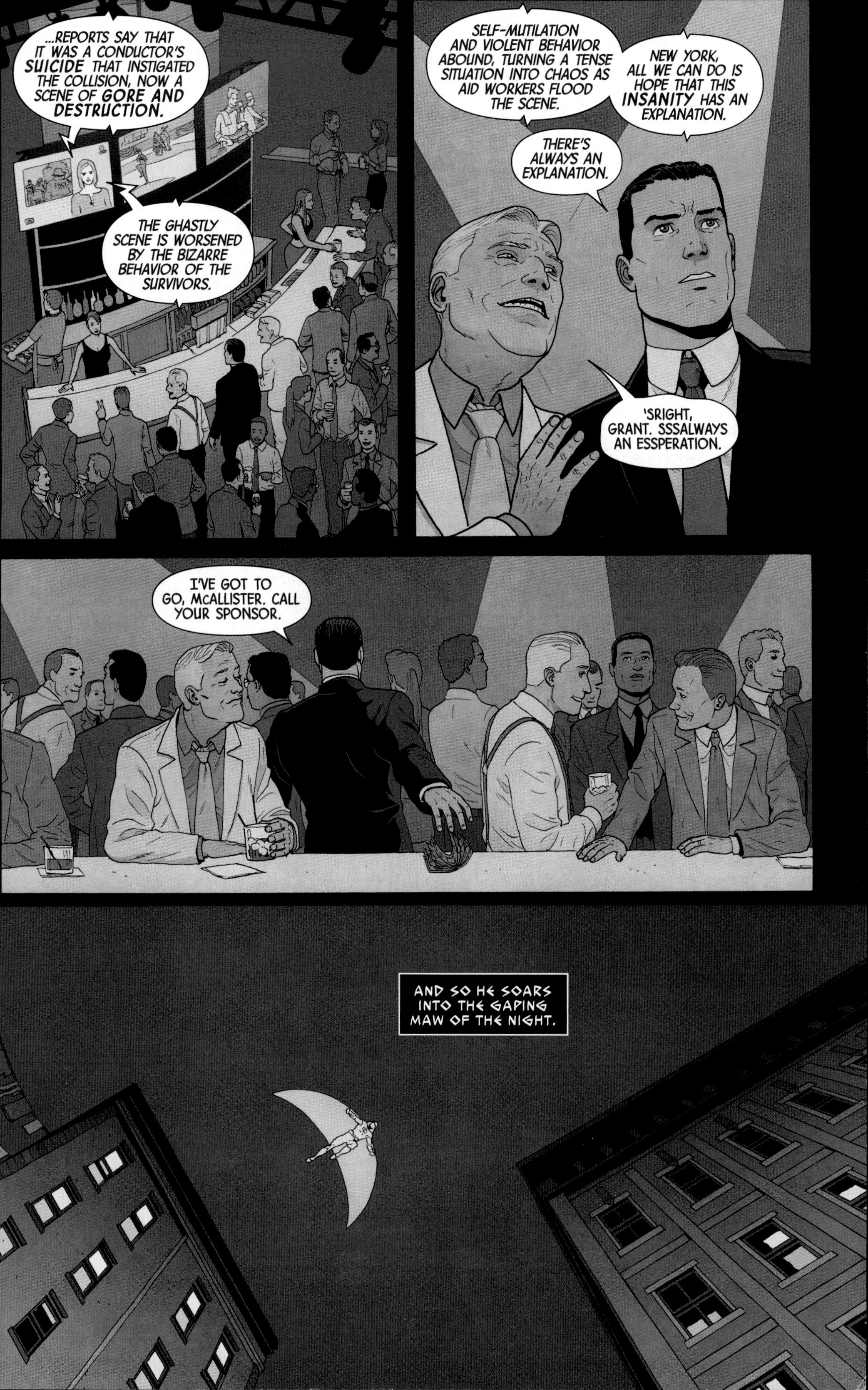
...REPORTS SAY THAT IT WAS A CONDUCTOR'S SUICIDE THAT INSTIGATED THE COLLISION, NOW A SCENE OF GORE AND DESTRUCTION.
THE GHASTLY SCENE IS WORSENED BY THE BIZARRE BEHAVIOR OF THE SURVIVORS.
SELF-MUTILATION AND VIOLENT BEHAVIOR ABOUND, TURNING A TENSE SITUATION INTO CHAOS AS AID WORKERS FLOOD THE SCENE.
NEW YORK, ALL WE CAN DO IS HOPE THAT THIS INSANITY HAS AN EXPLANATION.
THERE'S ALWAYS AN EXPLANATION.
'SRIGHT, GRANT. SSSALWAYS AN ESSPERATION.
I'VE GOT TO GO, McALLISTER. CALL YOUR SPONSOR.
AND SO HE SOARS INTO THE GAPING MAW OF THE NIGHT.

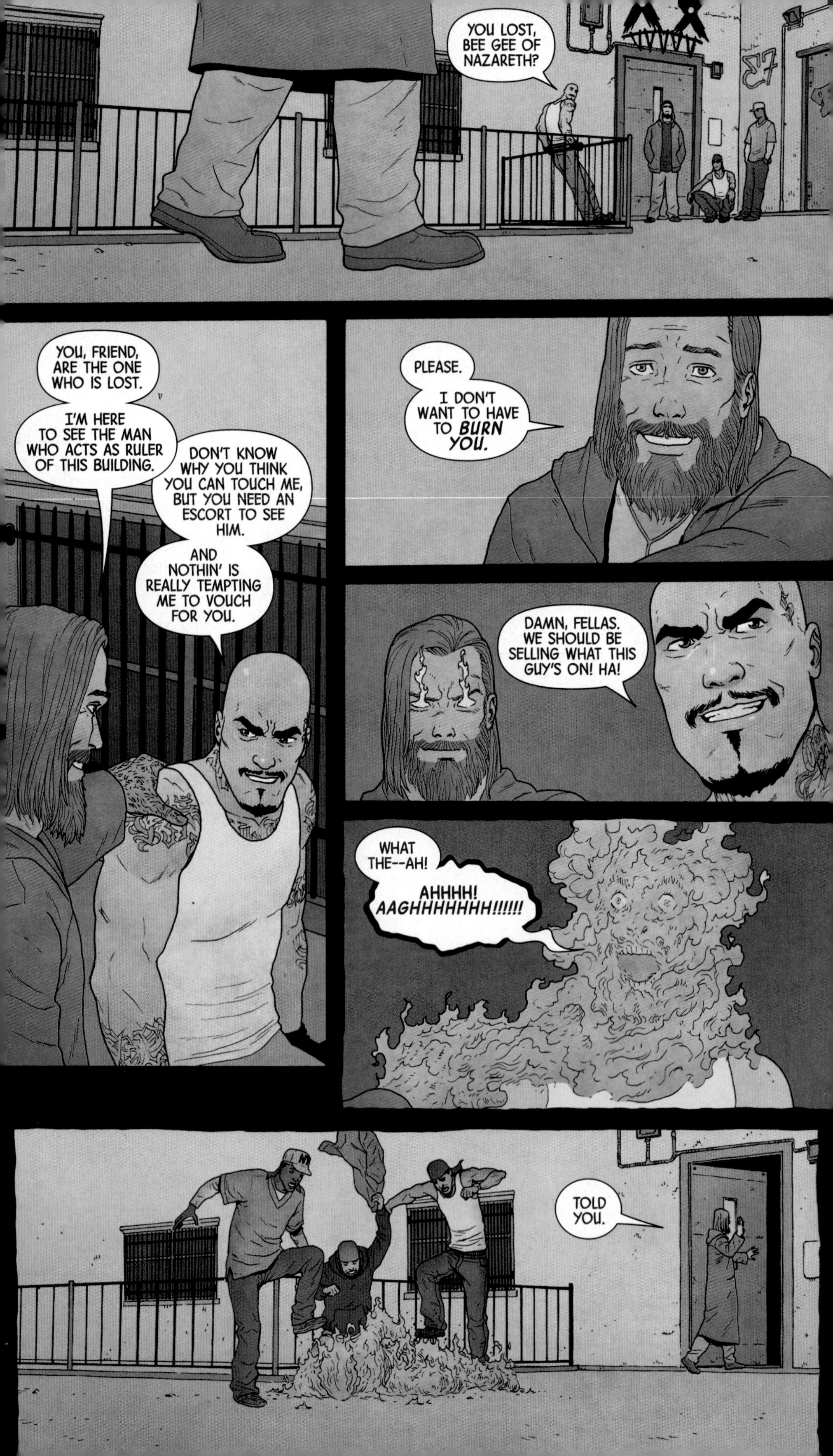
YOU LOST, BEE GEE OF NAZARETH?
YOU, FRIEND, ARE THE ONE WHO IS LOST.
I'M HERE TO SEE THE MAN WHO ACTS AS RULER OF THIS BUILDING.
DON'T KNOW WHY YOU THINK YOU CAN TOUCH ME, BUT YOU NEED AN ESCORT TO SEE HIM.
AND NOTHIN' IS REALLY TEMPTING ME TO VOUCH FOR YOU.
PLEASE.
I DON'T WANT TO HAVE TO **BURN YOU.**
DAMN, FELLAS. WE SHOULD BE SELLING WHAT THIS GUY'S ON! HA!
WHAT THE--AH!
AHHHH! AAGHHHHHHHH!!!!!!
TOLD YOU.

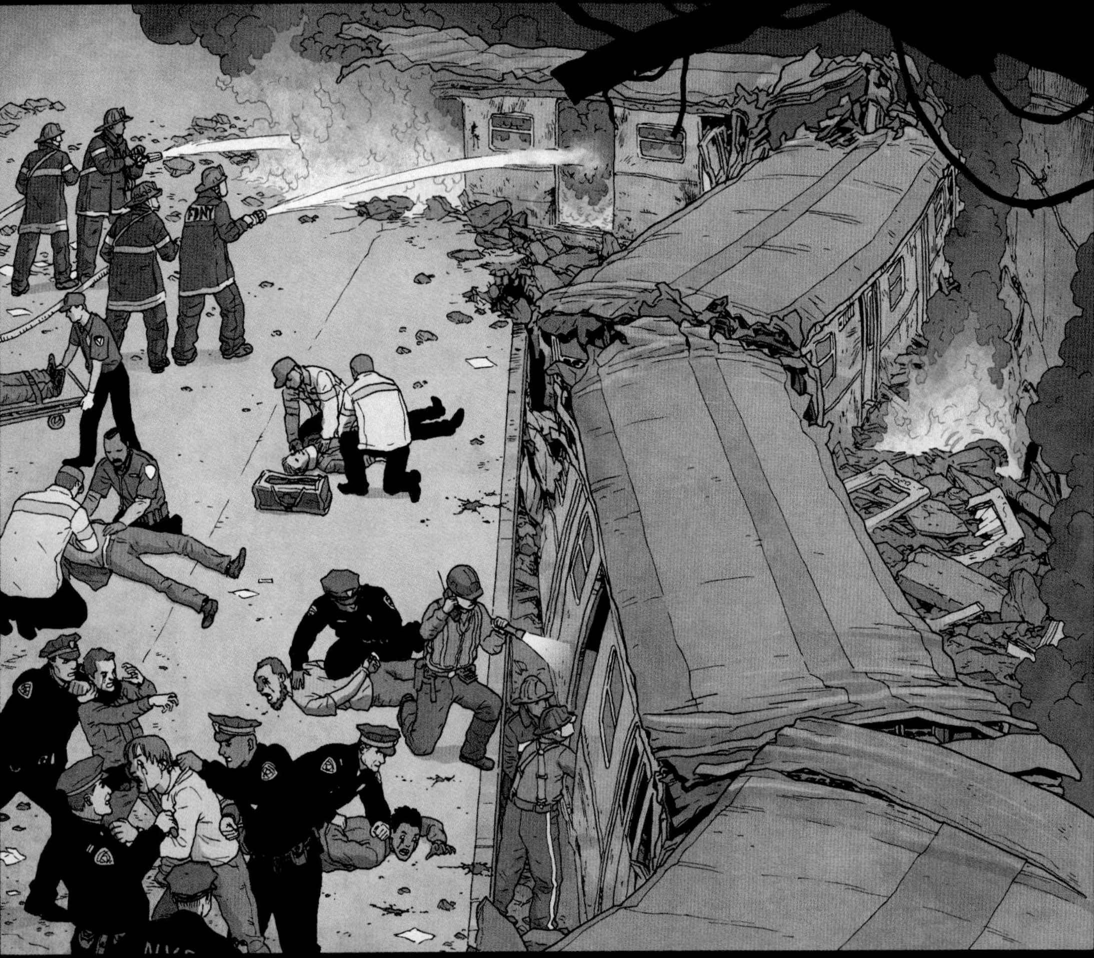
FDNY

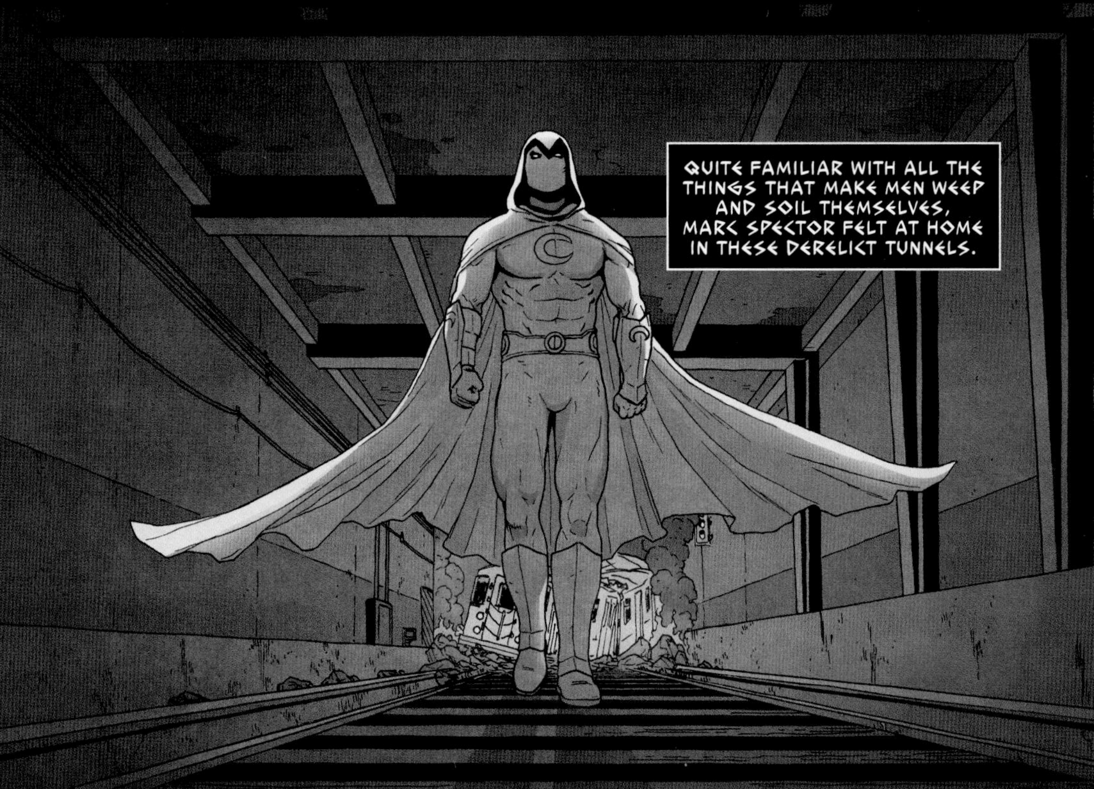
QUITE FAMILIAR WITH ALL THE THINGS THAT MAKE MEN WEEP AND SOIL THEMSELVES, MARC SPECTOR FELT AT HOME IN THESE DERELICT TUNNELS.

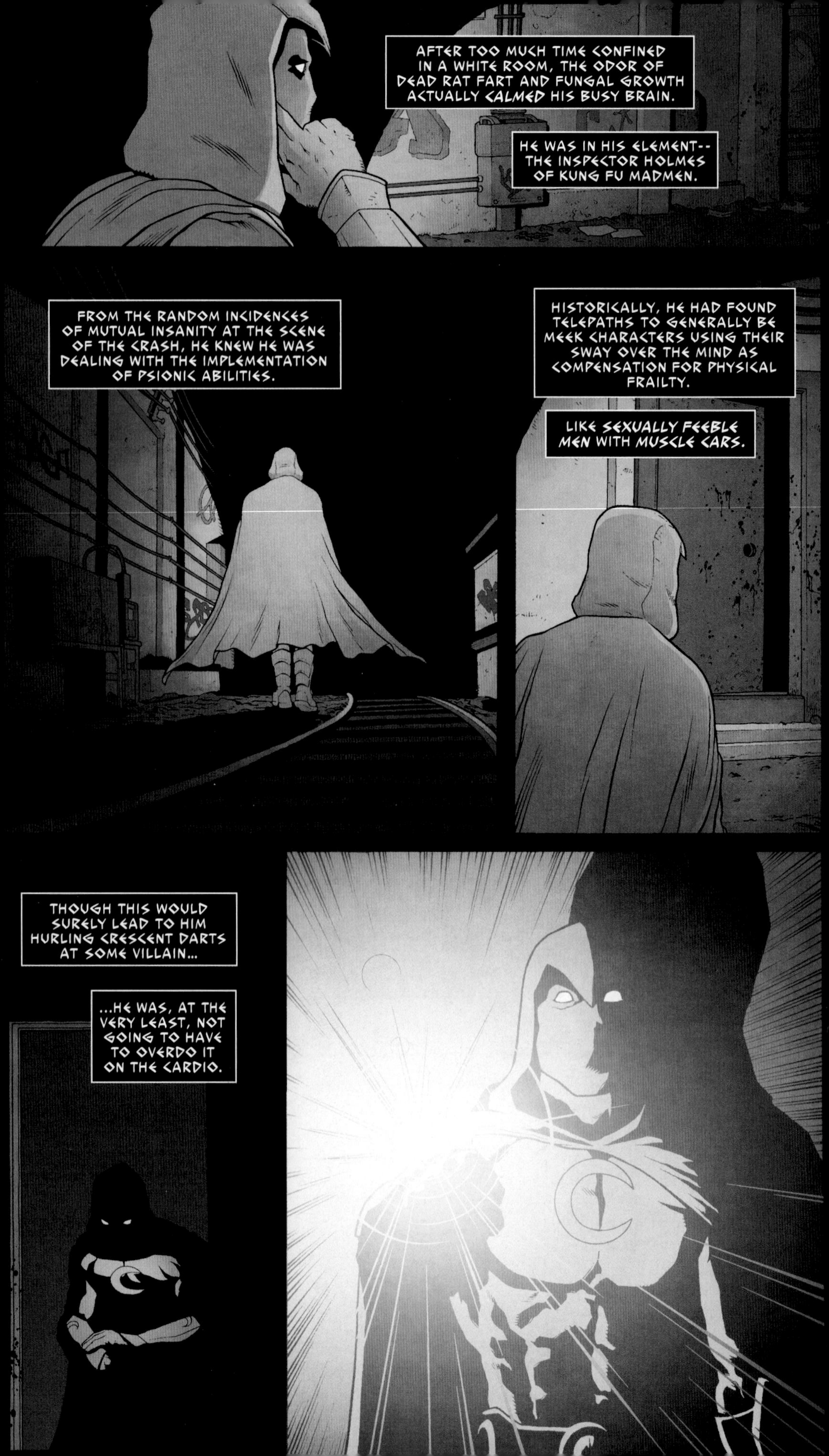
AFTER TOO MUCH TIME CONFINED IN A WHITE ROOM, THE ODOR OF DEAD RAT FART AND FUNGAL GROWTH ACTUALLY CALMED HIS BUSY BRAIN.
HE WAS IN HIS ELEMENT-- THE INSPECTOR HOLMES OF KUNG FU MADMEN.
FROM THE RANDOM INCIDENCES OF MUTUAL INSANITY AT THE SCENE OF THE CRASH, HE KNEW HE WAS DEALING WITH THE IMPLEMENTATION OF PSIONIC ABILITIES.
HISTORICALLY, HE HAD FOUND TELEPATHS TO GENERALLY BE MEEK CHARACTERS USING THEIR SWAY OVER THE MIND AS COMPENSATION FOR PHYSICAL FRAILTY.
LIKE SEXUALLY FEEBLE MEN WITH MUSCLE CARS.
THOUGH THIS WOULD SURELY LEAD TO HIM HURLING CRESCENT DARTS AT SOME VILLAIN...
...HE WAS, AT THE VERY LEAST, NOT GOING TO HAVE TO OVERDO IT ON THE CARDIO.

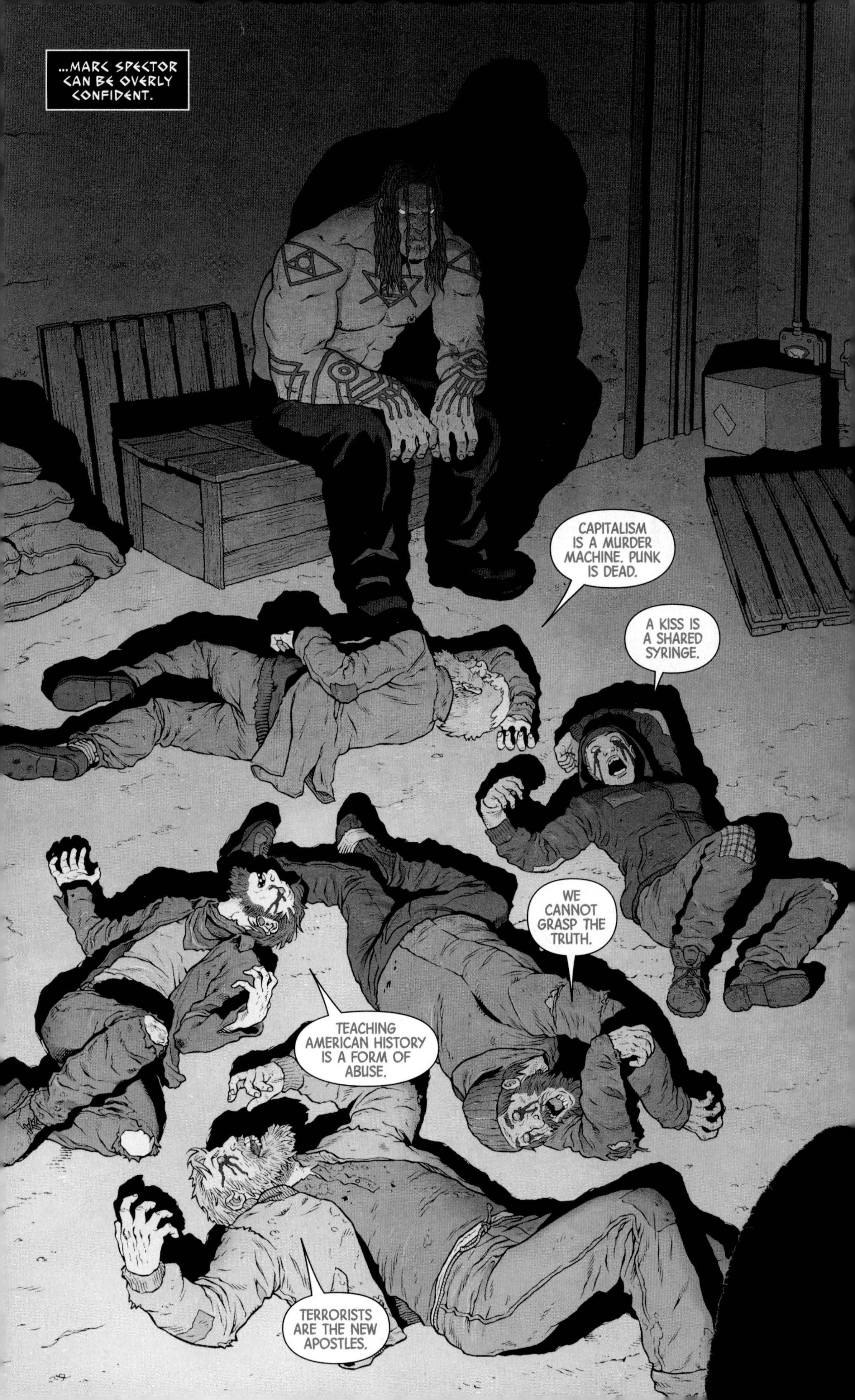
...MARC SPECTOR CAN BE OVERLY CONFIDENT.
CAPITALISM IS A MURDER MACHINE. PUNK IS DEAD.
A KISS IS A SHARED SYRINGE.
WE CANNOT GRASP THE TRUTH.
TEACHING AMERICAN HISTORY IS A FORM OF ABUSE.
TERRORISTS ARE THE NEW APOSTLES.

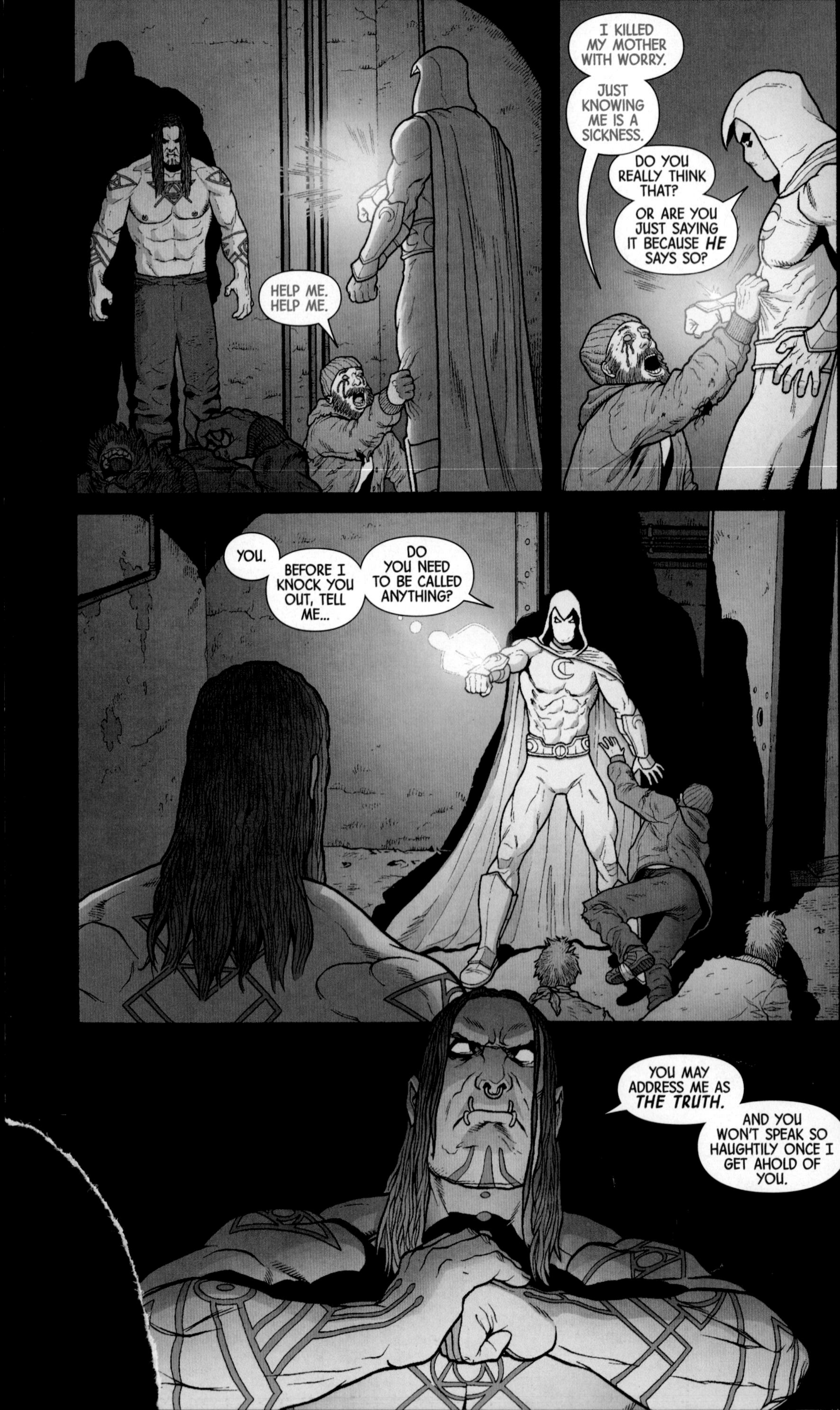
HELP ME. HELP ME.
I KILLED MY MOTHER WITH WORRY.
JUST KNOWING ME IS A SICKNESS.
DO YOU REALLY THINK THAT?
OR ARE YOU JUST SAYING IT BECAUSE *HE* SAYS SO?
YOU.
BEFORE I KNOCK YOU OUT, TELL ME...
DO YOU NEED TO BE CALLED ANYTHING?
YOU MAY ADDRESS ME AS *THE TRUTH.*
AND YOU WON'T SPEAK SO HAUGHTILY ONCE I GET AHOLD OF YOU.

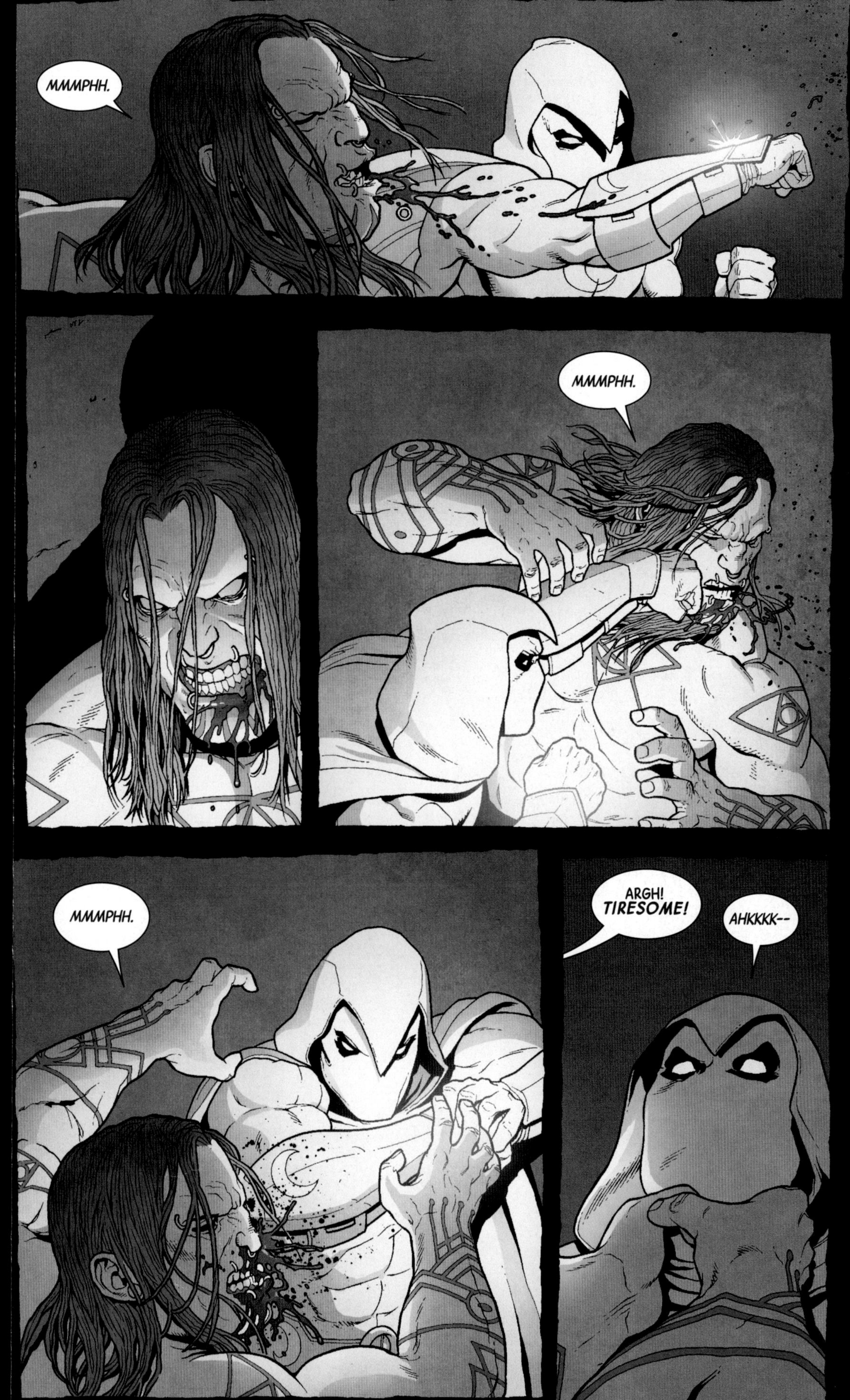
MMMPHH.
MMMPHH.
MMMPHH.
ARGH! TIRESOME!
AHKKKK--

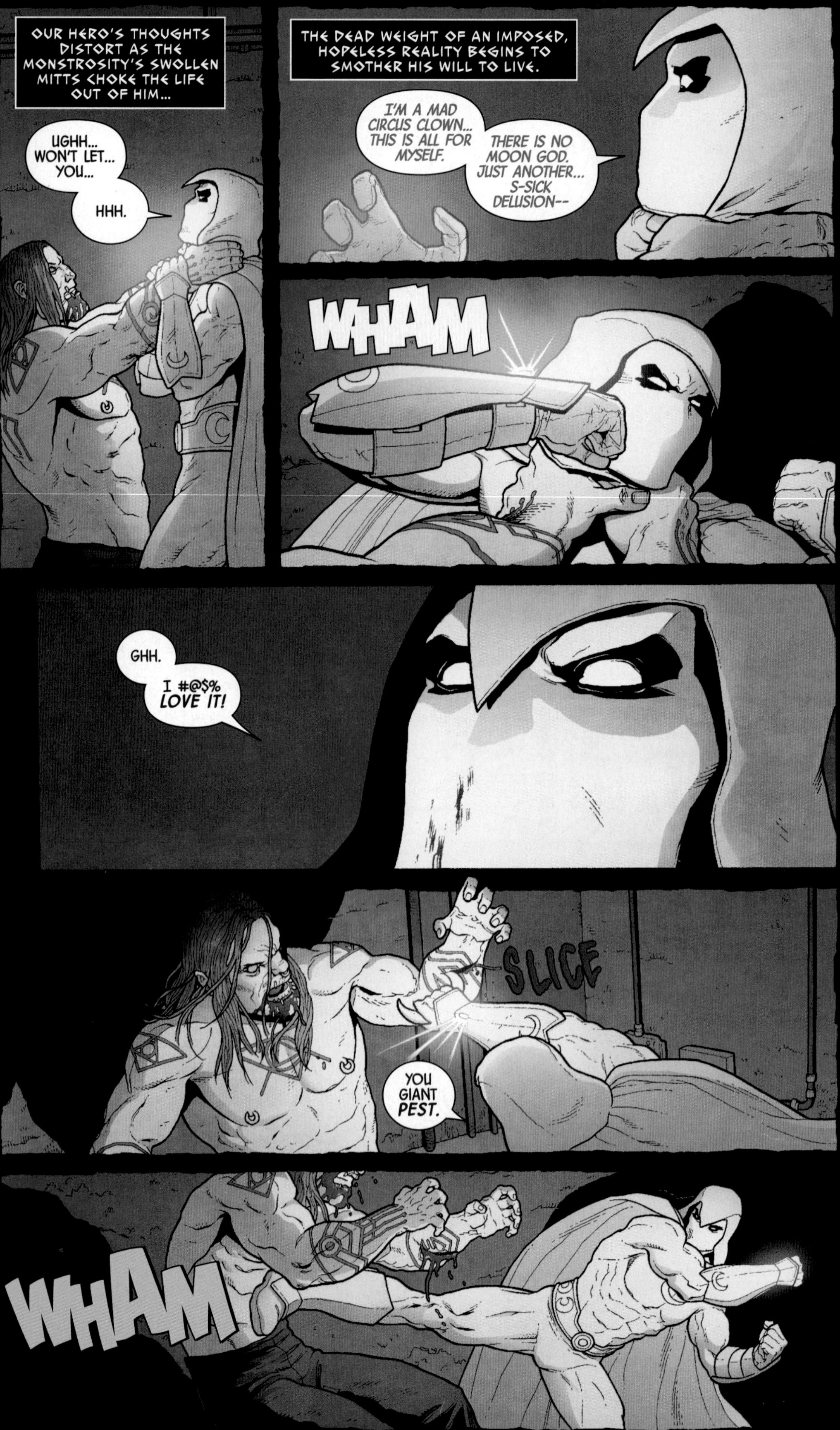
OUR HERO'S THOUGHTS DISTORT AS THE MONSTROSITY'S SWOLLEN MITTS CHOKE THE LIFE OUT OF HIM...
UGHH... WON'T LET... YOU...
HHH.
THE DEAD WEIGHT OF AN IMPOSED, HOPELESS REALITY BEGINS TO SMOTHER HIS WILL TO LIVE.
I'M A MAD CIRCUS CLOWN... THIS IS ALL FOR MYSELF.
THERE IS NO MOON GOD. JUST ANOTHER... S-SICK DELUSION--
WHAM
GHH.
I #@$% LOVE IT!
SLICE
YOU GIANT PEST.
WHAM

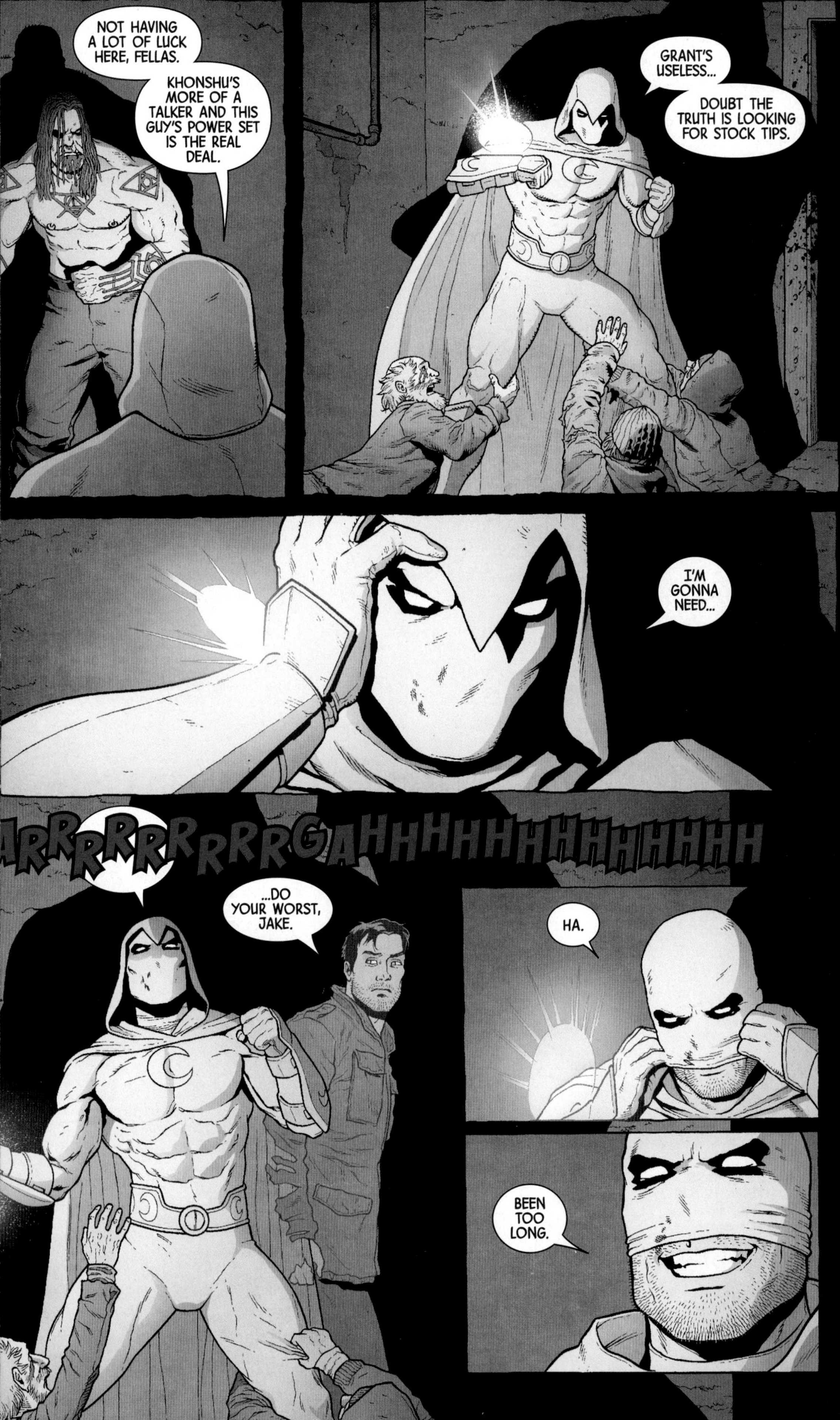
NOT HAVING A LOT OF LUCK HERE, FELLAS.
KHONSHU'S MORE OF A TALKER AND THIS GUY'S POWER SET IS THE REAL DEAL.
GRANT'S USELESS...
DOUBT THE TRUTH IS LOOKING FOR STOCK TIPS.
I'M GONNA NEED...
ARRRRRRRRRRGAHHHHHHHHHHHHHH
...DO YOUR WORST, JAKE.
HA.
BEEN TOO LONG.

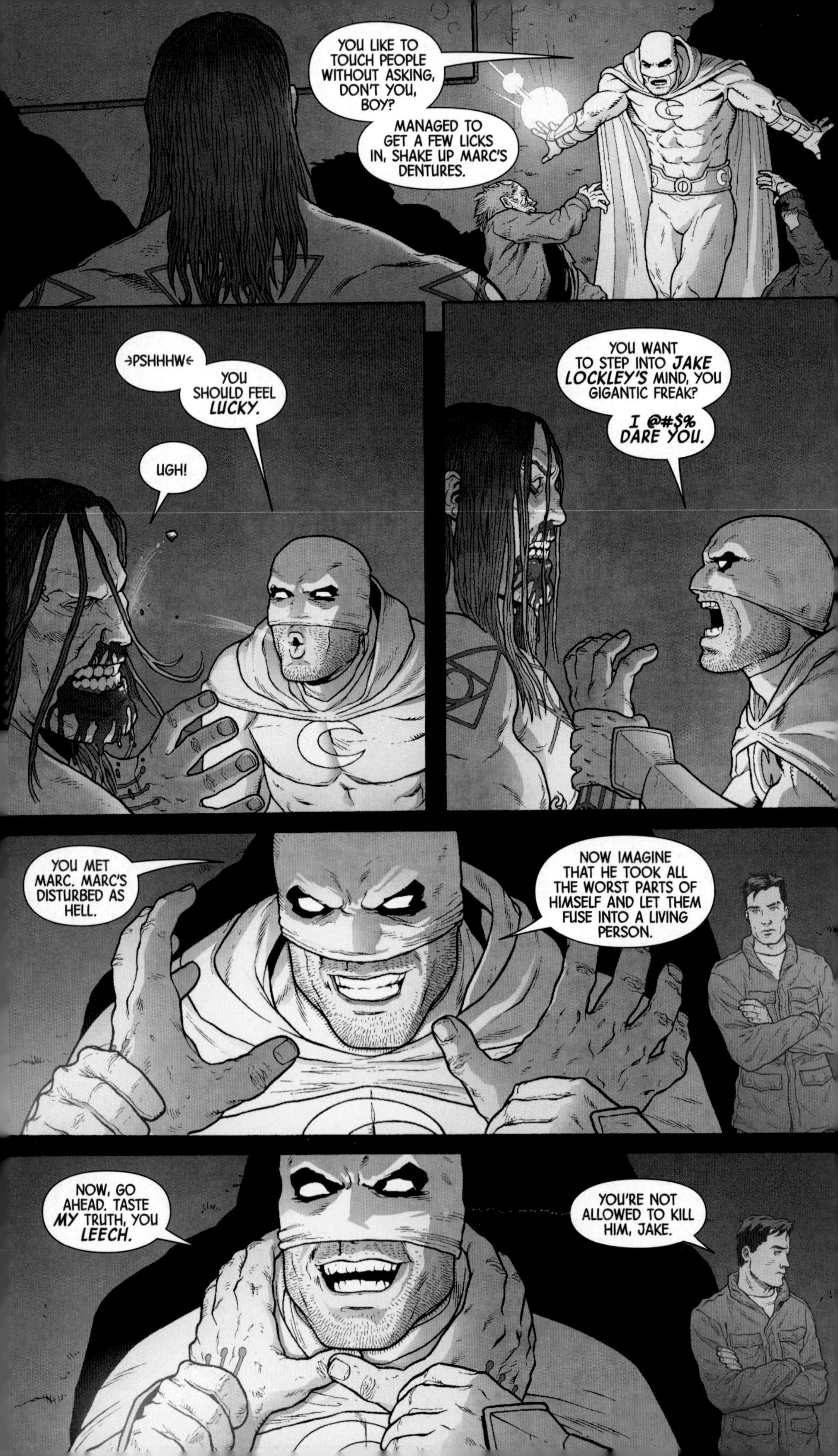

YOU LIKE TO TOUCH PEOPLE WITHOUT ASKING, DON'T YOU, BOY?
MANAGED TO GET A FEW LICKS IN, SHAKE UP MARC'S DENTURES.
→PSHHHW←
YOU SHOULD FEEL LUCKY.
UGH!
YOU WANT TO STEP INTO JAKE LOCKLEY'S MIND, YOU GIGANTIC FREAK?
I @#$% DARE YOU.
YOU MET MARC. MARC'S DISTURBED AS HELL.
NOW IMAGINE THAT HE TOOK ALL THE WORST PARTS OF HIMSELF AND LET THEM FUSE INTO A LIVING PERSON.
NOW, GO AHEAD. TASTE MY TRUTH, YOU LEECH.
YOU'RE NOT ALLOWED TO KILL HIM, JAKE.

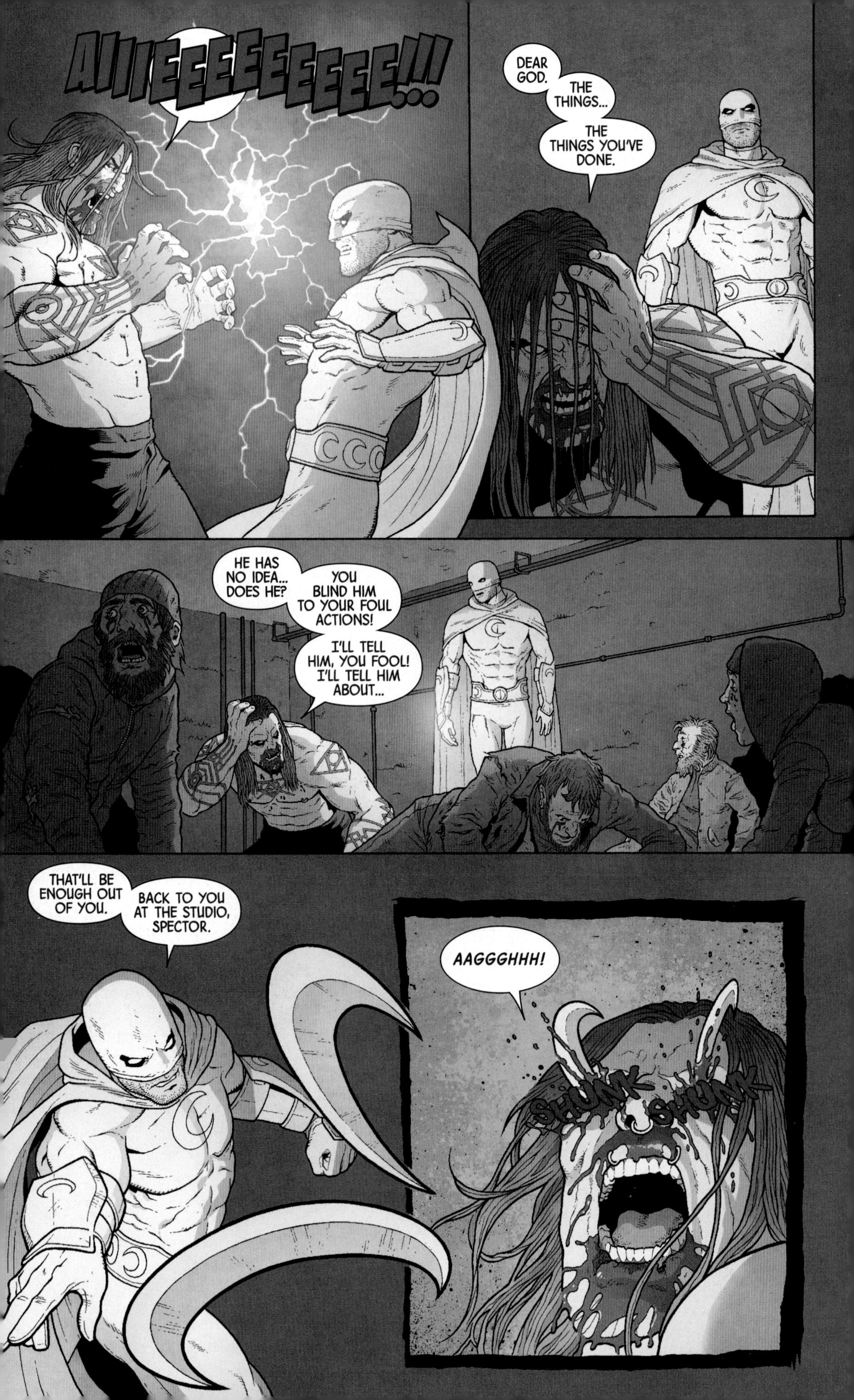
AIIIEEEEEEEEEE!!!...
DEAR GOD.
THE THINGS...
THE THINGS YOU'VE DONE.
HE HAS NO IDEA... DOES HE?
YOU BLIND HIM TO YOUR FOUL ACTIONS!
I'LL TELL HIM, YOU FOOL! I'LL TELL HIM ABOUT...
THAT'LL BE ENOUGH OUT OF YOU.
BACK TO YOU AT THE STUDIO, SPECTOR.
AAGGGHHH!
SHUNK
SHUNK

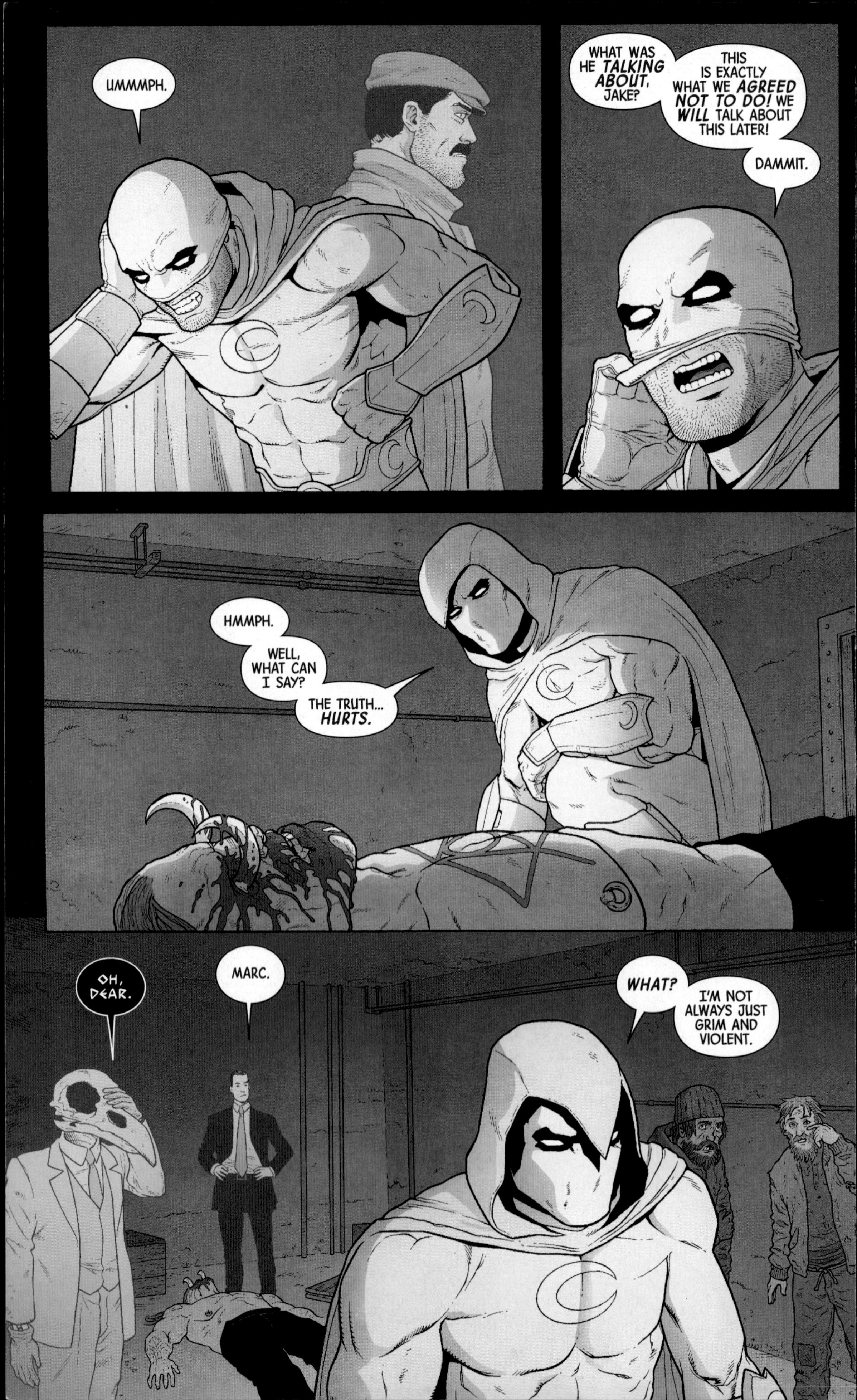
UMMMPH.
WHAT WAS HE TALKING ABOUT, JAKE?
THIS IS EXACTLY WHAT WE AGREED NOT TO DO! WE WILL TALK ABOUT THIS LATER!
DAMMIT.
HMMPH.
WELL, WHAT CAN I SAY?
THE TRUTH... HURTS.
OH, DEAR.
MARC.
WHAT?
I'M NOT ALWAYS JUST GRIM AND VIOLENT.

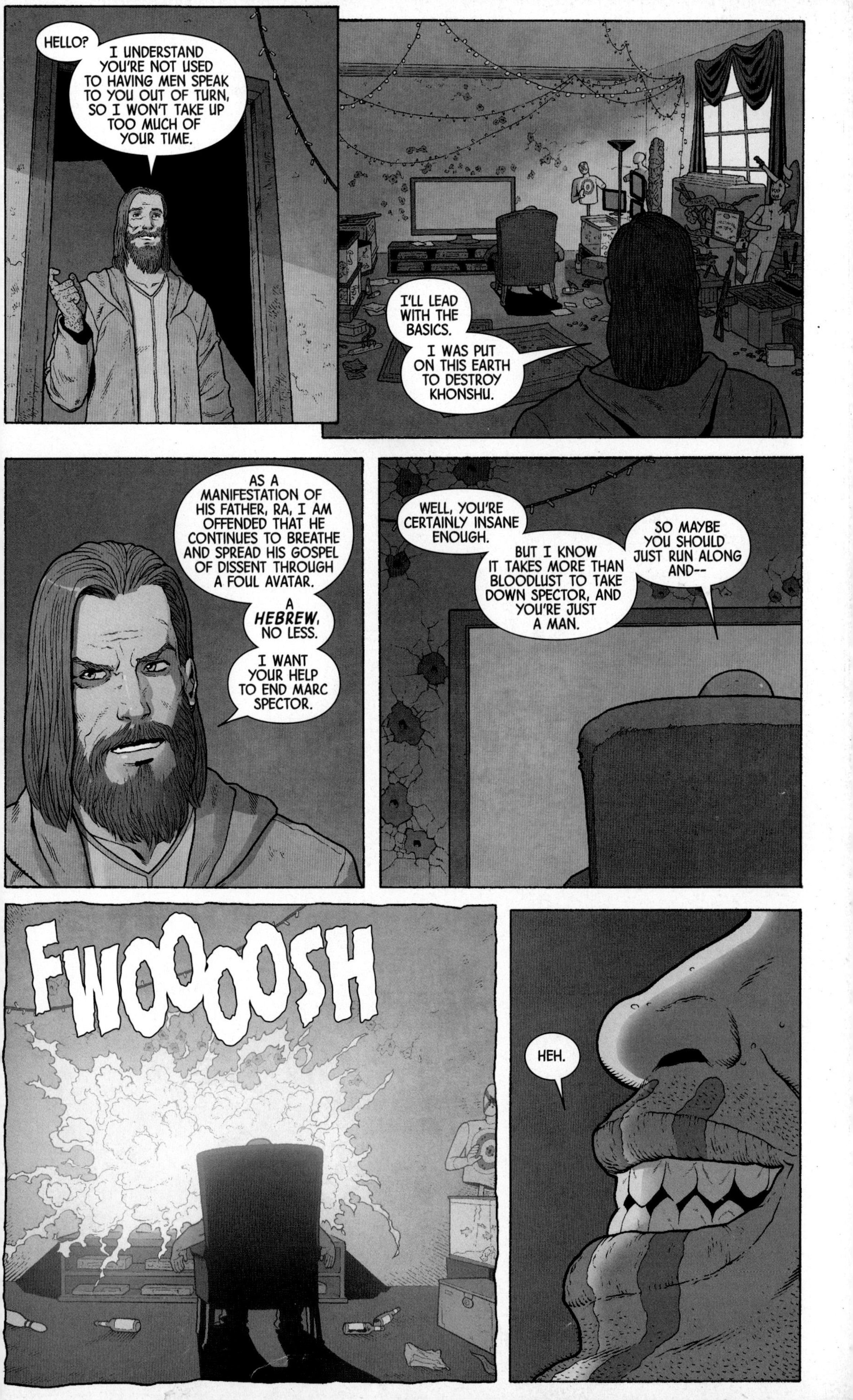
HELLO?
I UNDERSTAND YOU'RE NOT USED TO HAVING MEN SPEAK TO YOU OUT OF TURN, SO I WON'T TAKE UP TOO MUCH OF YOUR TIME.
I'LL LEAD WITH THE BASICS.
I WAS PUT ON THIS EARTH TO DESTROY KHONSHU.
AS A MANIFESTATION OF HIS FATHER, RA, I AM OFFENDED THAT HE CONTINUES TO BREATHE AND SPREAD HIS GOSPEL OF DISSENT THROUGH A FOUL AVATAR.
A *HEBREW*, NO LESS.
I WANT YOUR HELP TO END MARC SPECTOR.
WELL, YOU'RE CERTAINLY INSANE ENOUGH.
BUT I KNOW IT TAKES MORE THAN BLOODLUST TO TAKE DOWN SPECTOR, AND YOU'RE JUST A MAN.
SO MAYBE YOU SHOULD JUST RUN ALONG AND--
FWOOOOSH
HEH.

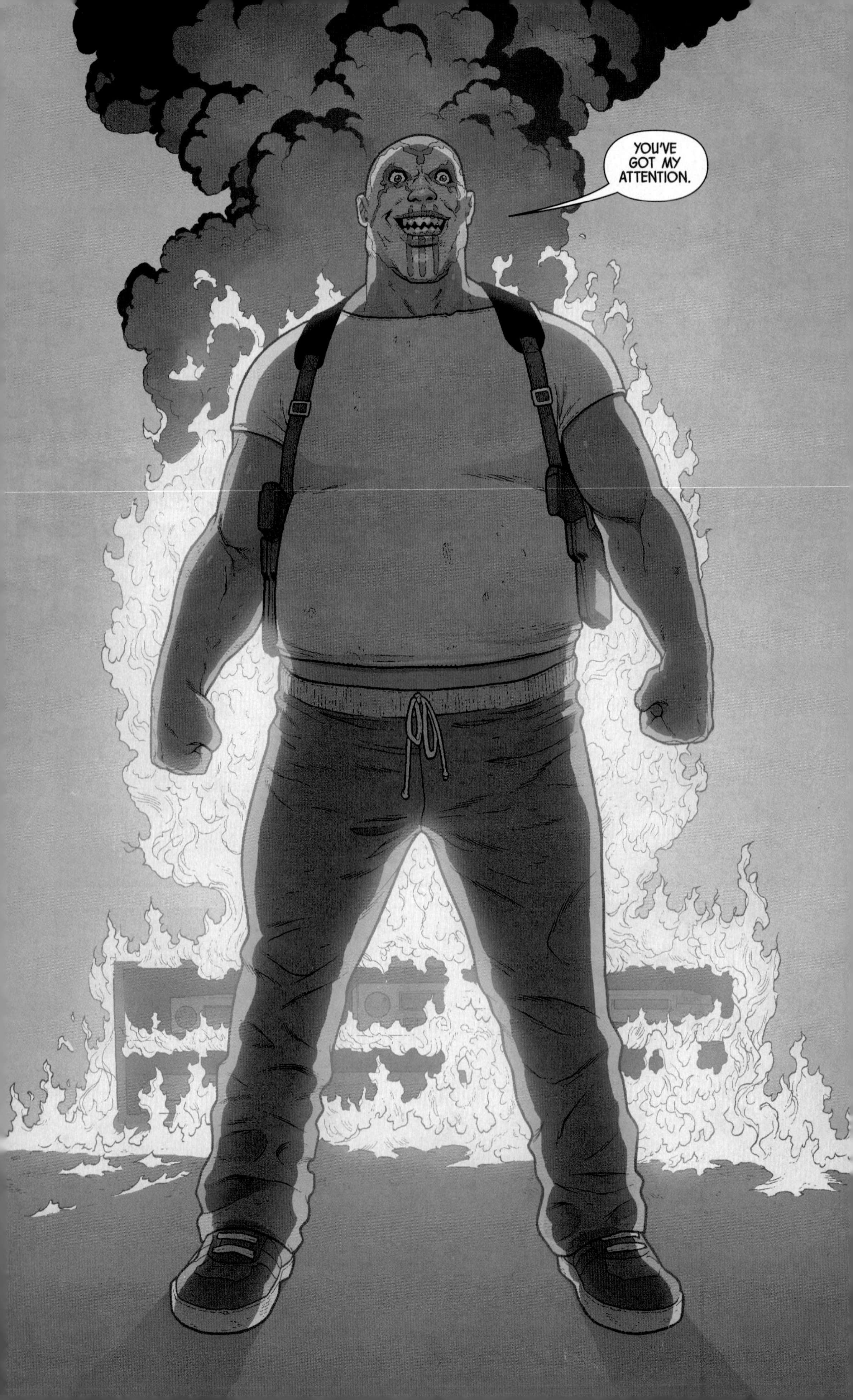
YOU'VE GOT MY ATTENTION.

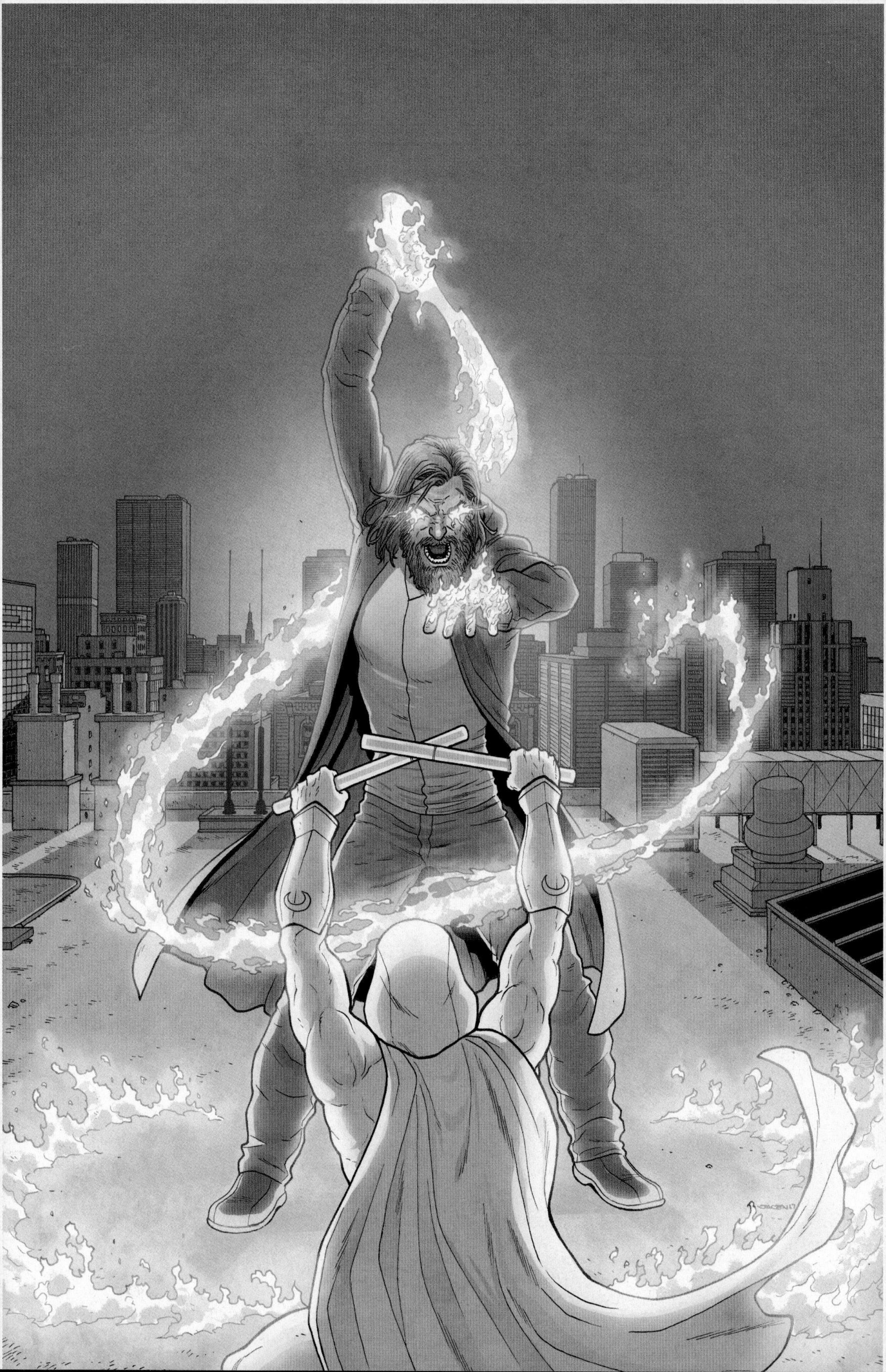

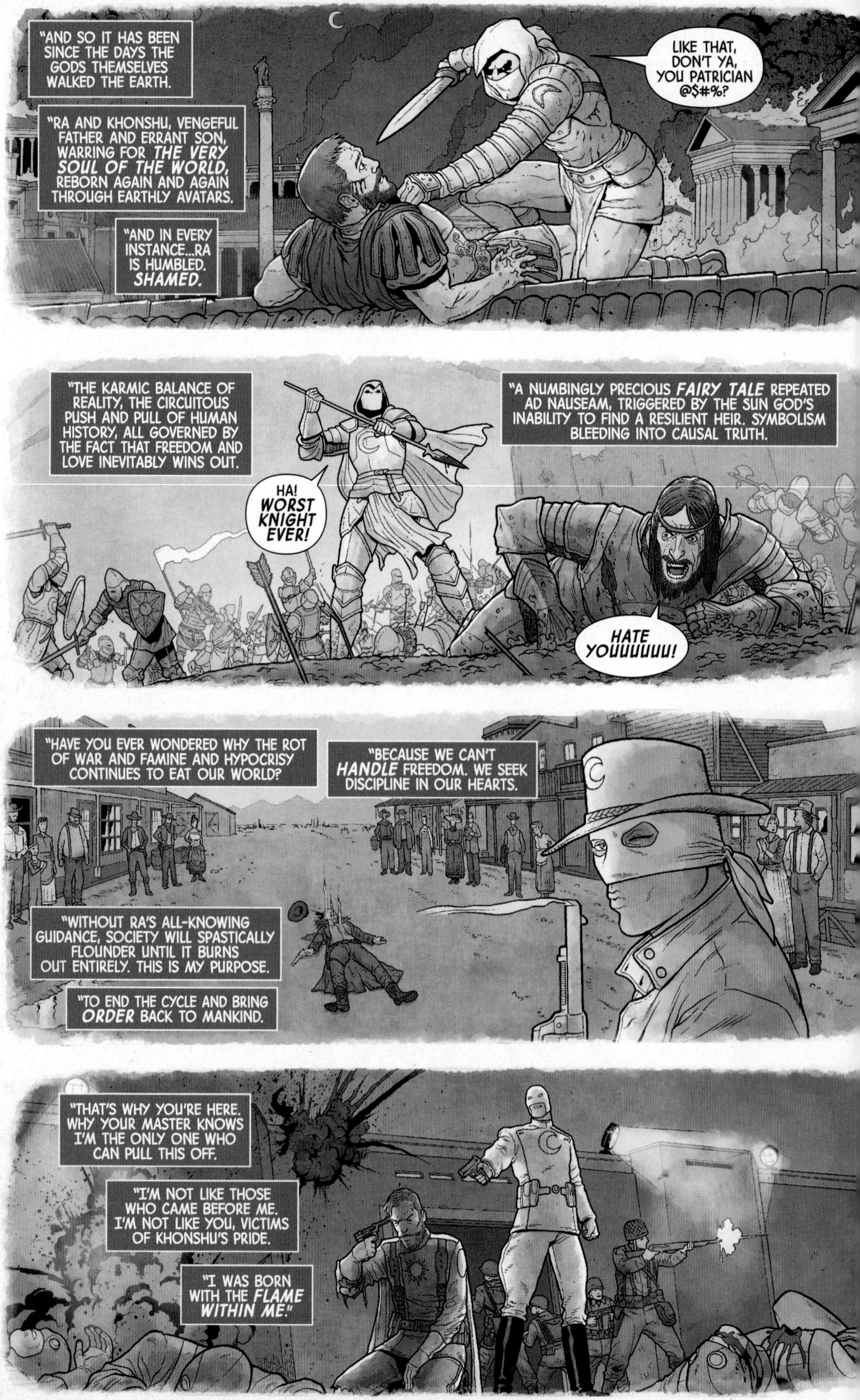
"AND SO IT HAS BEEN SINCE THE DAYS THE GODS THEMSELVES WALKED THE EARTH.
LIKE THAT, DON'T YA, YOU PATRICIAN @$#%?
"RA AND KHONSHU, VENGEFUL FATHER AND ERRANT SON, WARRING FOR THE VERY SOUL OF THE WORLD, REBORN AGAIN AND AGAIN THROUGH EARTHLY AVATARS.
"AND IN EVERY INSTANCE...RA IS HUMBLED. SHAMED.
"THE KARMIC BALANCE OF REALITY, THE CIRCUITOUS PUSH AND PULL OF HUMAN HISTORY, ALL GOVERNED BY THE FACT THAT FREEDOM AND LOVE INEVITABLY WINS OUT.
HA! WORST KNIGHT EVER!
"A NUMBINGLY PRECIOUS FAIRY TALE REPEATED AD NAUSEAM, TRIGGERED BY THE SUN GOD'S INABILITY TO FIND A RESILIENT HEIR. SYMBOLISM BLEEDING INTO CAUSAL TRUTH.
HATE YOUUUUUU!
"HAVE YOU EVER WONDERED WHY THE ROT OF WAR AND FAMINE AND HYPOCRISY CONTINUES TO EAT OUR WORLD?
"BECAUSE WE CAN'T HANDLE FREEDOM. WE SEEK DISCIPLINE IN OUR HEARTS.
"WITHOUT RA'S ALL-KNOWING GUIDANCE, SOCIETY WILL SPASTICALLY FLOUNDER UNTIL IT BURNS OUT ENTIRELY. THIS IS MY PURPOSE.
"TO END THE CYCLE AND BRING ORDER BACK TO MANKIND.
"THAT'S WHY YOU'RE HERE. WHY YOUR MASTER KNOWS I'M THE ONLY ONE WHO CAN PULL THIS OFF.
"I'M NOT LIKE THOSE WHO CAME BEFORE ME. I'M NOT LIKE YOU, VICTIMS OF KHONSHU'S PRIDE.
"I WAS BORN WITH THE FLAME WITHIN ME."

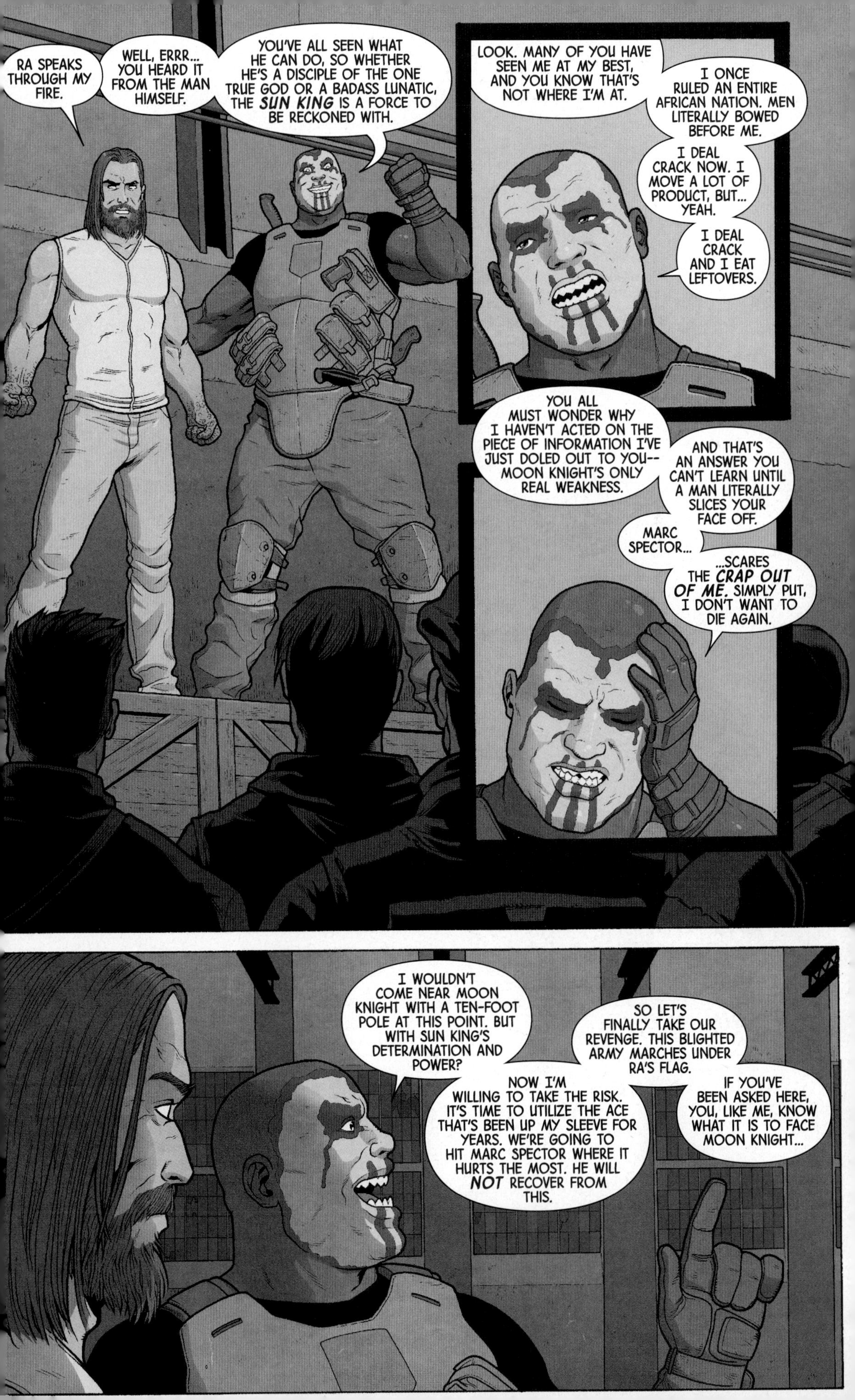
RA SPEAKS THROUGH MY FIRE.
WELL, ERRR... YOU HEARD IT FROM THE MAN HIMSELF.
YOU'VE ALL SEEN WHAT HE CAN DO, SO WHETHER HE'S A DISCIPLE OF THE ONE TRUE GOD OR A BADASS LUNATIC, THE SUN KING IS A FORCE TO BE RECKONED WITH.
LOOK. MANY OF YOU HAVE SEEN ME AT MY BEST, AND YOU KNOW THAT'S NOT WHERE I'M AT.
I ONCE RULED AN ENTIRE AFRICAN NATION. MEN LITERALLY BOWED BEFORE ME.
I DEAL CRACK NOW. I MOVE A LOT OF PRODUCT, BUT... YEAH.
I DEAL CRACK AND I EAT LEFTOVERS.
YOU ALL MUST WONDER WHY I HAVEN'T ACTED ON THE PIECE OF INFORMATION I'VE JUST DOLED OUT TO YOU-- MOON KNIGHT'S ONLY REAL WEAKNESS.
AND THAT'S AN ANSWER YOU CAN'T LEARN UNTIL A MAN LITERALLY SLICES YOUR FACE OFF.
MARC SPECTOR...
...SCARES THE CRAP OUT OF ME. SIMPLY PUT, I DON'T WANT TO DIE AGAIN.
I WOULDN'T COME NEAR MOON KNIGHT WITH A TEN-FOOT POLE AT THIS POINT. BUT WITH SUN KING'S DETERMINATION AND POWER?
NOW I'M WILLING TO TAKE THE RISK. IT'S TIME TO UTILIZE THE ACE THAT'S BEEN UP MY SLEEVE FOR YEARS. WE'RE GOING TO HIT MARC SPECTOR WHERE IT HURTS THE MOST. HE WILL NOT RECOVER FROM THIS.
SO LET'S FINALLY TAKE OUR REVENGE. THIS BLIGHTED ARMY MARCHES UNDER RA'S FLAG.
IF YOU'VE BEEN ASKED HERE, YOU, LIKE ME, KNOW WHAT IT IS TO FACE MOON KNIGHT...

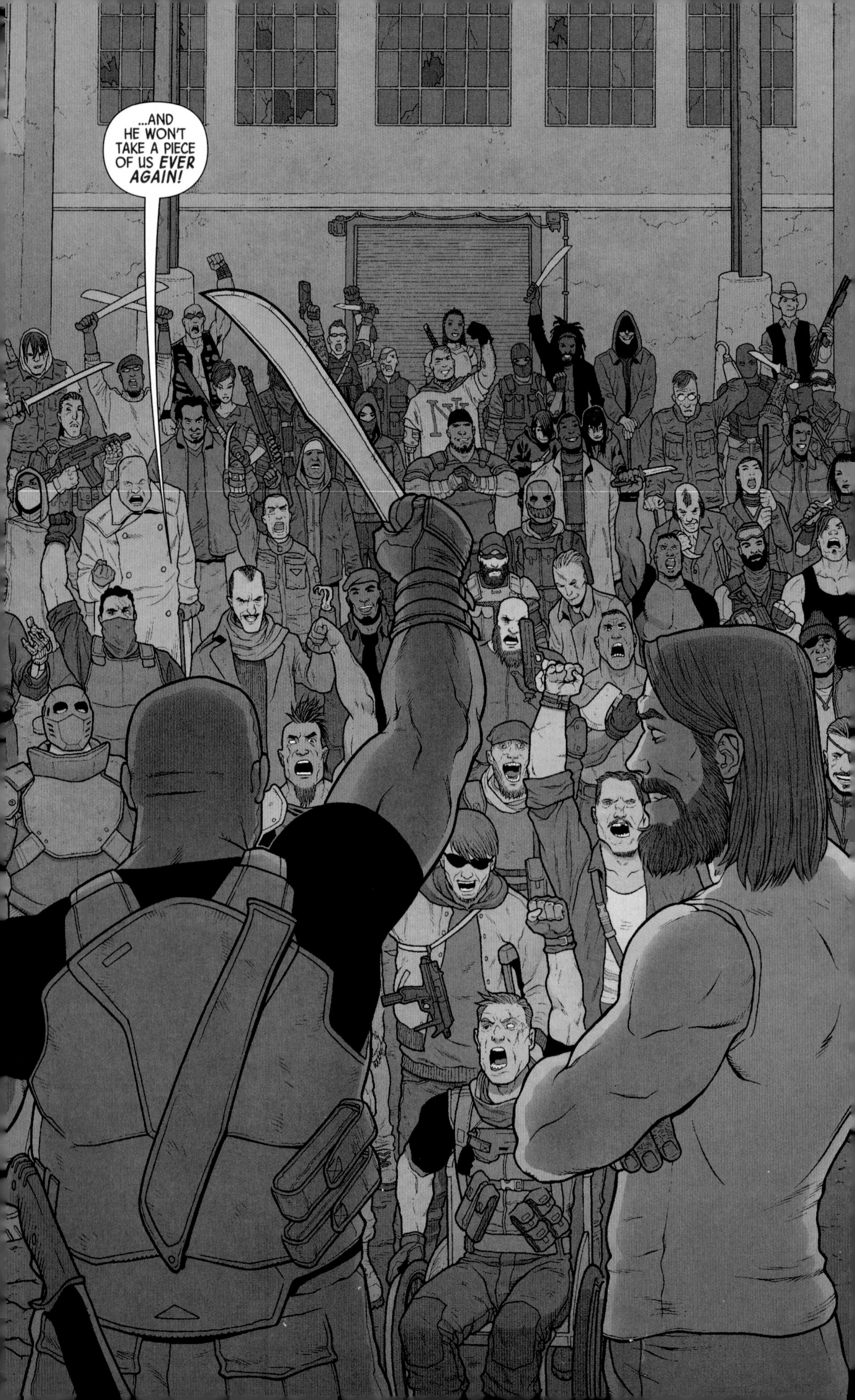
...AND HE WON'T TAKE A PIECE OF US EVER AGAIN!

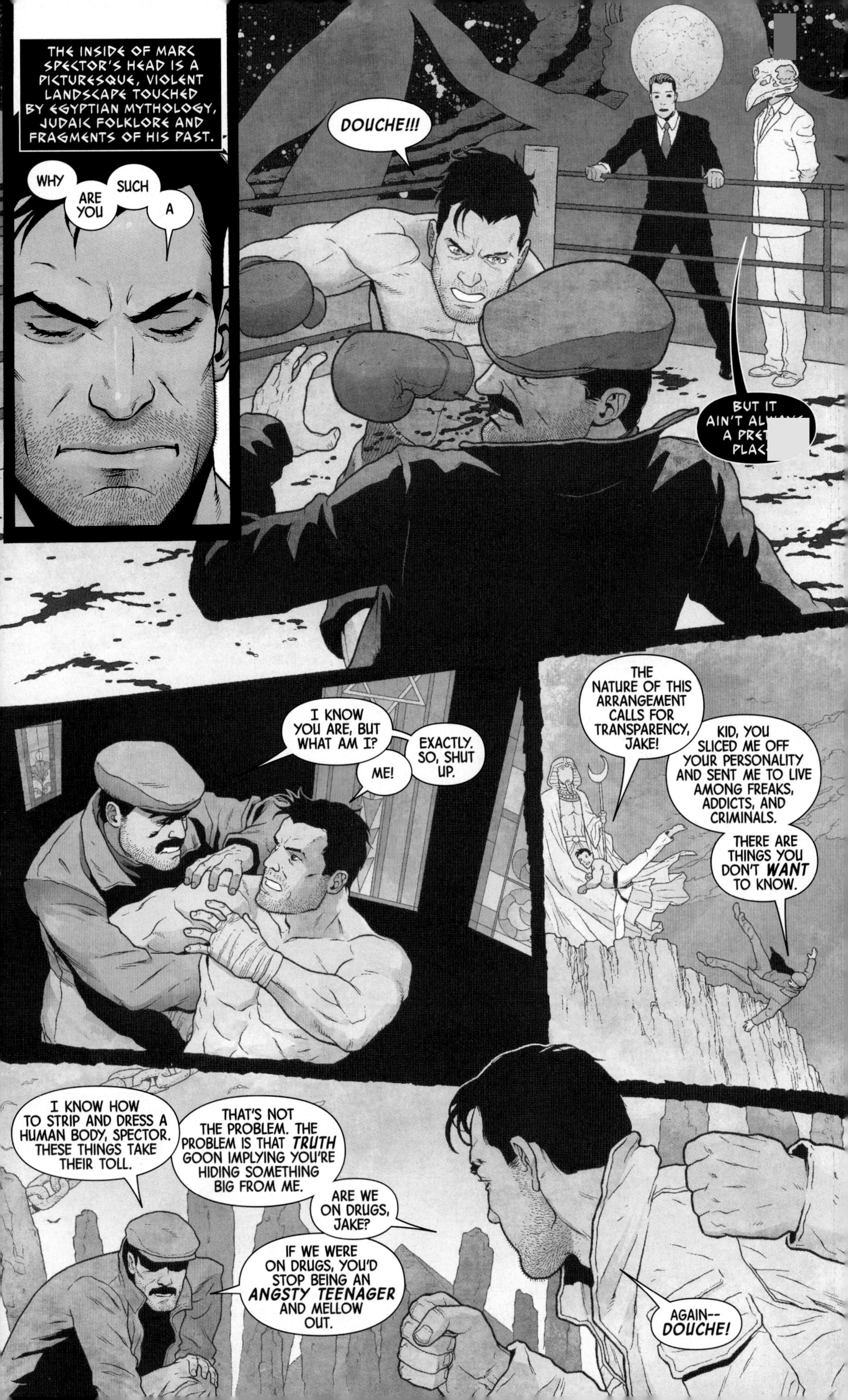
THE INSIDE OF MARC SPECTOR'S HEAD IS A PICTURESQUE, VIOLENT LANDSCAPE TOUCHED BY EGYPTIAN MYTHOLOGY, JUDAIC FOLKLORE AND FRAGMENTS OF HIS PAST.
WHY
ARE YOU
SUCH
A
DOUCHE!!!
BUT IT AIN'T ALW
A PRET
PLAC
I KNOW YOU ARE, BUT WHAT AM I?
ME!
EXACTLY. SO, SHUT UP.
THE NATURE OF THIS ARRANGEMENT CALLS FOR TRANSPARENCY, JAKE!
KID, YOU SLICED ME OFF YOUR PERSONALITY AND SENT ME TO LIVE AMONG FREAKS, ADDICTS, AND CRIMINALS.
THERE ARE THINGS YOU DON'T WANT TO KNOW.
I KNOW HOW TO STRIP AND DRESS A HUMAN BODY, SPECTOR. THESE THINGS TAKE THEIR TOLL.
THAT'S NOT THE PROBLEM. THE PROBLEM IS THAT TRUTH GOON IMPLYING YOU'RE HIDING SOMETHING BIG FROM ME.
ARE WE ON DRUGS, JAKE?
IF WE WERE ON DRUGS, YOU'D STOP BEING AN ANGSTY TEENAGER AND MELLOW OUT.
AGAIN-- DOUCHE!

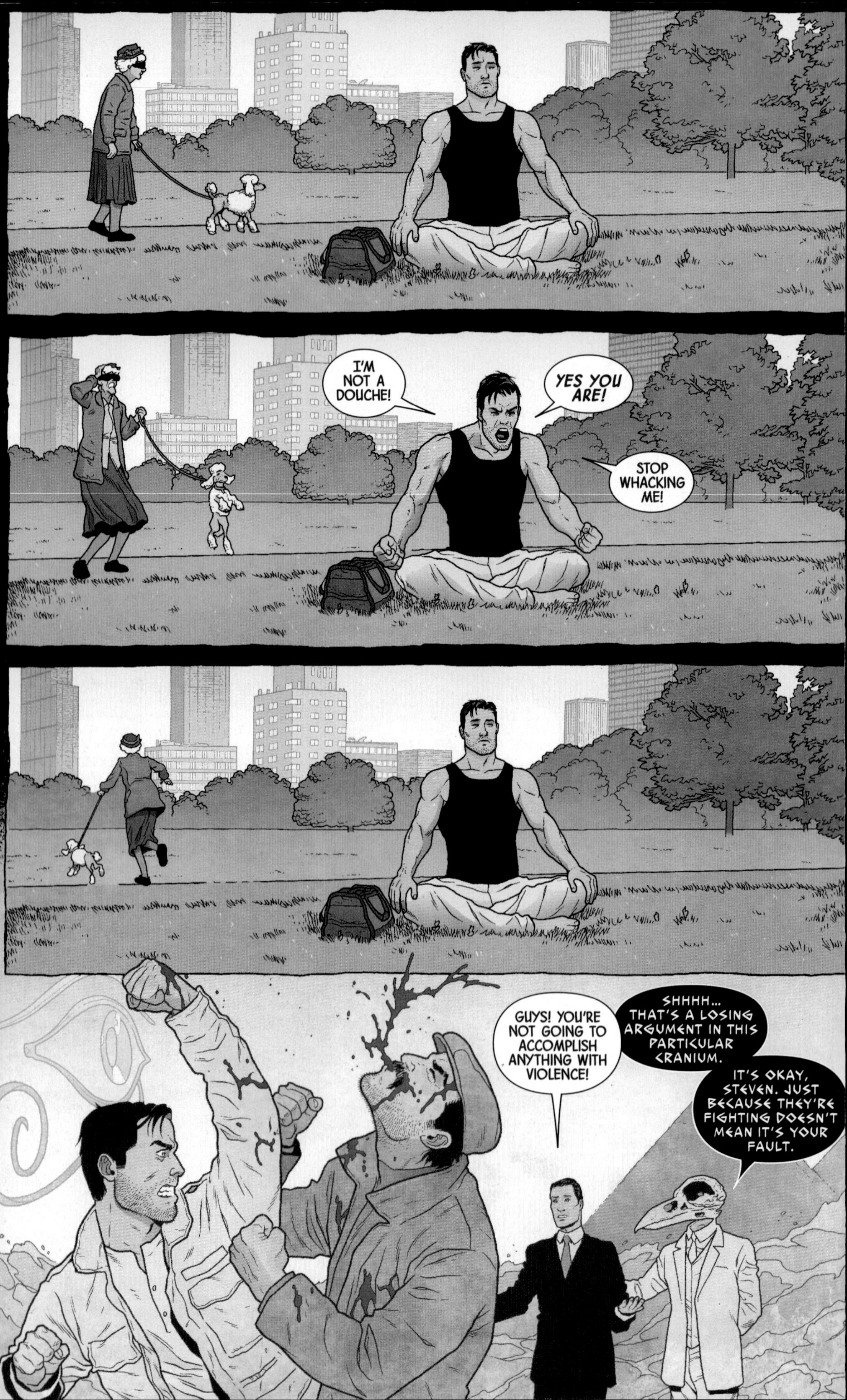
I'M NOT A DOUCHE!
YES YOU ARE!
STOP WHACKING ME!
GUYS! YOU'RE NOT GOING TO ACCOMPLISH ANYTHING WITH VIOLENCE!
SHHHH... THAT'S A LOSING ARGUMENT IN THIS PARTICULAR CRANIUM.
IT'S OKAY, STEVEN. JUST BECAUSE THEY'RE FIGHTING DOESN'T MEAN IT'S YOUR FAULT.

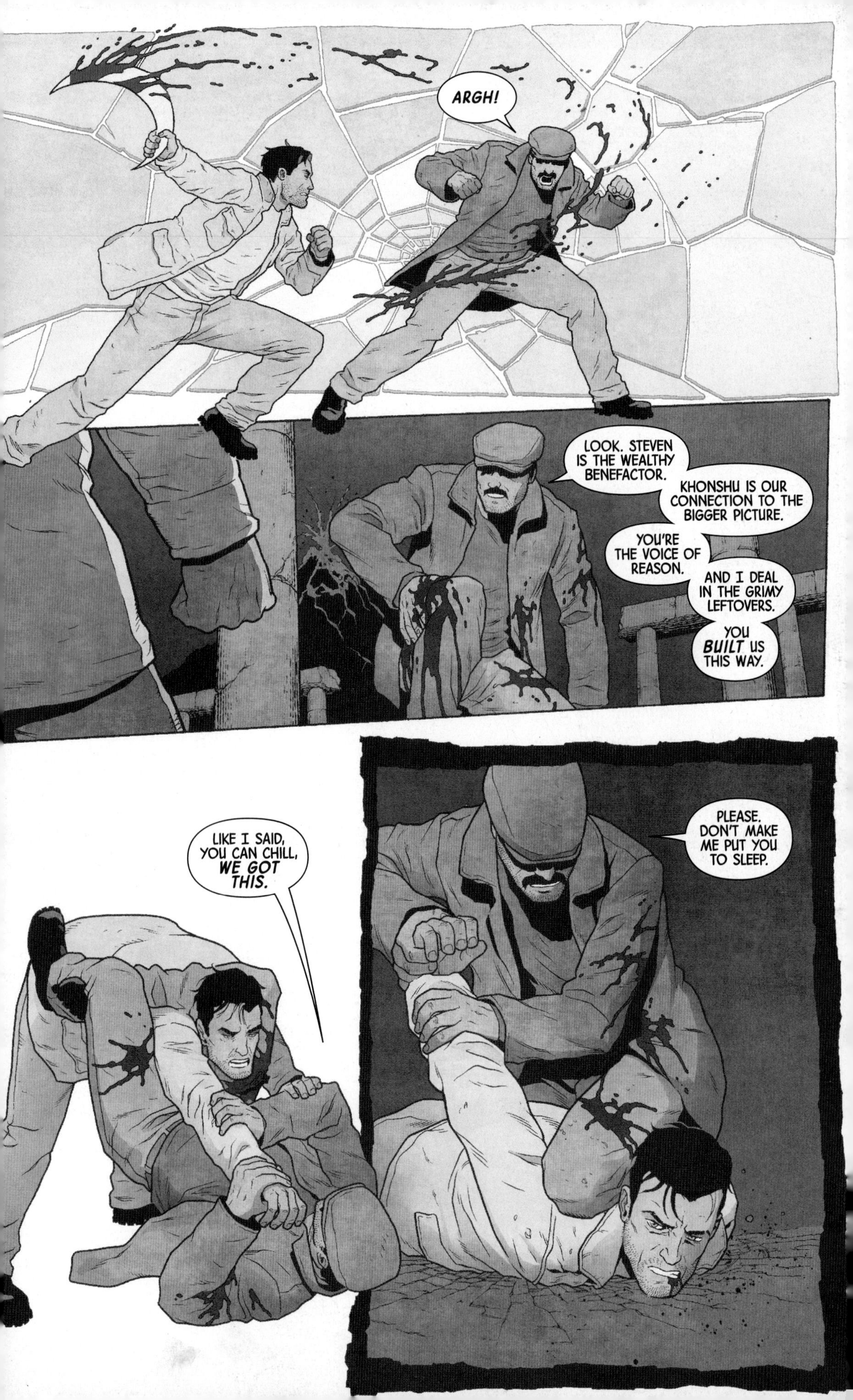

ARGH!
LOOK. STEVEN IS THE WEALTHY BENEFACTOR.
KHONSHU IS OUR CONNECTION TO THE BIGGER PICTURE.
YOU'RE THE VOICE OF REASON.
AND I DEAL IN THE GRIMY LEFTOVERS.
YOU *BUILT* US THIS WAY.
LIKE I SAID, YOU CAN CHILL, ***WE GOT THIS.***
PLEASE. DON'T MAKE ME PUT YOU TO SLEEP.

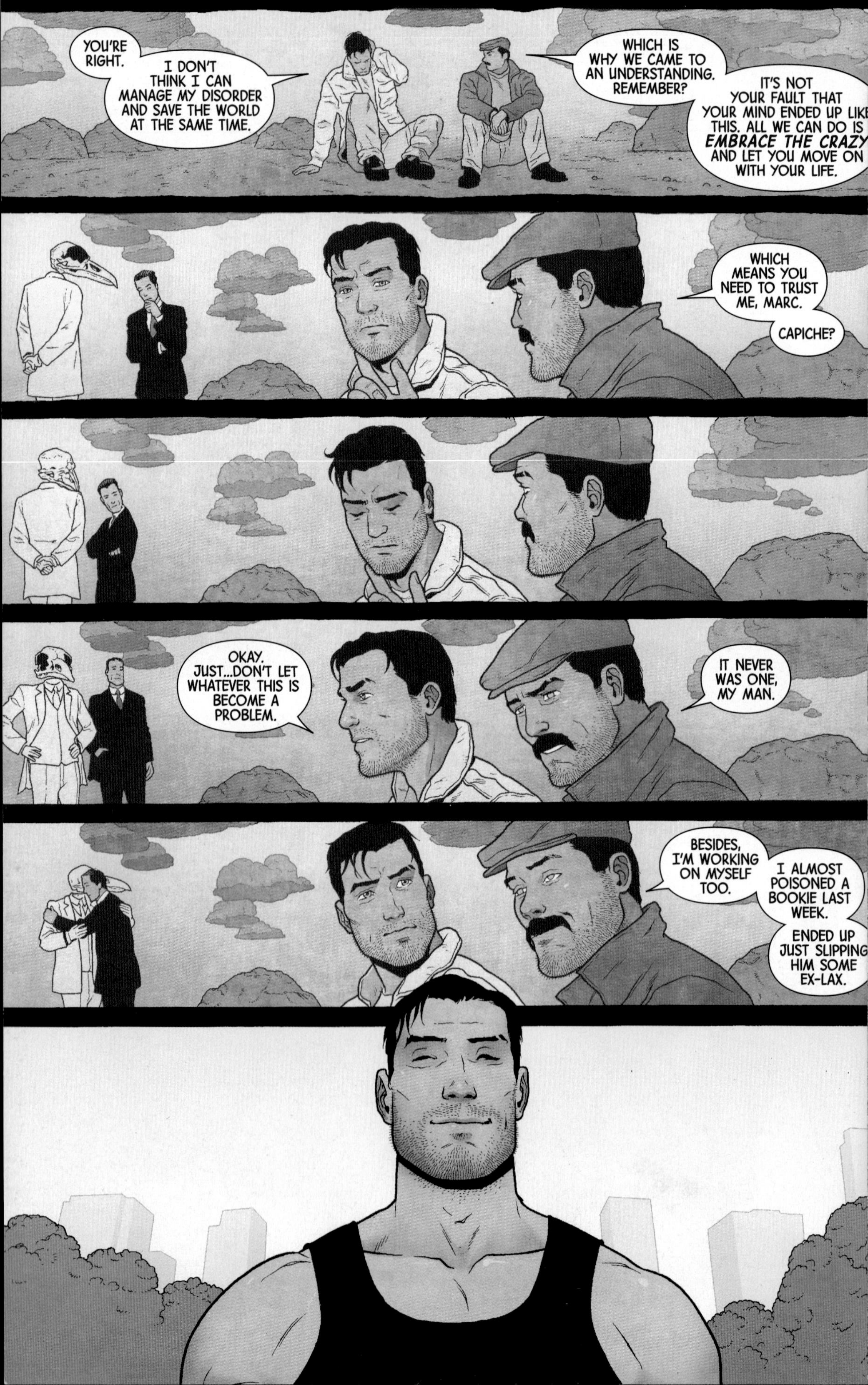
YOU'RE RIGHT.
I DON'T THINK I CAN MANAGE MY DISORDER AND SAVE THE WORLD AT THE SAME TIME.
WHICH IS WHY WE CAME TO AN UNDERSTANDING. REMEMBER?
IT'S NOT YOUR FAULT THAT YOUR MIND ENDED UP LIKE THIS. ALL WE CAN DO IS EMBRACE THE CRAZY AND LET YOU MOVE ON WITH YOUR LIFE.
WHICH MEANS YOU NEED TO TRUST ME, MARC.
CAPICHE?
OKAY. JUST...DON'T LET WHATEVER THIS IS BECOME A PROBLEM.
IT NEVER WAS ONE, MY MAN.
BESIDES, I'M WORKING ON MYSELF TOO.
I ALMOST POISONED A BOOKIE LAST WEEK.
ENDED UP JUST SLIPPING HIM SOME EX-LAX.

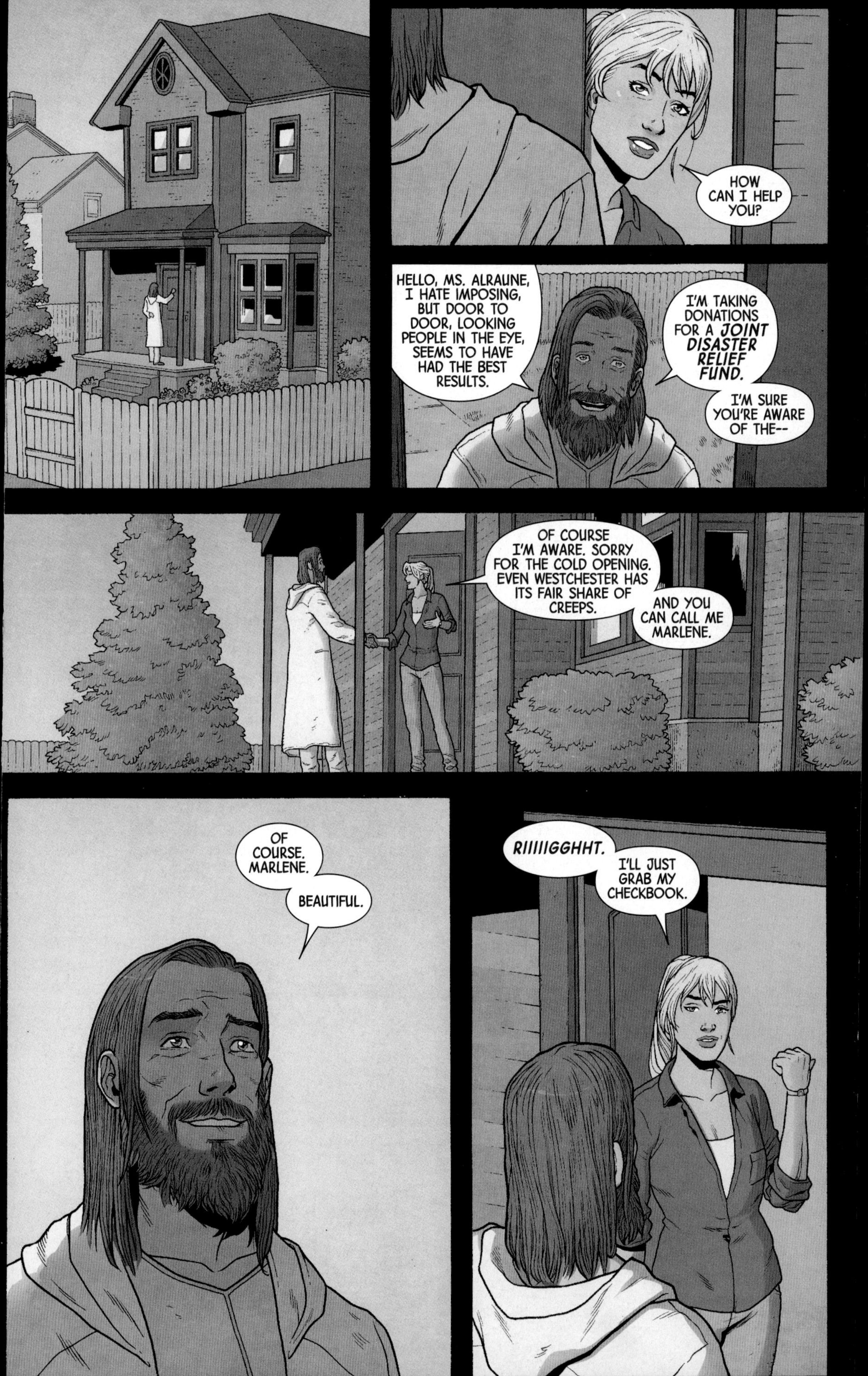
HOW CAN I HELP YOU?
HELLO, MS. ALRAUNE, I HATE IMPOSING, BUT DOOR TO DOOR, LOOKING PEOPLE IN THE EYE, SEEMS TO HAVE HAD THE BEST RESULTS.
I'M TAKING DONATIONS FOR A JOINT DISASTER RELIEF FUND.
I'M SURE YOU'RE AWARE OF THE--
OF COURSE I'M AWARE. SORRY FOR THE COLD OPENING. EVEN WESTCHESTER HAS ITS FAIR SHARE OF CREEPS.
AND YOU CAN CALL ME MARLENE.
OF COURSE. MARLENE.
BEAUTIFUL.
RIIIIIGGHHT.
I'LL JUST GRAB MY CHECKBOOK.

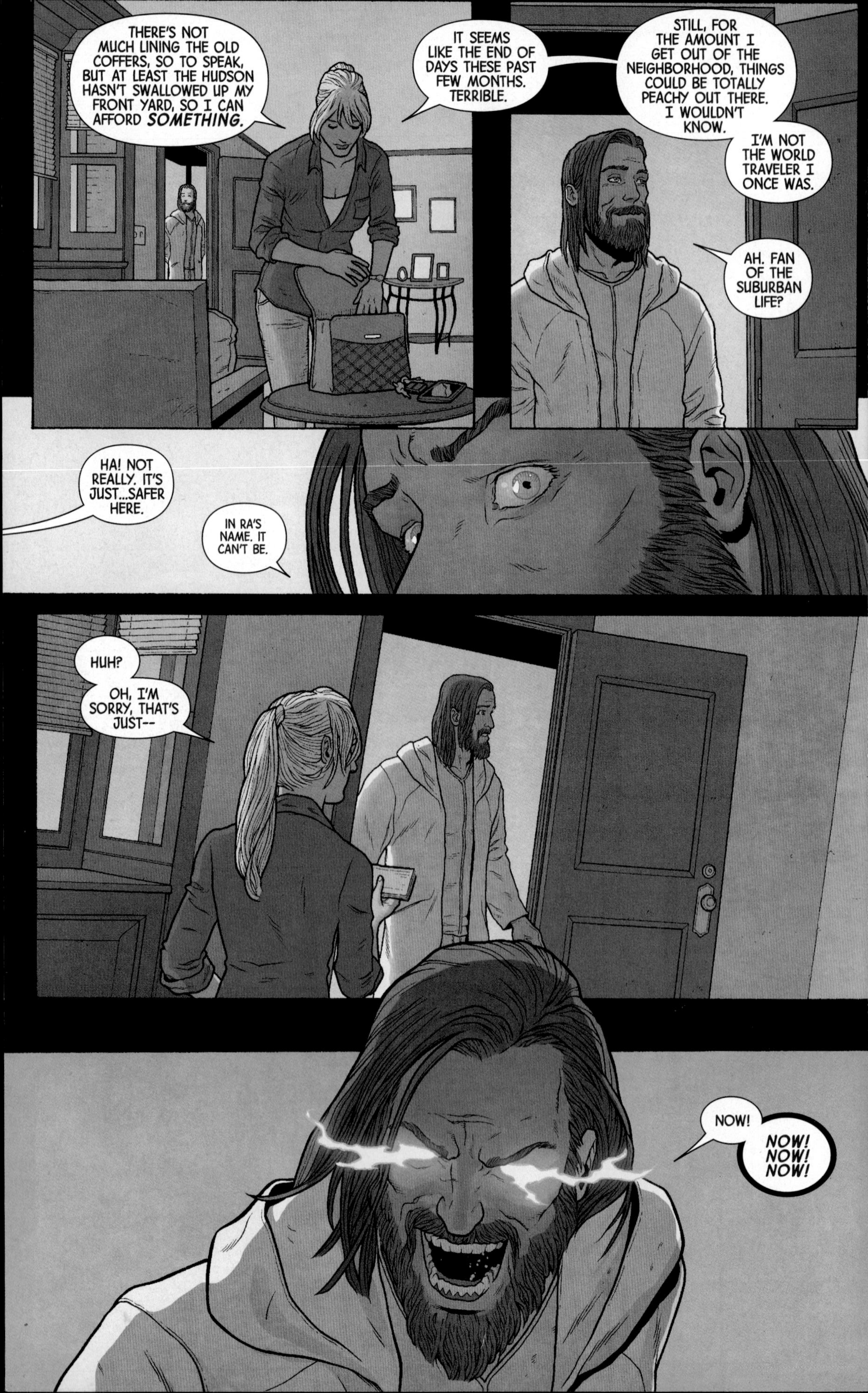
THERE'S NOT MUCH LINING THE OLD COFFERS, SO TO SPEAK, BUT AT LEAST THE HUDSON HASN'T SWALLOWED UP MY FRONT YARD, SO I CAN AFFORD SOMETHING.
IT SEEMS LIKE THE END OF DAYS THESE PAST FEW MONTHS. TERRIBLE.
STILL, FOR THE AMOUNT I GET OUT OF THE NEIGHBORHOOD, THINGS COULD BE TOTALLY PEACHY OUT THERE. I WOULDN'T KNOW.
I'M NOT THE WORLD TRAVELER I ONCE WAS.
AH. FAN OF THE SUBURBAN LIFE?
HA! NOT REALLY. IT'S JUST...SAFER HERE.
IN RA'S NAME. IT CAN'T BE.
HUH?
OH, I'M SORRY, THAT'S JUST--
NOW!
NOW! NOW! NOW!

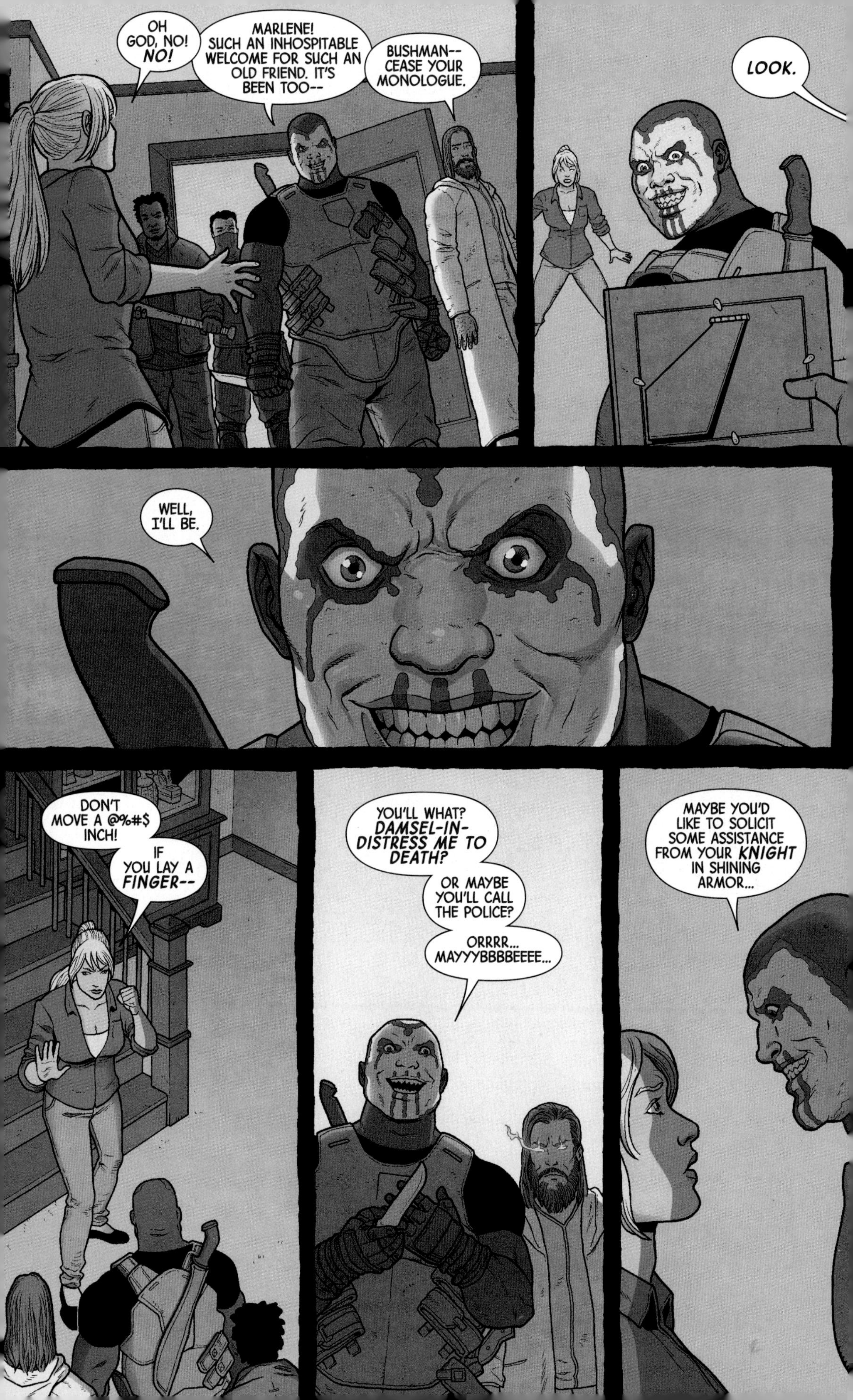
OH GOD, NO! NO!
MARLENE! SUCH AN INHOSPITABLE WELCOME FOR SUCH AN OLD FRIEND. IT'S BEEN TOO--
BUSHMAN-- CEASE YOUR MONOLOGUE.
LOOK.
WELL, I'LL BE.
DON'T MOVE A @%#$ INCH!
IF YOU LAY A FINGER--
YOU'LL WHAT? DAMSEL-IN-DISTRESS ME TO DEATH?
OR MAYBE YOU'LL CALL THE POLICE?
ORRRR... MAYYYBBBBEEEE...
MAYBE YOU'D LIKE TO SOLICIT SOME ASSISTANCE FROM YOUR KNIGHT IN SHINING ARMOR...

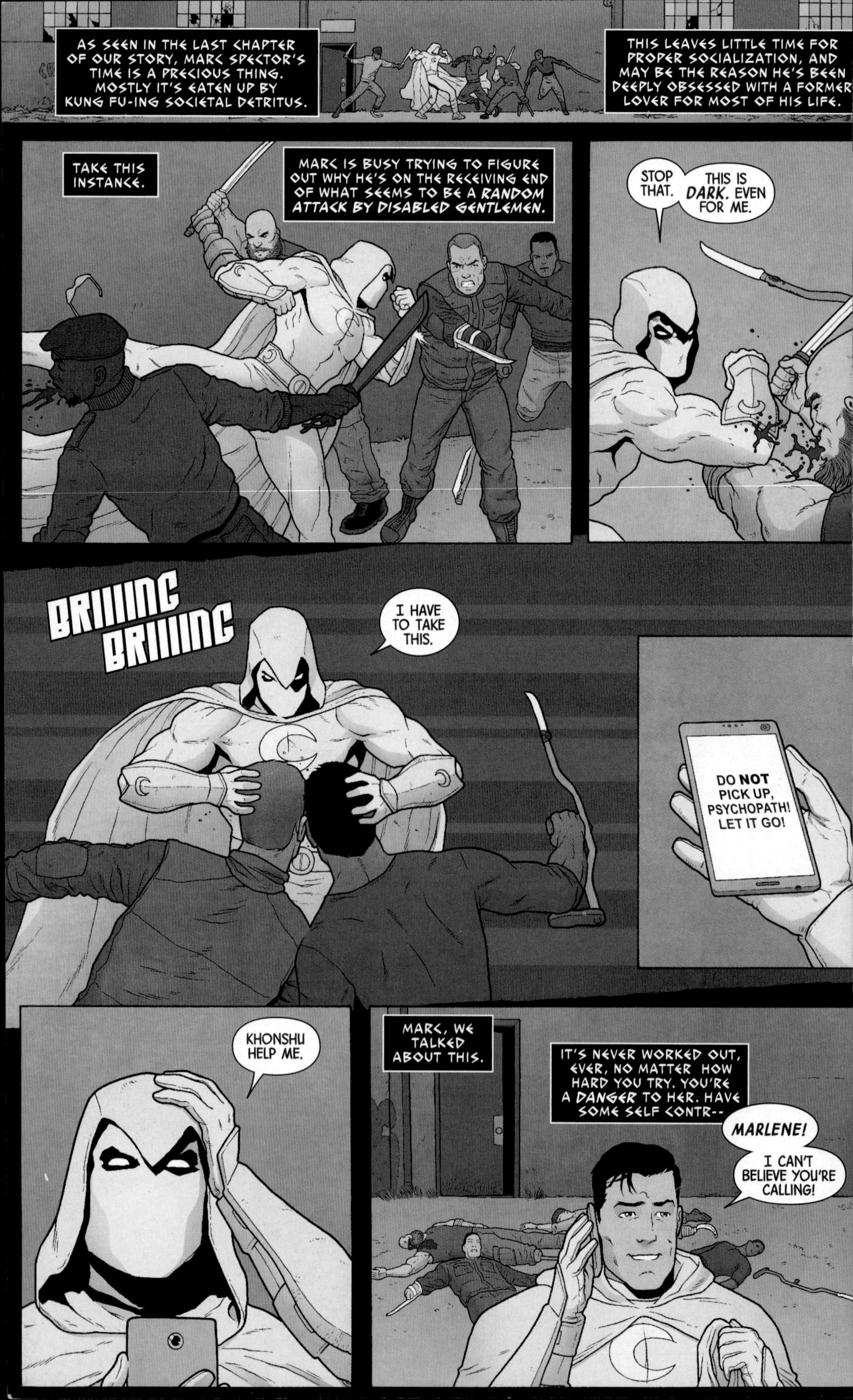
AS SEEN IN THE LAST CHAPTER OF OUR STORY, MARC SPECTOR'S TIME IS A PRECIOUS THING. MOSTLY IT'S EATEN UP BY KUNG FU-ING SOCIETAL DETRITUS.
THIS LEAVES LITTLE TIME FOR PROPER SOCIALIZATION, AND MAY BE THE REASON HE'S BEEN DEEPLY OBSESSED WITH A FORMER LOVER FOR MOST OF HIS LIFE.
TAKE THIS INSTANCE.
MARC IS BUSY TRYING TO FIGURE OUT WHY HE'S ON THE RECEIVING END OF WHAT SEEMS TO BE A RANDOM ATTACK BY DISABLED GENTLEMEN.
STOP THAT.
THIS IS DARK. EVEN FOR ME.
BRIIIING BRIIIING
I HAVE TO TAKE THIS.
DO NOT PICK UP, PSYCHOPATH! LET IT GO!
KHONSHU HELP ME.
MARC, WE TALKED ABOUT THIS.
IT'S NEVER WORKED OUT, EVER, NO MATTER HOW HARD YOU TRY. YOU'RE A DANGER TO HER. HAVE SOME SELF CONTR--
MARLENE!
I CAN'T BELIEVE YOU'RE CALLING!

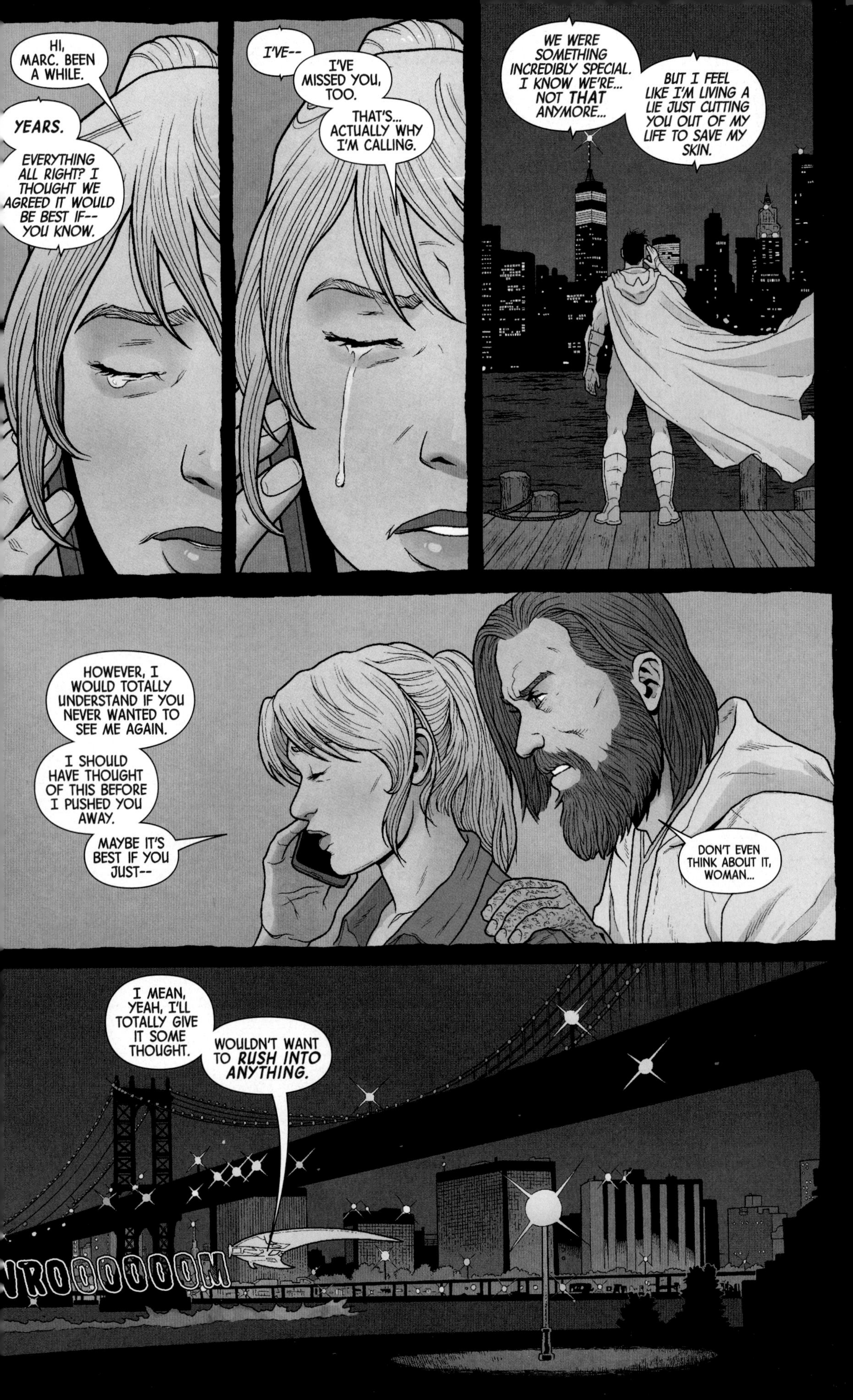

HI, MARC. BEEN A WHILE.
YEARS.
EVERYTHING ALL RIGHT? I THOUGHT WE AGREED IT WOULD BE BEST IF-- YOU KNOW.
I'VE--
I'VE MISSED YOU, TOO.
THAT'S... ACTUALLY WHY I'M CALLING.
WE WERE SOMETHING INCREDIBLY SPECIAL. I KNOW WE'RE... NOT THAT ANYMORE...
BUT I FEEL LIKE I'M LIVING A LIE JUST CUTTING YOU OUT OF MY LIFE TO SAVE MY SKIN.
HOWEVER, I WOULD TOTALLY UNDERSTAND IF YOU NEVER WANTED TO SEE ME AGAIN.
I SHOULD HAVE THOUGHT OF THIS BEFORE I PUSHED YOU AWAY.
MAYBE IT'S BEST IF YOU JUST--
DON'T EVEN THINK ABOUT IT, WOMAN...
I MEAN, YEAH, I'LL TOTALLY GIVE IT SOME THOUGHT.
WOULDN'T WANT TO RUSH INTO ANYTHING.
VROOOOOOOM

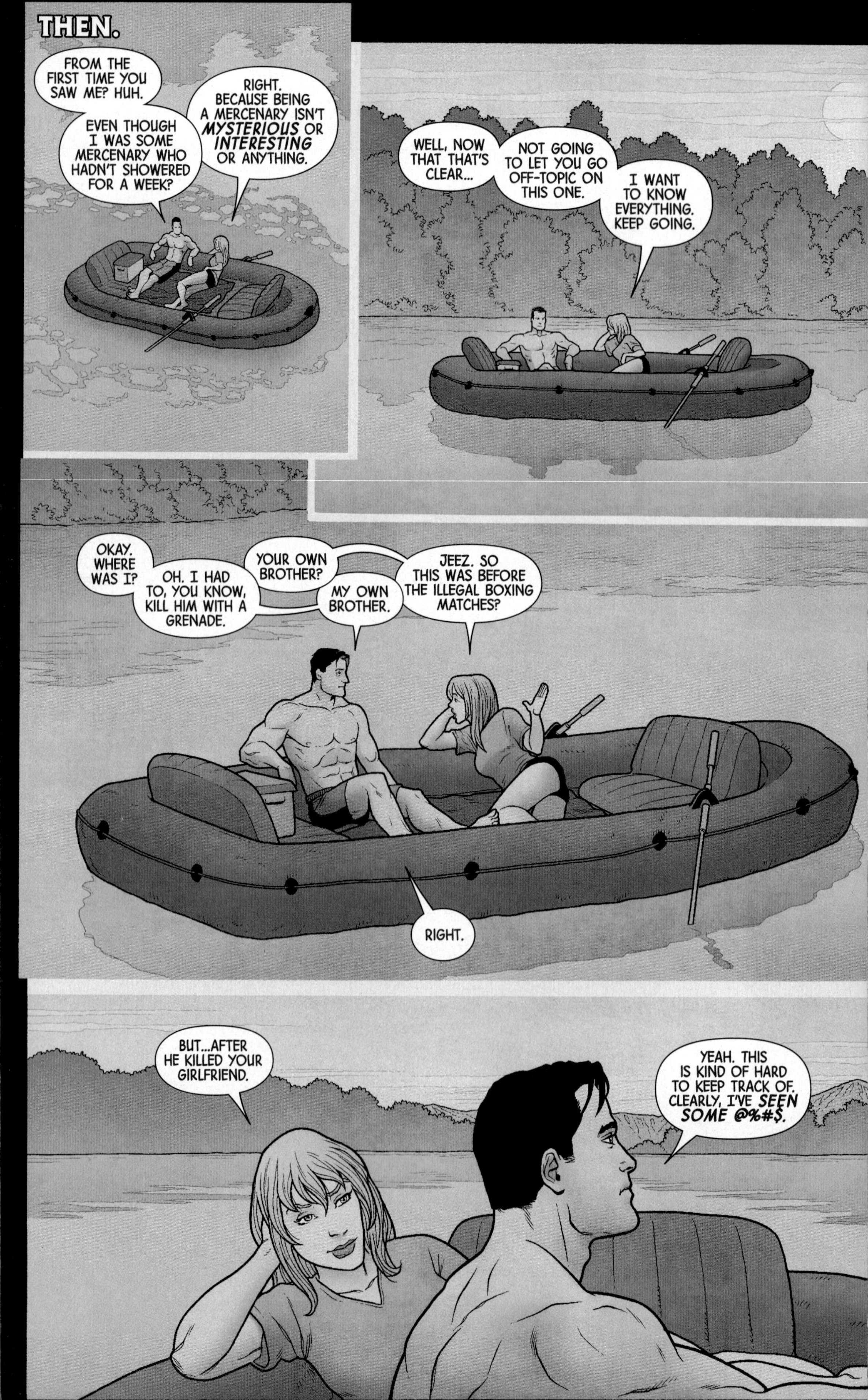
THEN.
FROM THE FIRST TIME YOU SAW ME? HUH.
EVEN THOUGH I WAS SOME MERCENARY WHO HADN'T SHOWERED FOR A WEEK?
RIGHT. BECAUSE BEING A MERCENARY ISN'T *MYSTERIOUS* OR *INTERESTING* OR ANYTHING.
WELL, NOW THAT THAT'S CLEAR...
NOT GOING TO LET YOU GO OFF-TOPIC ON THIS ONE.
I WANT TO KNOW EVERYTHING. KEEP GOING.
OKAY. WHERE WAS I?
OH. I HAD TO, YOU KNOW, KILL HIM WITH A GRENADE.
YOUR OWN BROTHER?
MY OWN BROTHER.
JEEZ. SO THIS WAS BEFORE THE ILLEGAL BOXING MATCHES?
RIGHT.
BUT...AFTER HE KILLED YOUR GIRLFRIEND.
YEAH. THIS IS KIND OF HARD TO KEEP TRACK OF. CLEARLY, I'VE *SEEN SOME* @%#$.

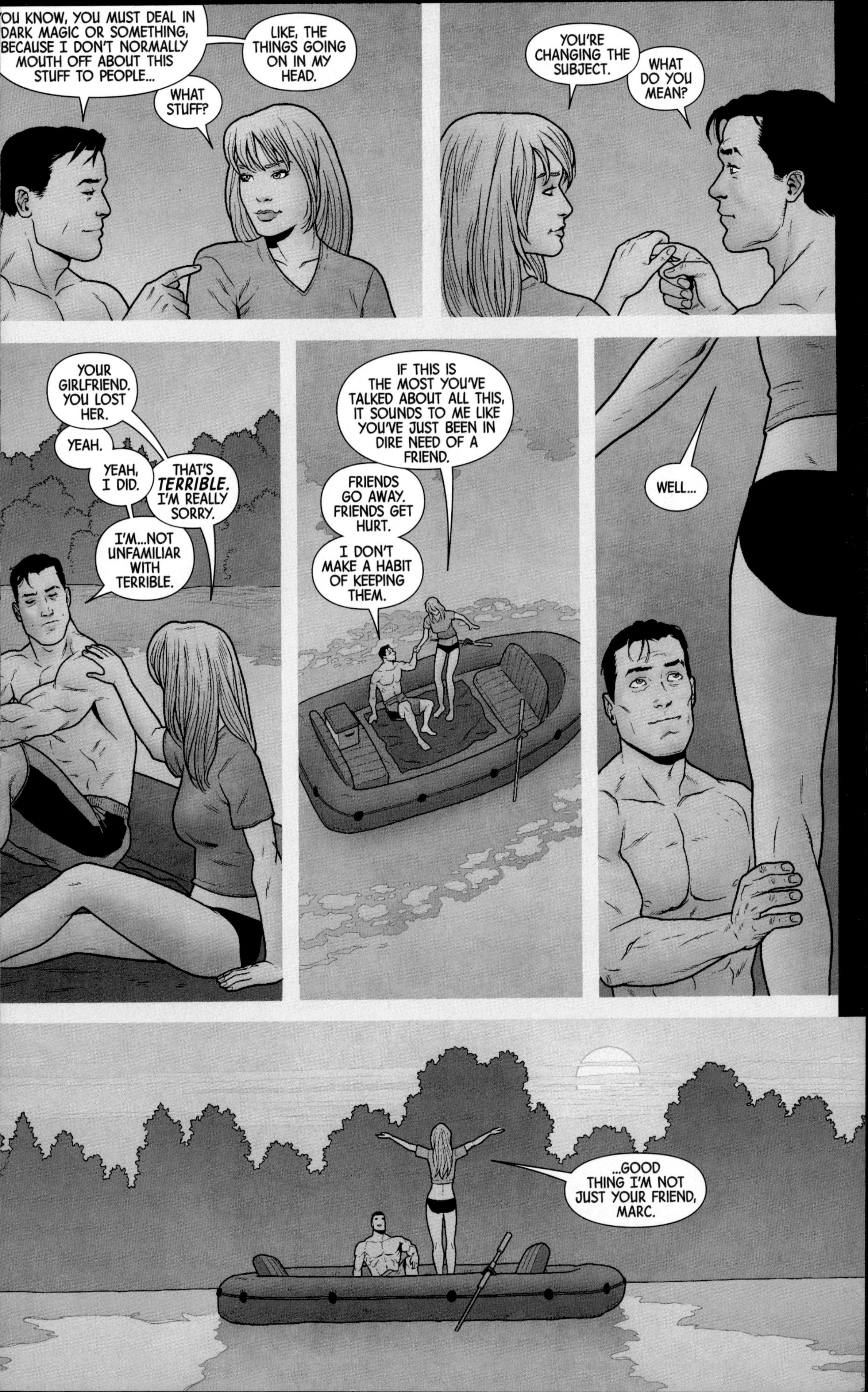
YOU KNOW, YOU MUST DEAL IN DARK MAGIC OR SOMETHING, BECAUSE I DON'T NORMALLY MOUTH OFF ABOUT THIS STUFF TO PEOPLE...
LIKE, THE THINGS GOING ON IN MY HEAD.
WHAT STUFF?
YOU'RE CHANGING THE SUBJECT.
WHAT DO YOU MEAN?
YOUR GIRLFRIEND. YOU LOST HER.
YEAH.
YEAH, I DID.
THAT'S *TERRIBLE.* I'M REALLY SORRY.
I'M...NOT UNFAMILIAR WITH TERRIBLE.
IF THIS IS THE MOST YOU'VE TALKED ABOUT ALL THIS, IT SOUNDS TO ME LIKE YOU'VE JUST BEEN IN DIRE NEED OF A FRIEND.
FRIENDS GO AWAY. FRIENDS GET HURT.
I DON'T MAKE A HABIT OF KEEPING THEM.
WELL...
...GOOD THING I'M NOT JUST YOUR FRIEND, MARC.

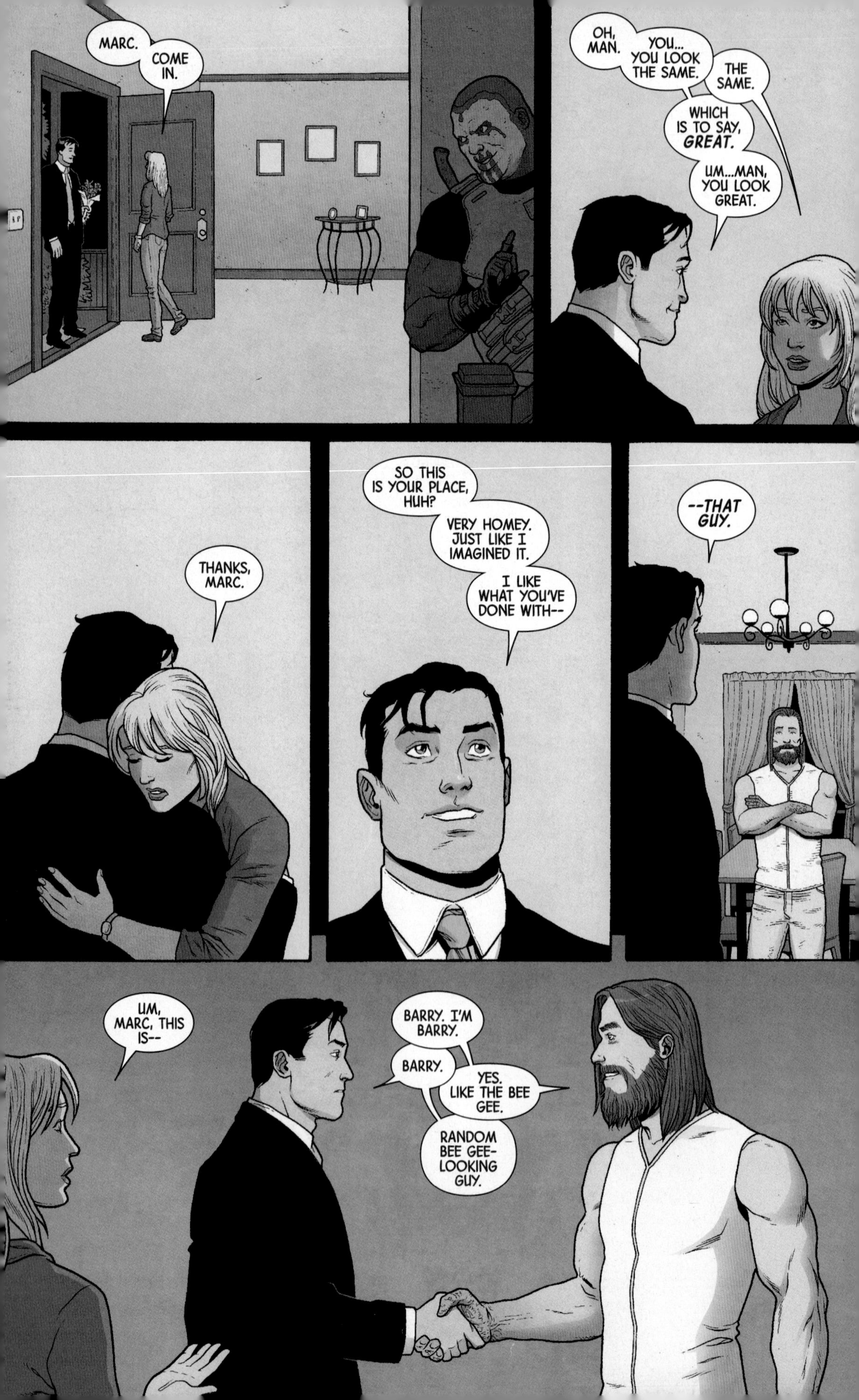
MARC.
COME IN.
OH, MAN.
YOU... YOU LOOK THE SAME.
THE SAME.
WHICH IS TO SAY, *GREAT.*
UM...MAN, YOU LOOK GREAT.
THANKS, MARC.
SO THIS IS YOUR PLACE, HUH?
VERY HOMEY. JUST LIKE I IMAGINED IT.
I LIKE WHAT YOU'VE DONE WITH--
--THAT GUY.
UM, MARC, THIS IS--
BARRY. I'M BARRY.
BARRY.
YES. LIKE THE BEE GEE.
RANDOM BEE GEE-LOOKING GUY.

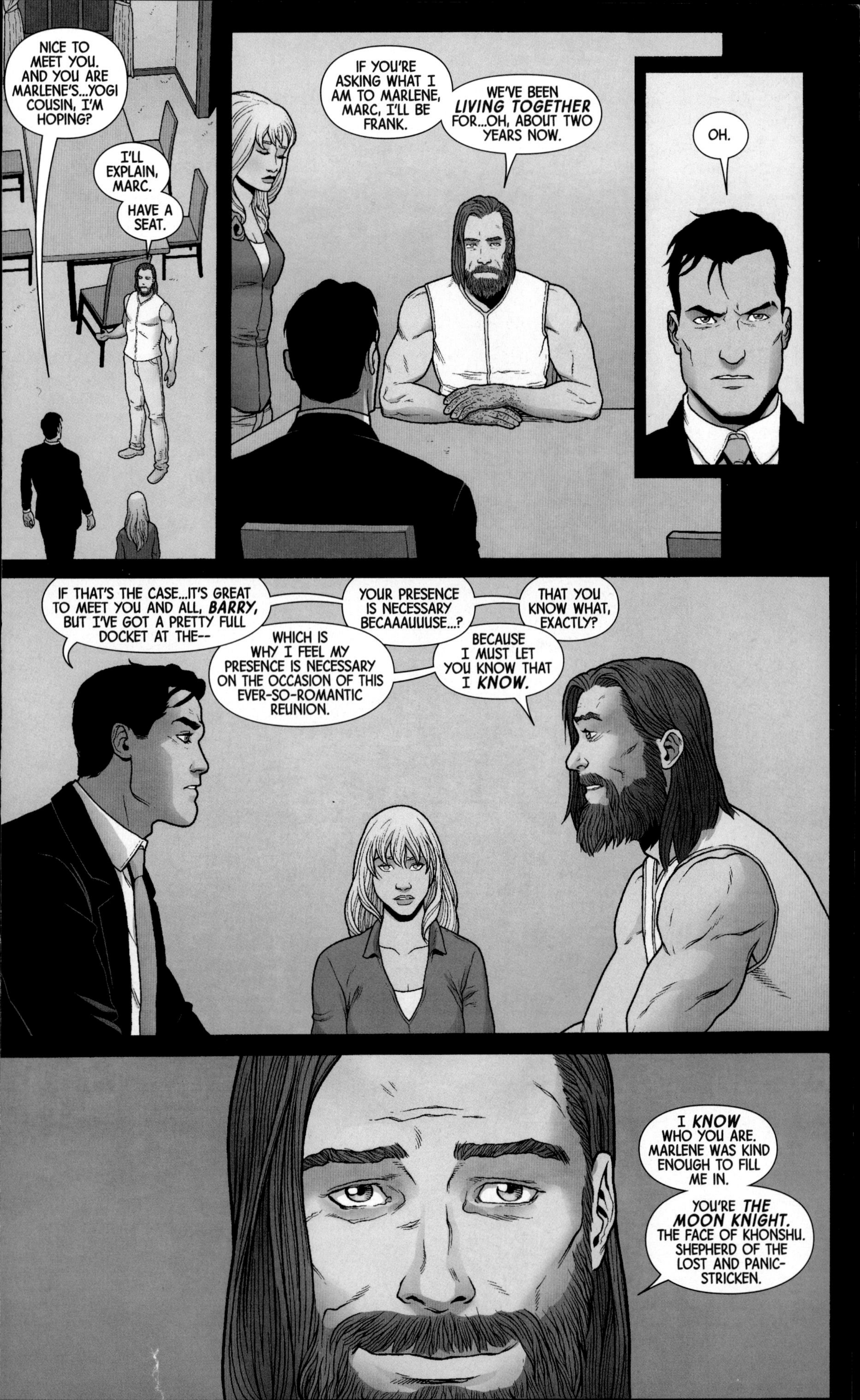

NICE TO MEET YOU. AND YOU ARE MARLENE'S...YOGI COUSIN, I'M HOPING?
I'LL EXPLAIN, MARC.
HAVE A SEAT.
IF YOU'RE ASKING WHAT I AM TO MARLENE, MARC, I'LL BE FRANK.
WE'VE BEEN LIVING TOGETHER FOR...OH, ABOUT TWO YEARS NOW.
OH.
IF THAT'S THE CASE...IT'S GREAT TO MEET YOU AND ALL, BARRY, BUT I'VE GOT A PRETTY FULL DOCKET AT THE--
WHICH IS WHY I FEEL MY PRESENCE IS NECESSARY ON THE OCCASION OF THIS EVER-SO-ROMANTIC REUNION.
YOUR PRESENCE IS NECESSARY BECAAAUUUSE...?
BECAUSE I MUST LET YOU KNOW THAT I KNOW.
THAT YOU KNOW WHAT, EXACTLY?
I KNOW WHO YOU ARE. MARLENE WAS KIND ENOUGH TO FILL ME IN.
YOU'RE THE MOON KNIGHT. THE FACE OF KHONSHU. SHEPHERD OF THE LOST AND PANIC-STRICKEN.

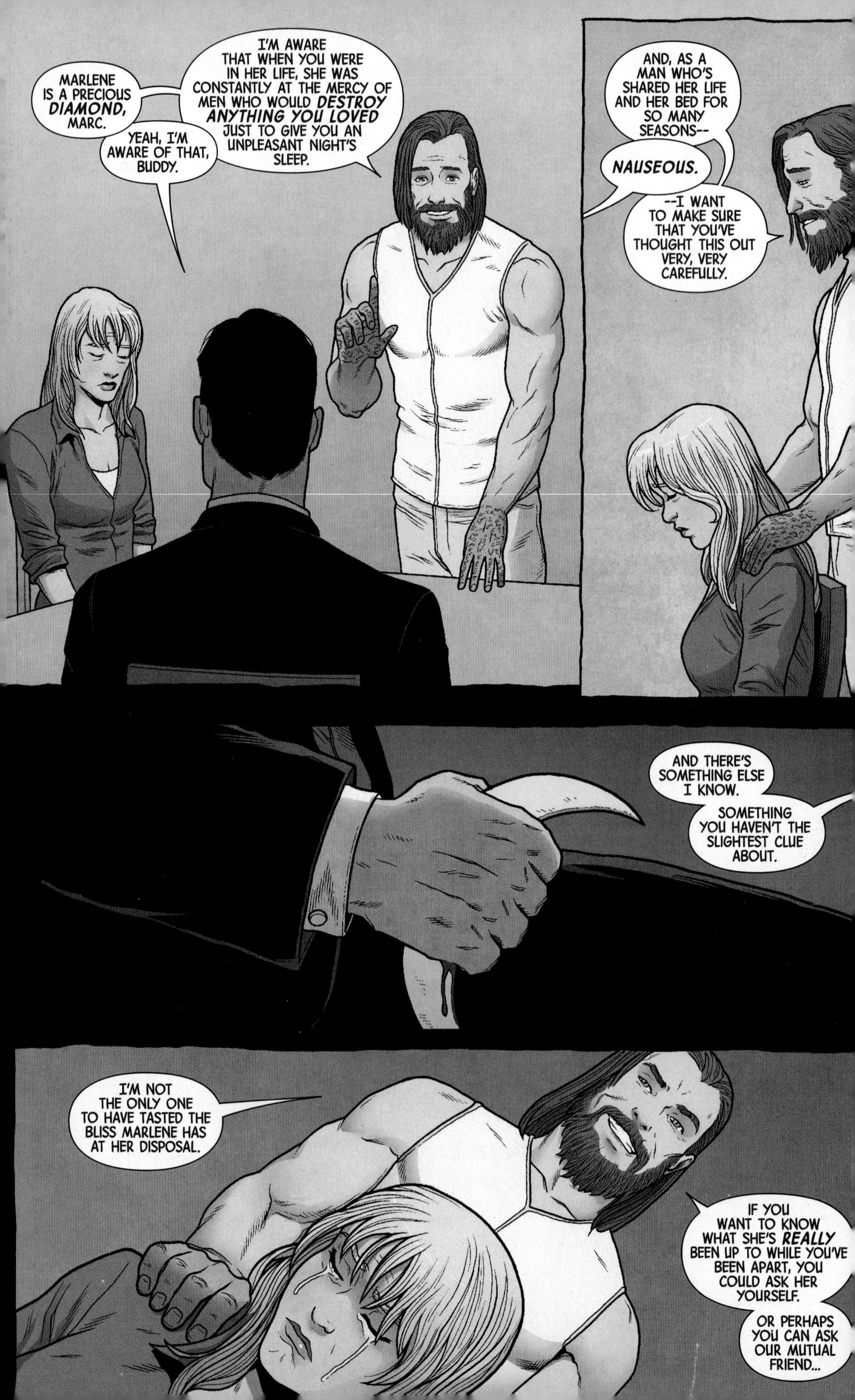
MARLENE IS A PRECIOUS DIAMOND, MARC.
YEAH, I'M AWARE OF THAT, BUDDY.
I'M AWARE THAT WHEN YOU WERE IN HER LIFE, SHE WAS CONSTANTLY AT THE MERCY OF MEN WHO WOULD DESTROY ANYTHING YOU LOVED JUST TO GIVE YOU AN UNPLEASANT NIGHT'S SLEEP.
AND, AS A MAN WHO'S SHARED HER LIFE AND HER BED FOR SO MANY SEASONS--
NAUSEOUS.
--I WANT TO MAKE SURE THAT YOU'VE THOUGHT THIS OUT VERY, VERY CAREFULLY.
AND THERE'S SOMETHING ELSE I KNOW.
SOMETHING YOU HAVEN'T THE SLIGHTEST CLUE ABOUT.
I'M NOT THE ONLY ONE TO HAVE TASTED THE BLISS MARLENE HAS AT HER DISPOSAL.
IF YOU WANT TO KNOW WHAT SHE'S REALLY BEEN UP TO WHILE YOU'VE BEEN APART, YOU COULD ASK HER YOURSELF.
OR PERHAPS YOU CAN ASK OUR MUTUAL FRIEND...

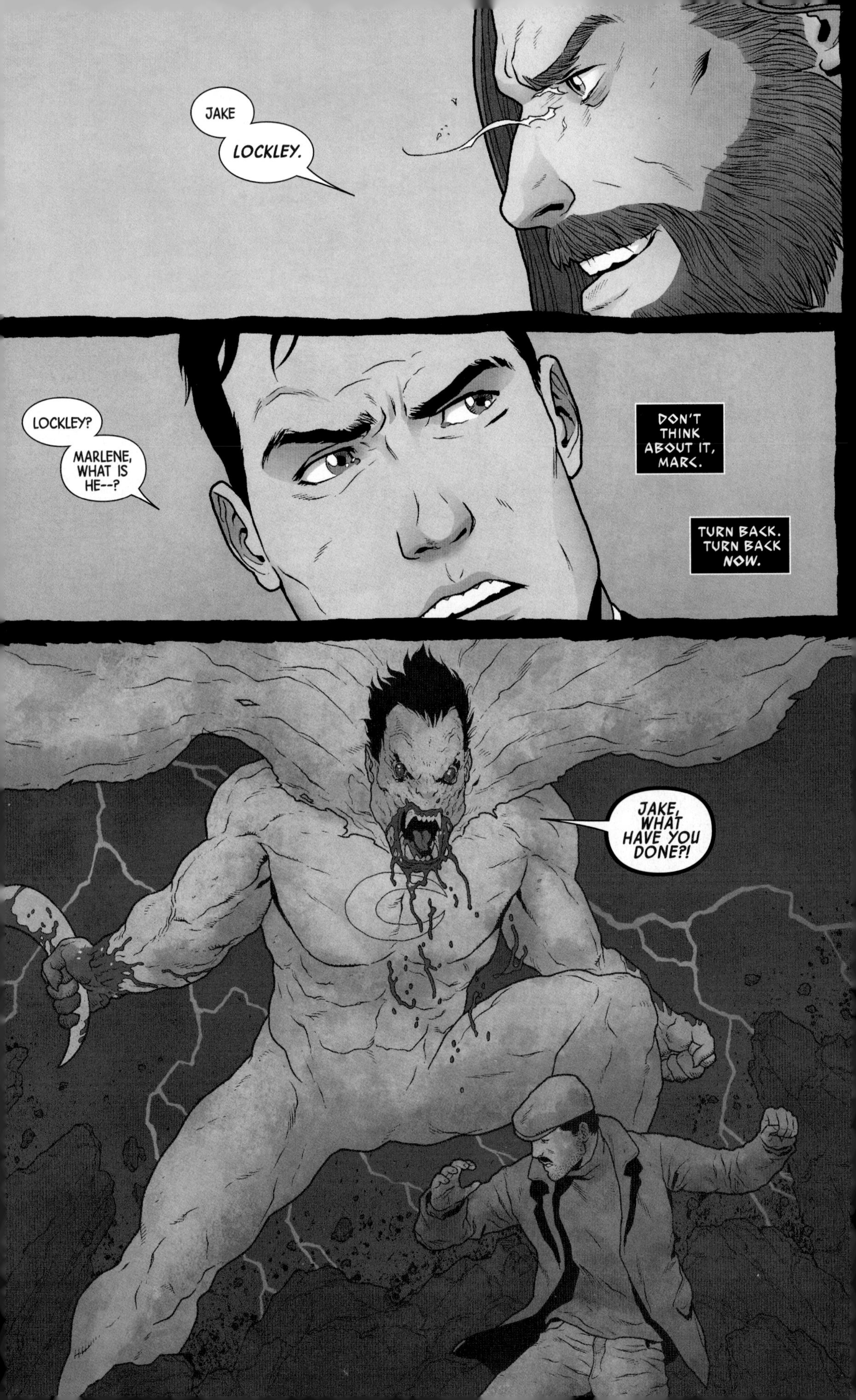
JAKE
LOCKLEY.
LOCKLEY?
MARLENE, WHAT IS HE--?
DON'T THINK ABOUT IT, MARC.
TURN BACK. TURN BACK NOW.
JAKE, WHAT HAVE YOU DONE?!

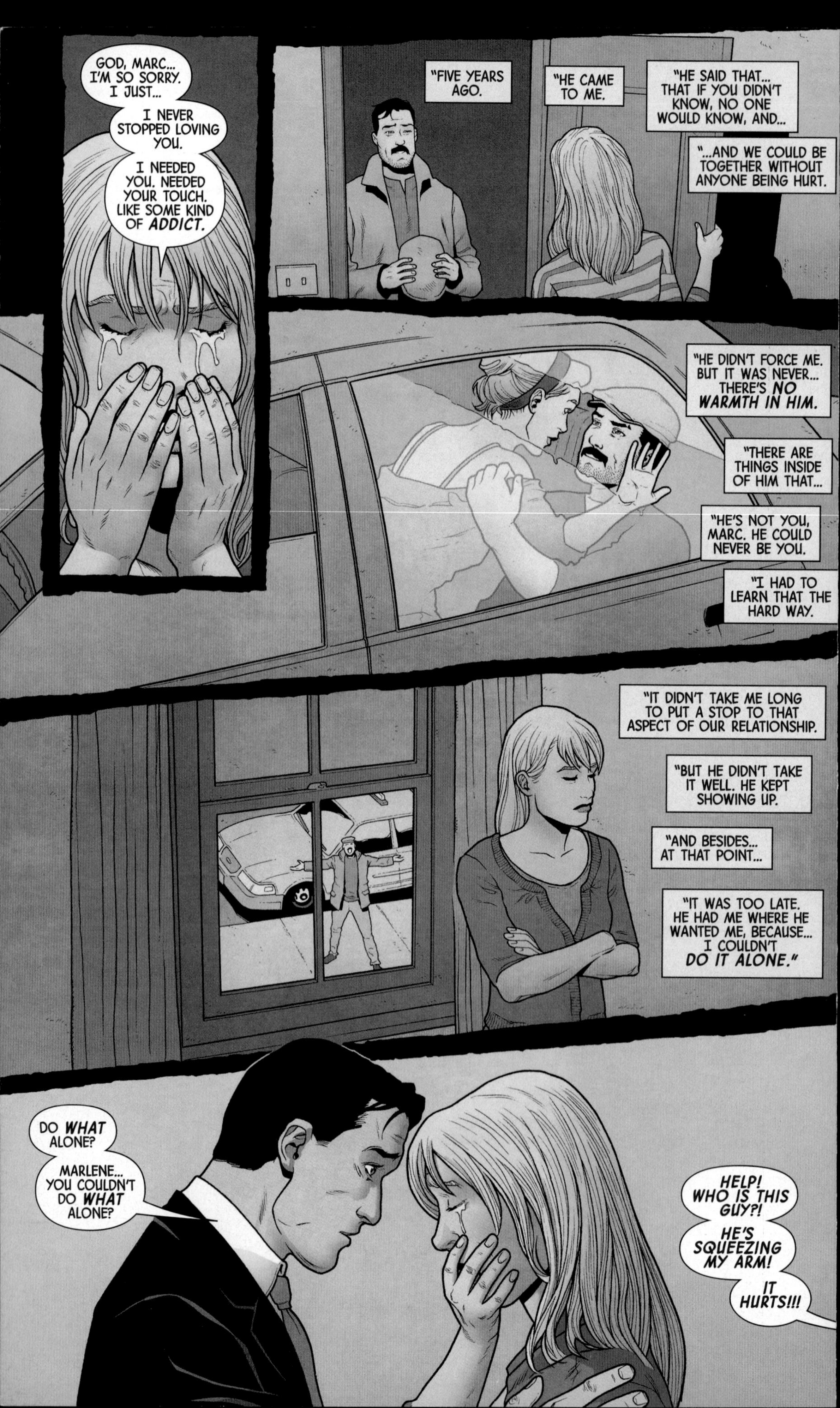
GOD, MARC... I'M SO SORRY. I JUST...
I NEVER STOPPED LOVING YOU.
I NEEDED YOU. NEEDED YOUR TOUCH. LIKE SOME KIND OF ADDICT.
"FIVE YEARS AGO.
"HE CAME TO ME.
"HE SAID THAT... THAT IF YOU DIDN'T KNOW, NO ONE WOULD KNOW, AND...
"...AND WE COULD BE TOGETHER WITHOUT ANYONE BEING HURT.
"HE DIDN'T FORCE ME. BUT IT WAS NEVER... THERE'S NO WARMTH IN HIM.
"THERE ARE THINGS INSIDE OF HIM THAT...
"HE'S NOT YOU, MARC. HE COULD NEVER BE YOU.
"I HAD TO LEARN THAT THE HARD WAY.
"IT DIDN'T TAKE ME LONG TO PUT A STOP TO THAT ASPECT OF OUR RELATIONSHIP.
"BUT HE DIDN'T TAKE IT WELL. HE KEPT SHOWING UP.
"AND BESIDES... AT THAT POINT...
"IT WAS TOO LATE. HE HAD ME WHERE HE WANTED ME, BECAUSE... I COULDN'T DO IT ALONE."
DO WHAT ALONE?
MARLENE... YOU COULDN'T DO WHAT ALONE?
HELP! WHO IS THIS GUY?!
HE'S SQUEEZING MY ARM!
IT HURTS!!!

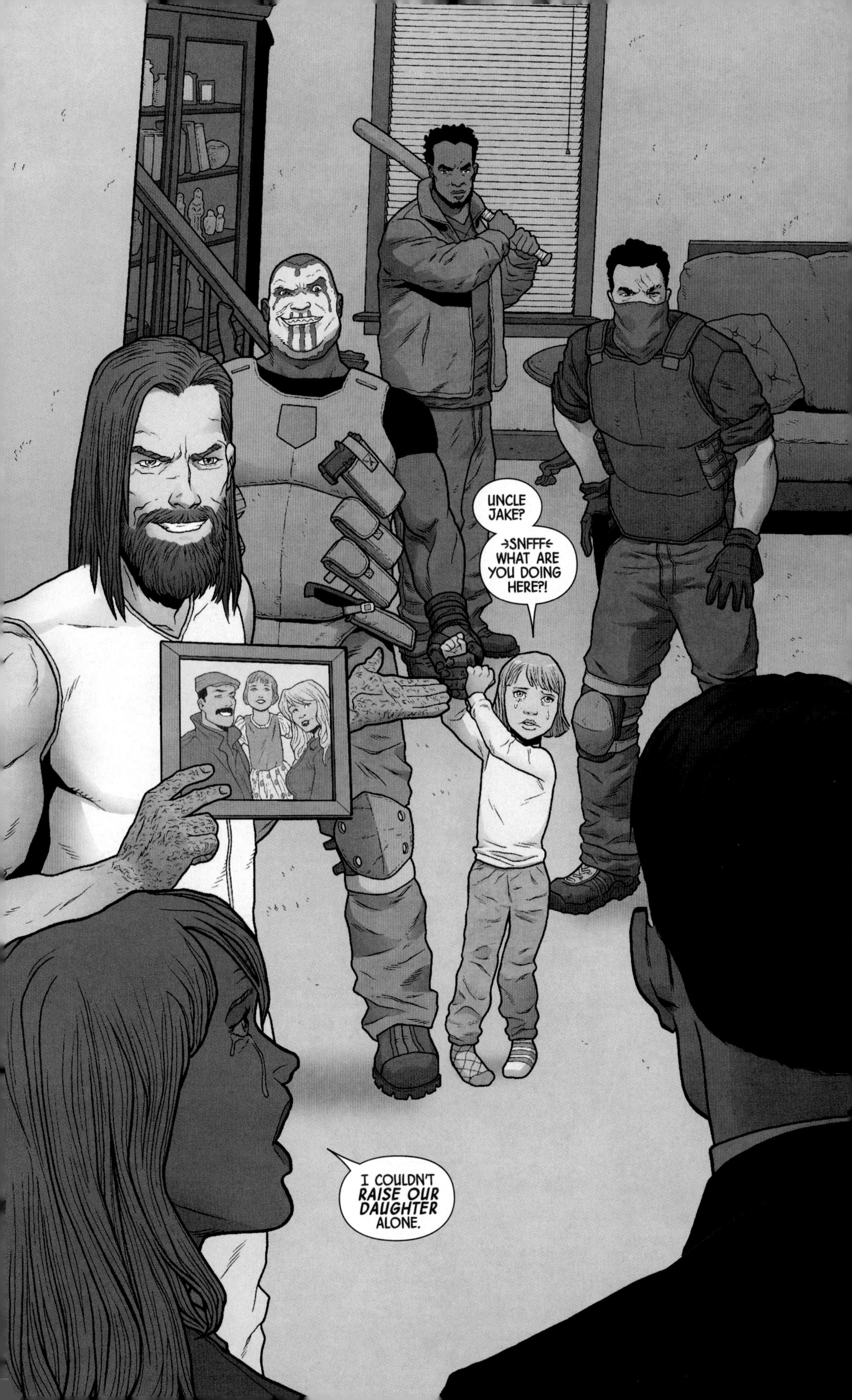
UNCLE JAKE?
→SNFFF← WHAT ARE YOU DOING HERE?!
I COULDN'T RAISE OUR DAUGHTER ALONE.

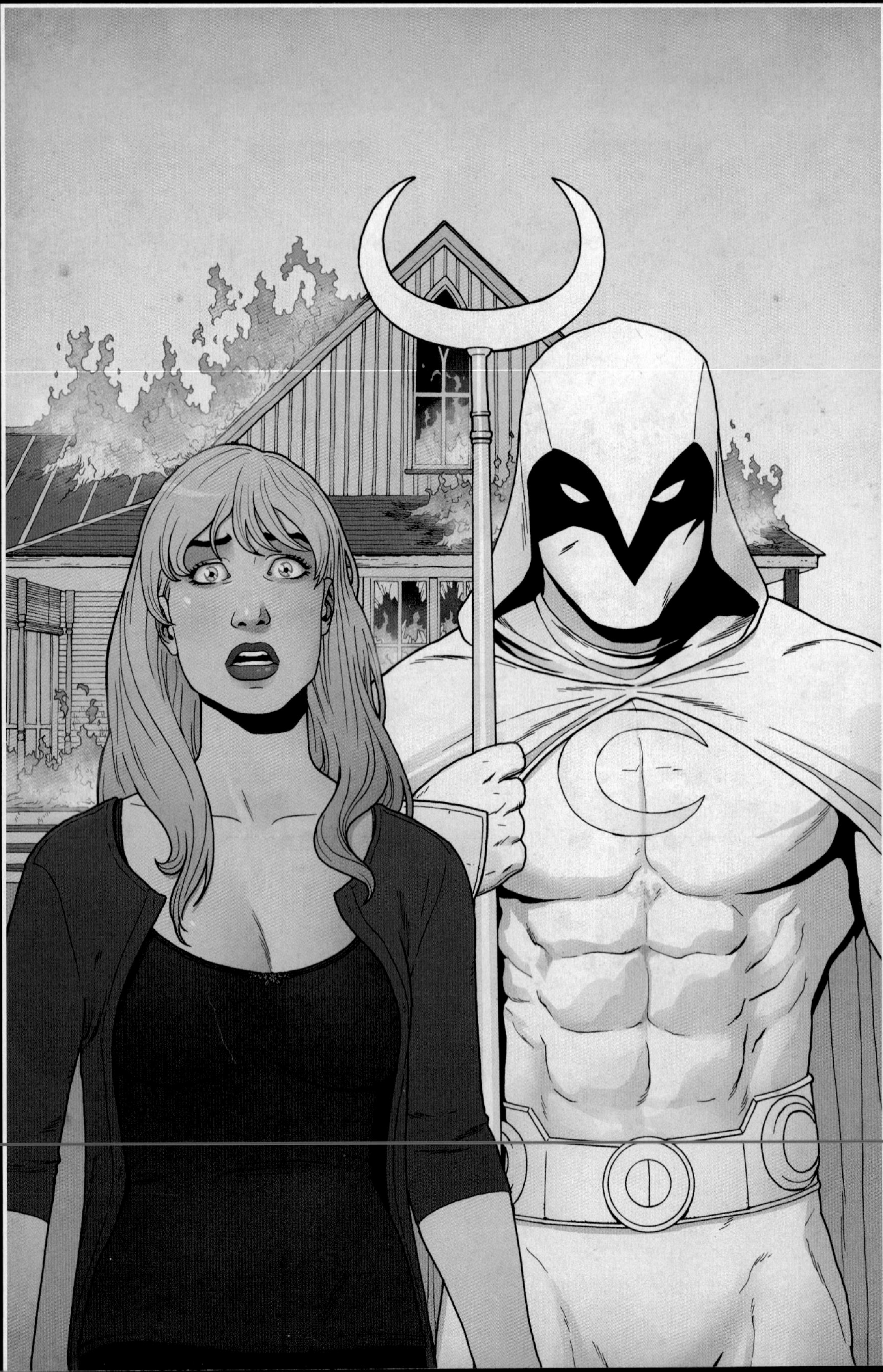

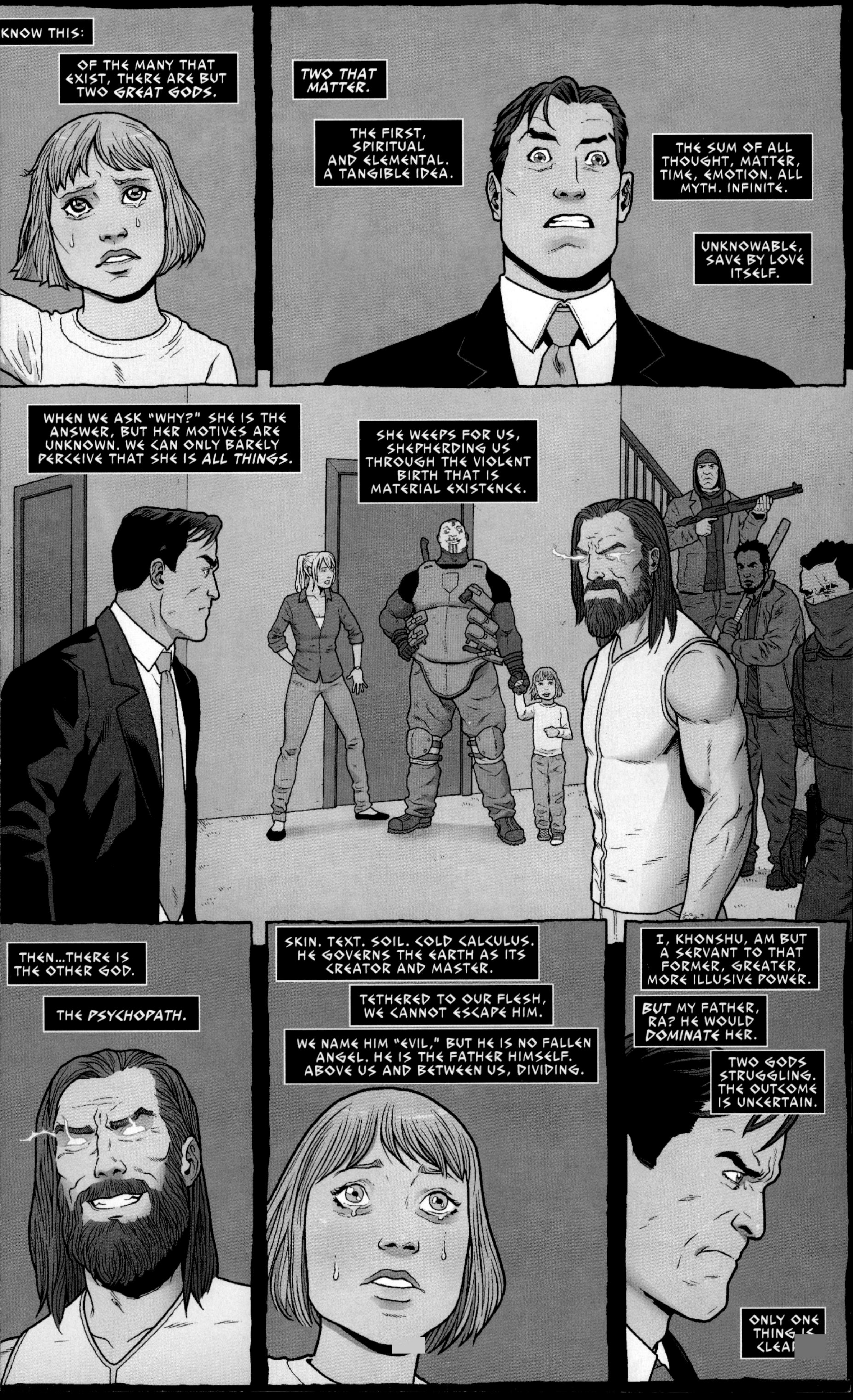

KNOW THIS:
OF THE MANY THAT EXIST, THERE ARE BUT TWO *GREAT GODS.*
TWO THAT MATTER.
THE FIRST, SPIRITUAL AND ELEMENTAL. A TANGIBLE IDEA.
THE SUM OF ALL THOUGHT, MATTER, TIME, EMOTION. ALL MYTH. INFINITE.
UNKNOWABLE, SAVE BY LOVE ITSELF.
WHEN WE ASK "WHY?" SHE IS THE ANSWER, BUT HER MOTIVES ARE UNKNOWN. WE CAN ONLY BARELY PERCEIVE THAT SHE IS *ALL THINGS.*
SHE WEEPS FOR US, SHEPHERDING US THROUGH THE VIOLENT BIRTH THAT IS MATERIAL EXISTENCE.
THEN...THERE IS THE OTHER GOD.
THE *PSYCHOPATH.*
SKIN. TEXT. SOIL. COLD CALCULUS. HE GOVERNS THE EARTH AS ITS CREATOR AND MASTER.
TETHERED TO OUR FLESH, WE CANNOT ESCAPE HIM.
WE NAME HIM "EVIL," BUT HE IS NO FALLEN ANGEL. HE IS THE FATHER HIMSELF. ABOVE US AND BETWEEN US, DIVIDING.
I, KHONSHU, AM BUT A SERVANT TO THAT FORMER, GREATER, MORE ILLUSIVE POWER.
BUT MY FATHER, RA? HE WOULD *DOMINATE* HER.
TWO GODS STRUGGLING. THE OUTCOME IS UNCERTAIN.
ONLY ONE THING IS CLEA

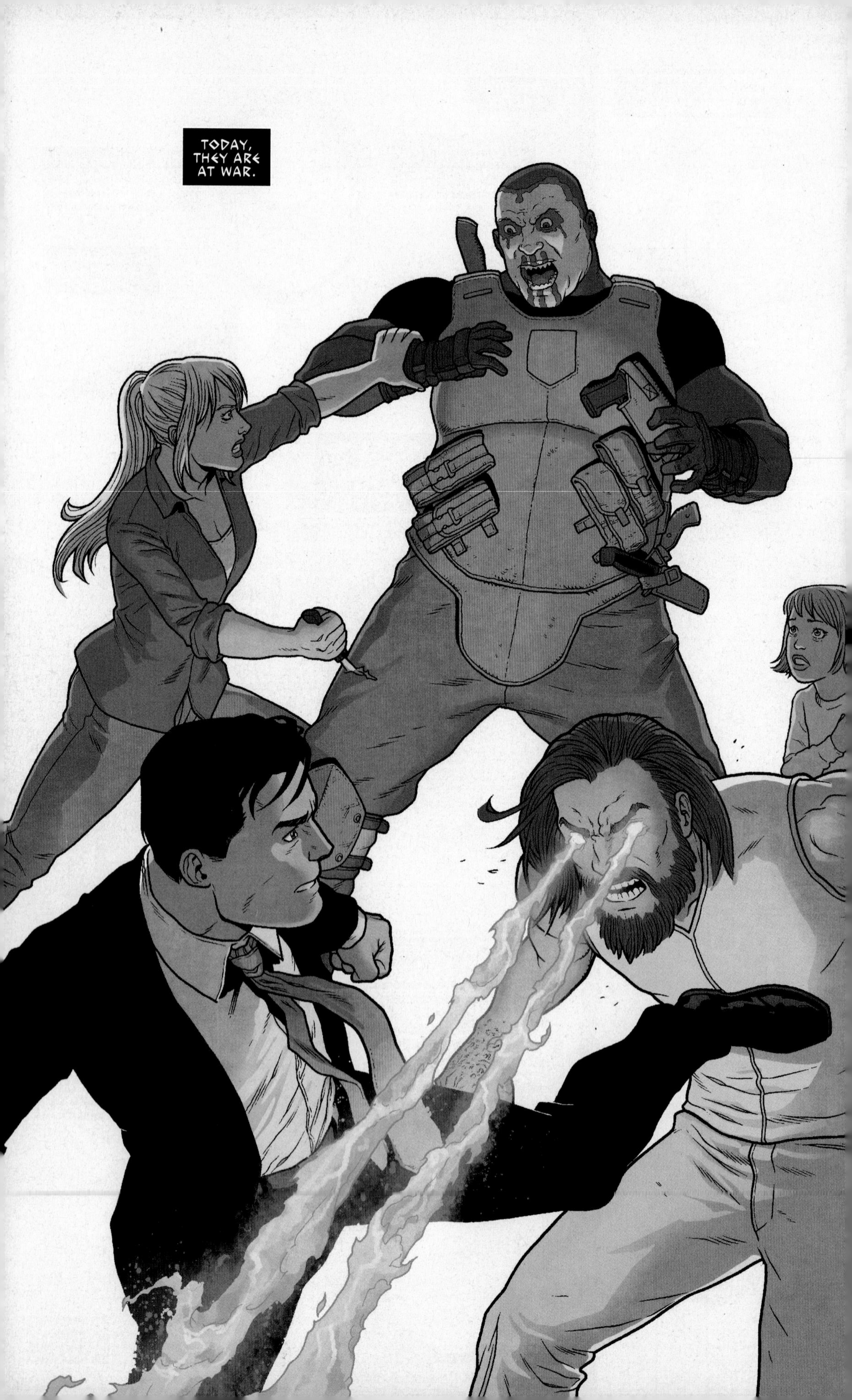
TODAY, THEY ARE AT WAR.

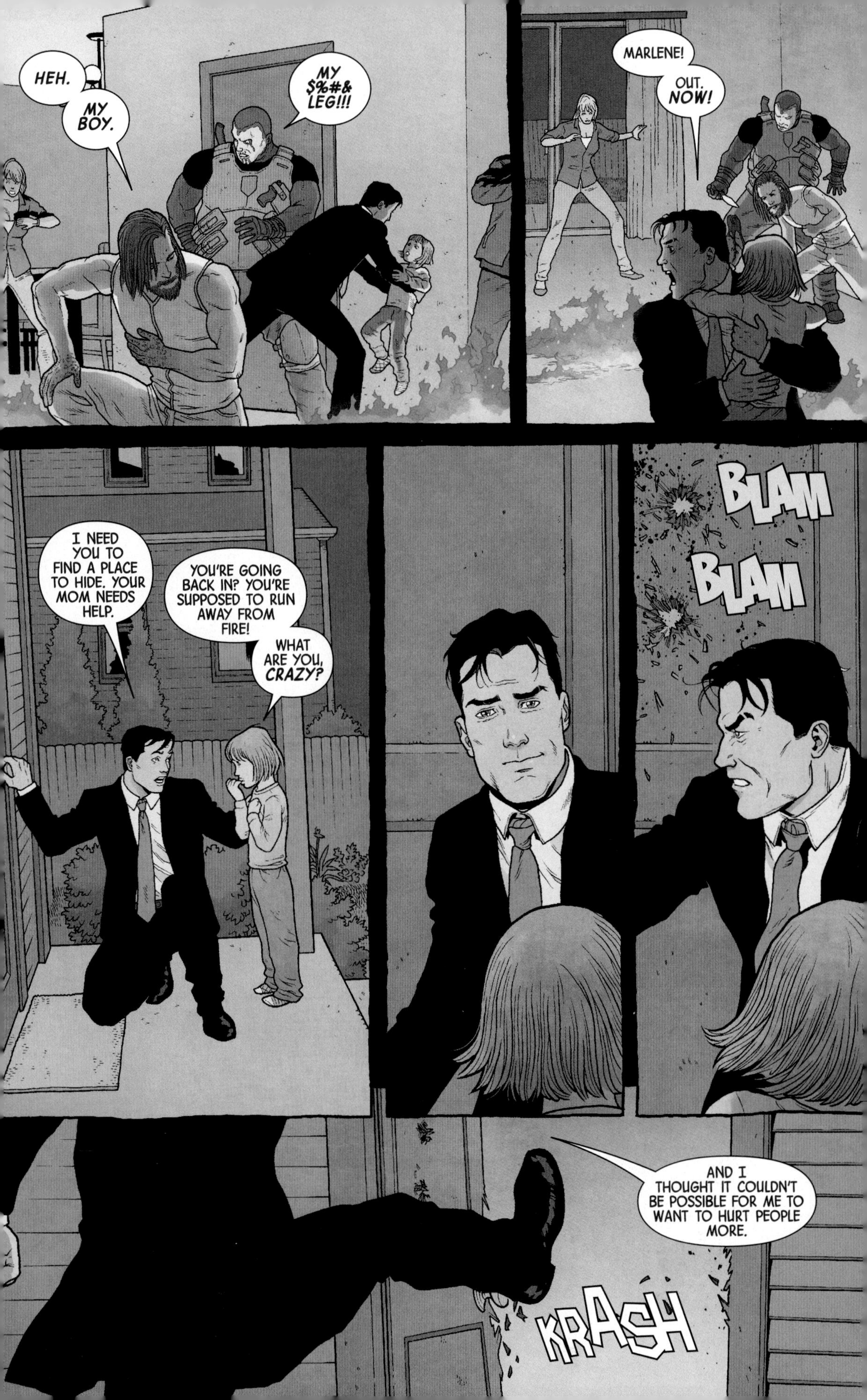

HEH.
MY BOY.
MY $%#& LEG!!!
MARLENE!
OUT. NOW!
I NEED YOU TO FIND A PLACE TO HIDE. YOUR MOM NEEDS HELP.
YOU'RE GOING BACK IN? YOU'RE SUPPOSED TO RUN AWAY FROM FIRE!
WHAT ARE YOU, CRAZY?
BLAM
BLAM
AND I THOUGHT IT COULDN'T BE POSSIBLE FOR ME TO WANT TO HURT PEOPLE MORE.
KRASH

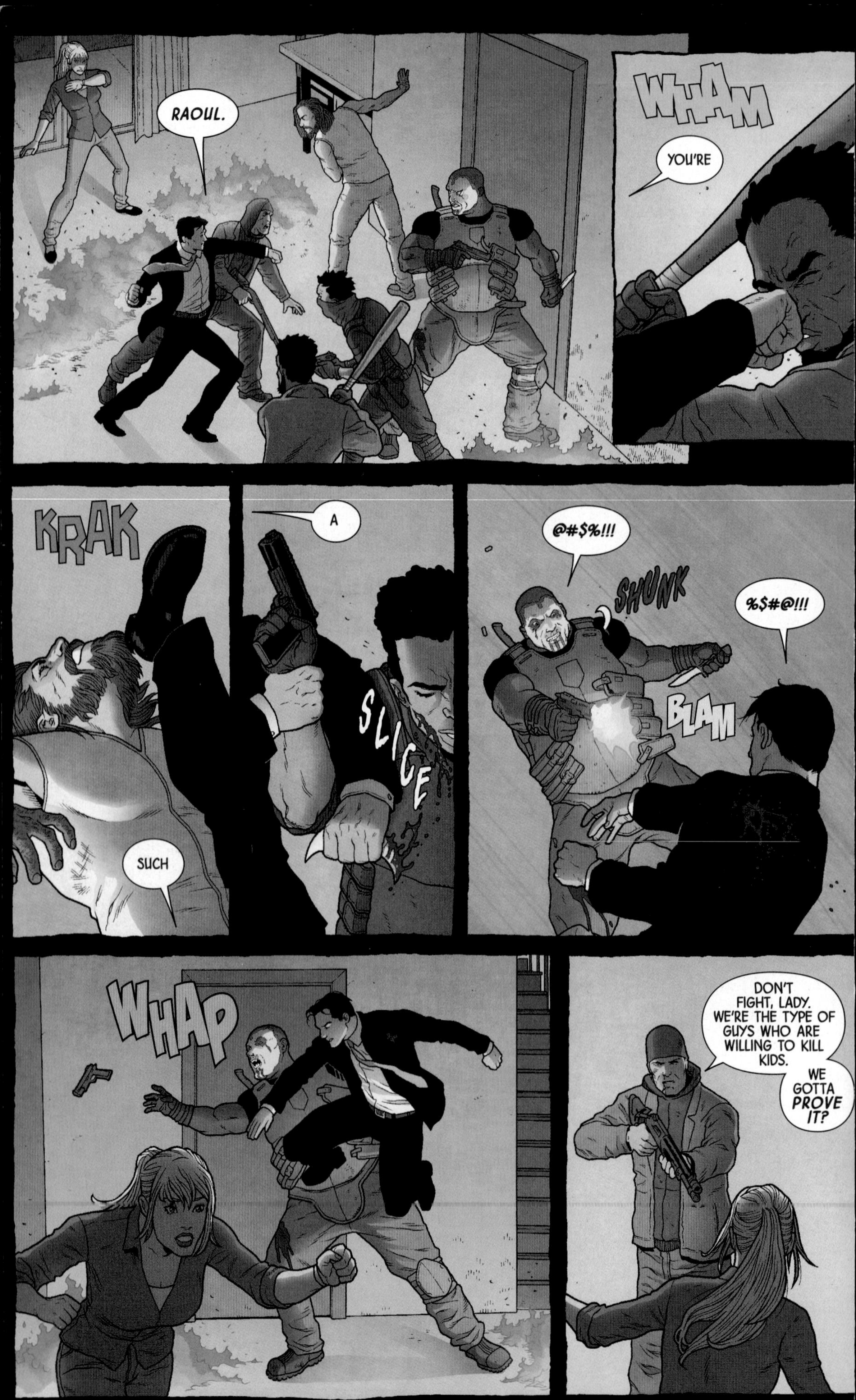
RAOUL.
WHAM
YOU'RE
KRAK
SUCH
A
SLICE
@#$%!!!
SHUNK
%$#@!!!
BLAM
WHAP
DON'T FIGHT, LADY. WE'RE THE TYPE OF GUYS WHO ARE WILLING TO KILL KIDS.
WE GOTTA *PROVE* IT?

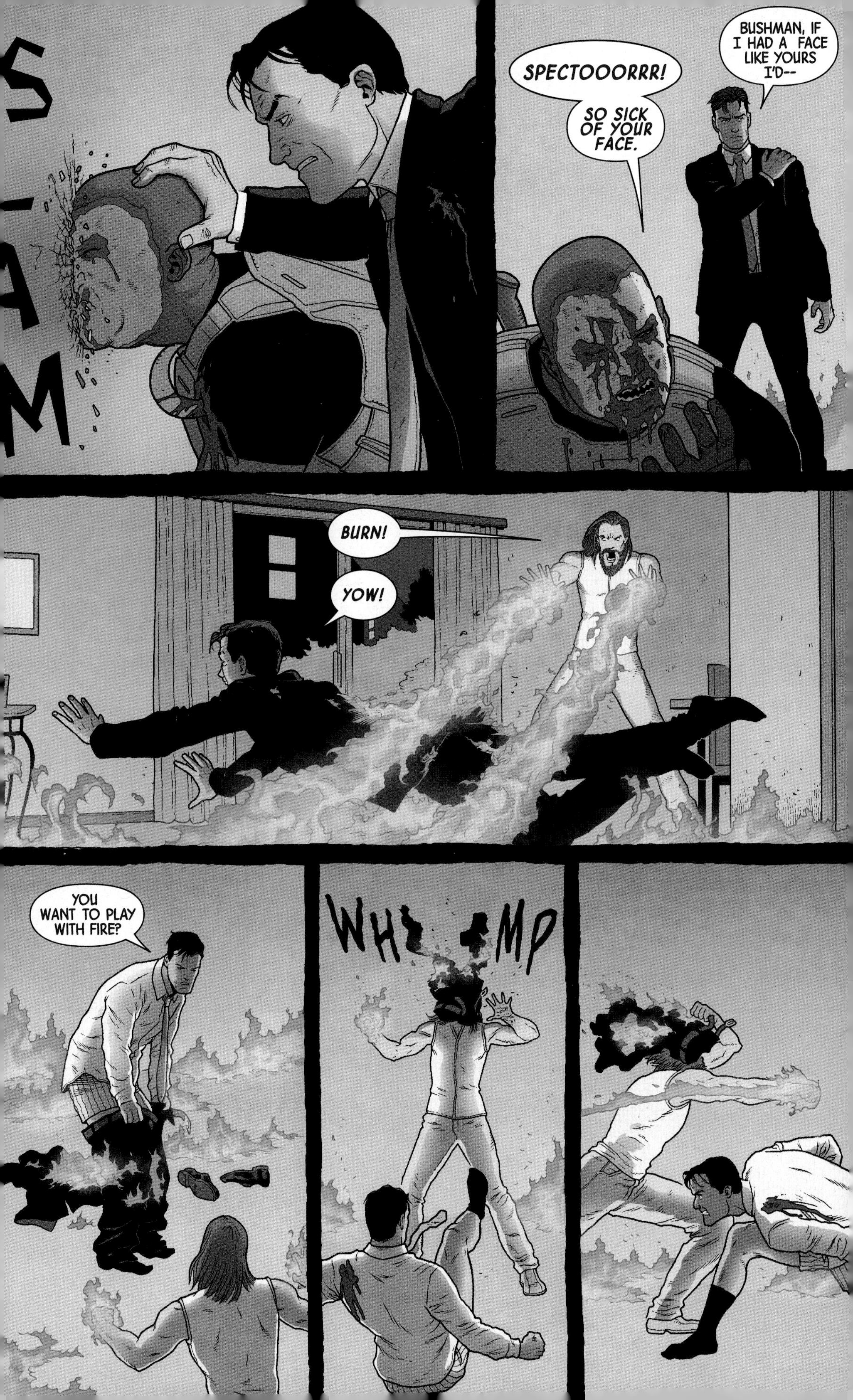
SLAM
SPECTOOOORRR!
SO SICK OF YOUR FACE.
BUSHMAN, IF I HAD A FACE LIKE YOURS I'D--
BURN!
YOW!
YOU WANT TO PLAY WITH FIRE?
WH MP

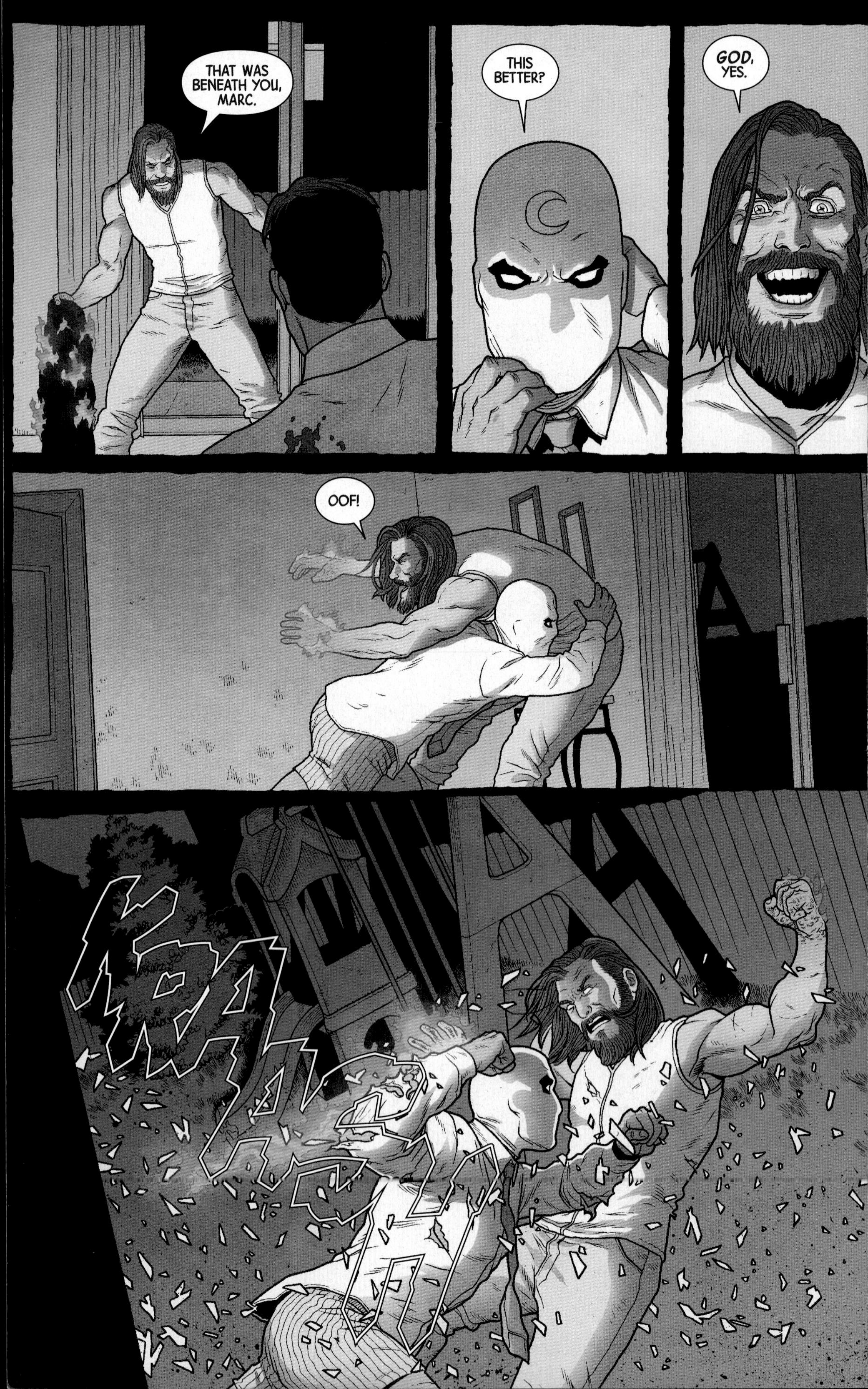
THAT WAS BENEATH YOU, MARC.
THIS BETTER?
GOD, YES.
OOF!

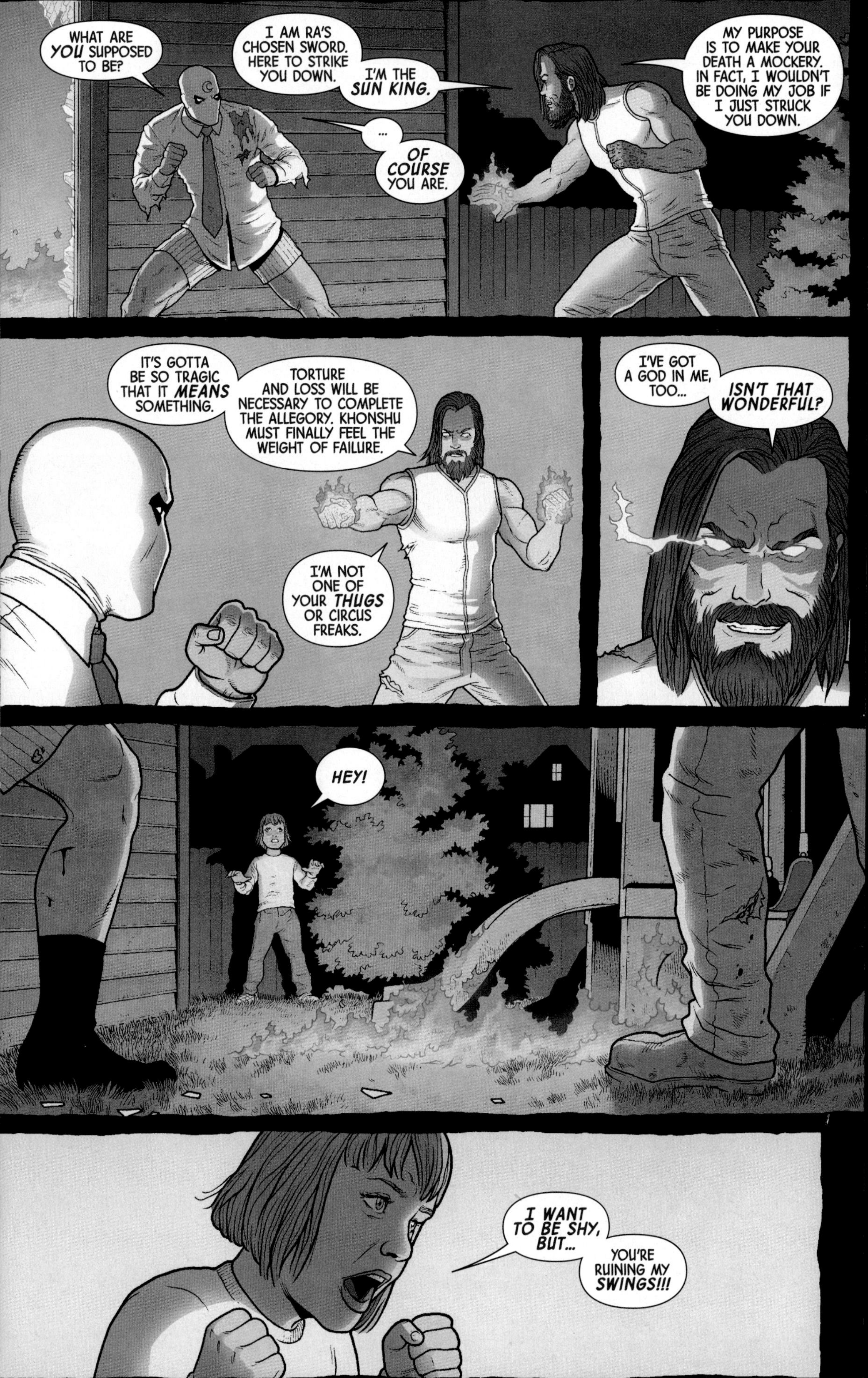
WHAT ARE YOU SUPPOSED TO BE?
I AM RA'S CHOSEN SWORD. HERE TO STRIKE YOU DOWN.
I'M THE SUN KING.
...
OF COURSE YOU ARE.
MY PURPOSE IS TO MAKE YOUR DEATH A MOCKERY. IN FACT, I WOULDN'T BE DOING MY JOB IF I JUST STRUCK YOU DOWN.
IT'S GOTTA BE SO TRAGIC THAT IT MEANS SOMETHING.
TORTURE AND LOSS WILL BE NECESSARY TO COMPLETE THE ALLEGORY. KHONSHU MUST FINALLY FEEL THE WEIGHT OF FAILURE.
I'M NOT ONE OF YOUR THUGS OR CIRCUS FREAKS.
I'VE GOT A GOD IN ME, TOO...
ISN'T THAT WONDERFUL?
HEY!
I WANT TO BE SHY, BUT...
YOU'RE RUINING MY SWINGS!!!

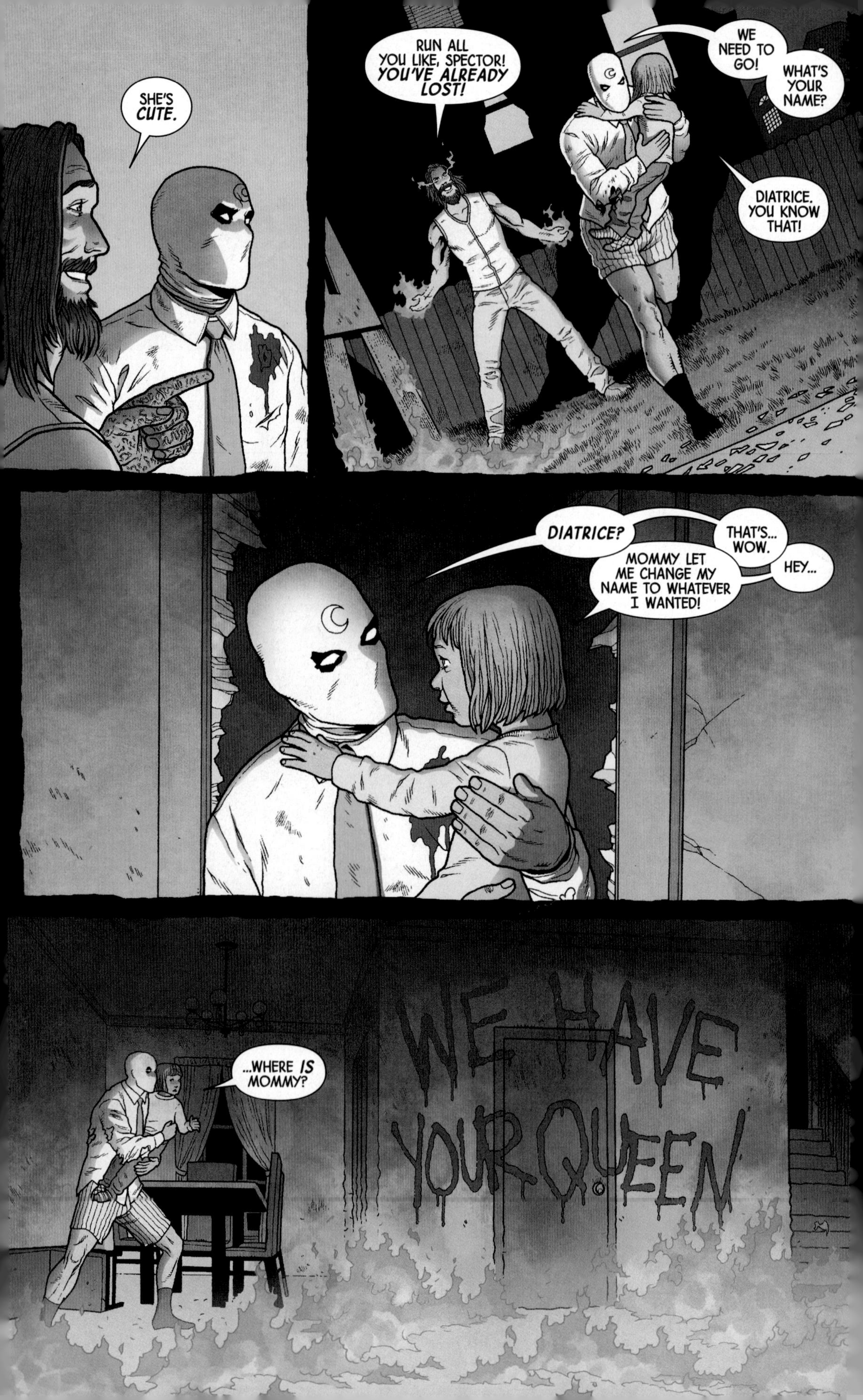
SHE'S CUTE.
RUN ALL YOU LIKE, SPECTOR! YOU'VE ALREADY LOST!
WE NEED TO GO!
WHAT'S YOUR NAME?
DIATRICE. YOU KNOW THAT!
DIATRICE?
THAT'S... WOW.
MOMMY LET ME CHANGE MY NAME TO WHATEVER I WANTED!
HEY...
...WHERE IS MOMMY?
WE HAVE YOUR QUEEN

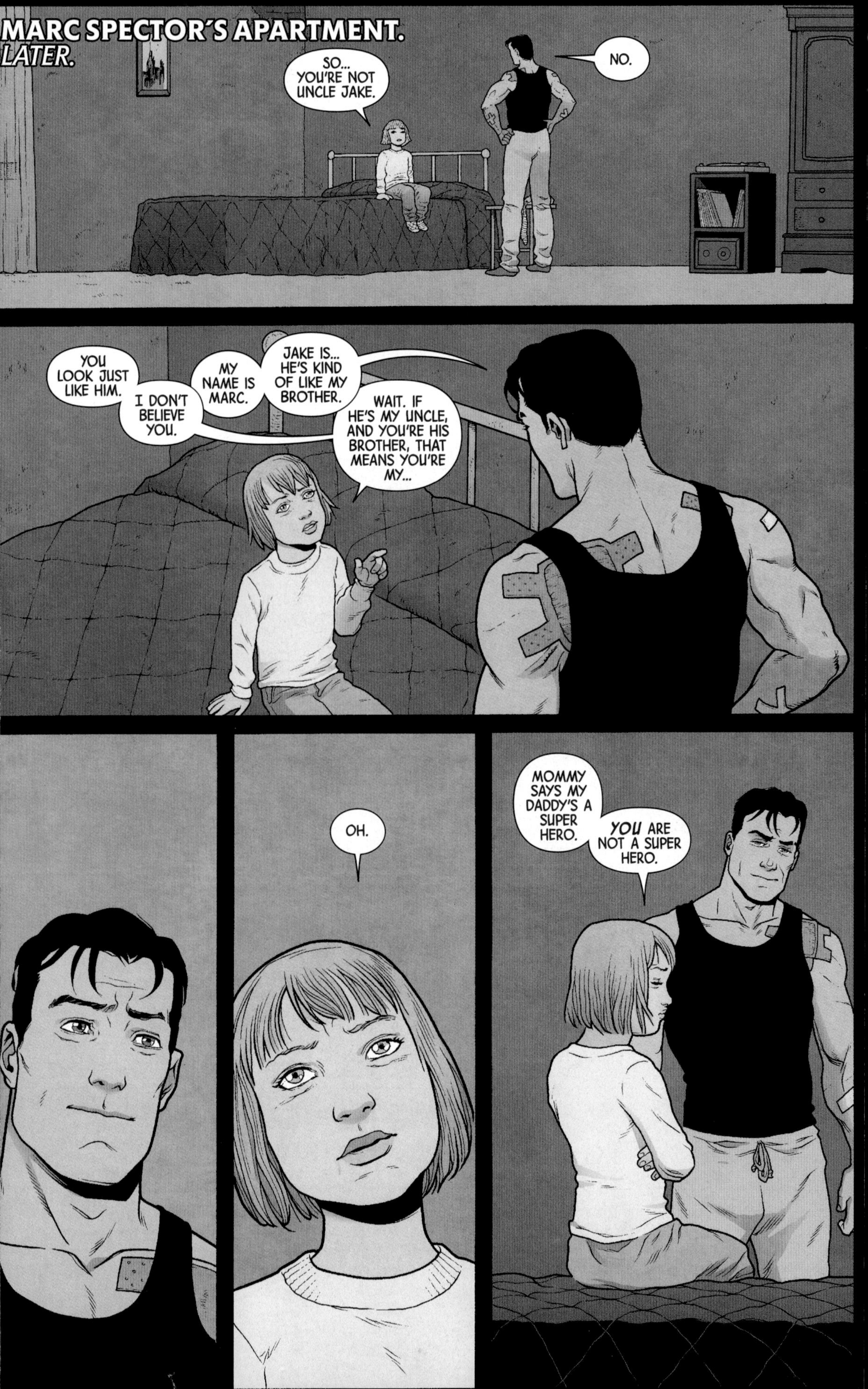
MARC SPECTOR'S APARTMENT. LATER.
SO... YOU'RE NOT UNCLE JAKE.
NO.
YOU LOOK JUST LIKE HIM.
MY NAME IS MARC.
JAKE IS... HE'S KIND OF LIKE MY BROTHER.
I DON'T BELIEVE YOU.
WAIT. IF HE'S MY UNCLE, AND YOU'RE HIS BROTHER, THAT MEANS YOU'RE MY...
OH.
MOMMY SAYS MY DADDY'S A SUPER HERO.
YOU ARE NOT A SUPER HERO.

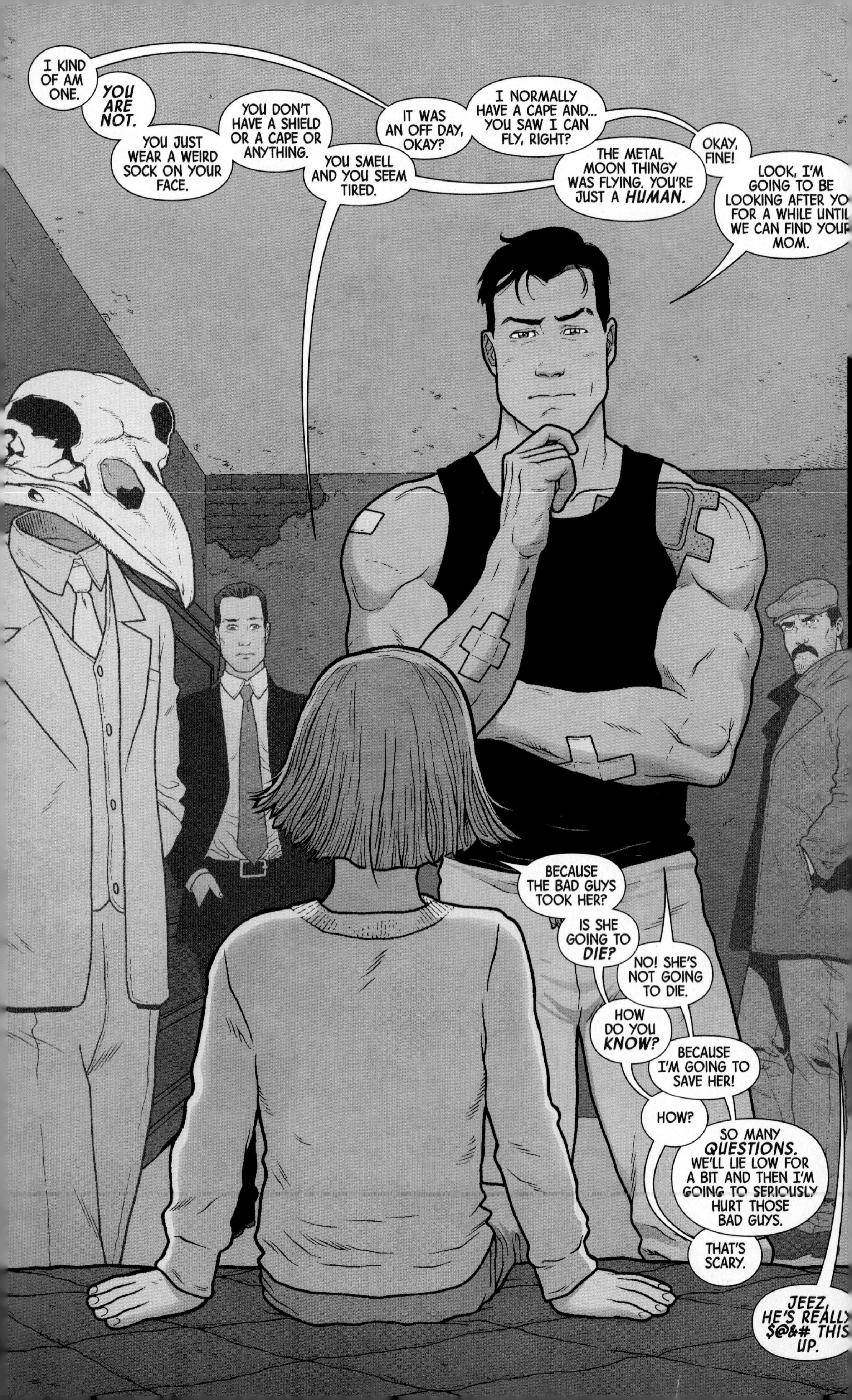
I KIND OF AM ONE.
YOU ARE NOT.
YOU JUST WEAR A WEIRD SOCK ON YOUR FACE.
YOU DON'T HAVE A SHIELD OR A CAPE OR ANYTHING.
IT WAS AN OFF DAY, OKAY?
I NORMALLY HAVE A CAPE AND... YOU SAW I CAN FLY, RIGHT?
YOU SMELL AND YOU SEEM TIRED.
THE METAL MOON THINGY WAS FLYING. YOU'RE JUST A HUMAN.
OKAY, FINE!
LOOK, I'M GOING TO BE LOOKING AFTER YO FOR A WHILE UNTIL WE CAN FIND YOUR MOM.
BECAUSE THE BAD GUYS TOOK HER?
IS SHE GOING TO DIE?
NO! SHE'S NOT GOING TO DIE.
HOW DO YOU KNOW?
BECAUSE I'M GOING TO SAVE HER!
HOW?
SO MANY QUESTIONS. WE'LL LIE LOW FOR A BIT AND THEN I'M GOING TO SERIOUSLY HURT THOSE BAD GUYS.
THAT'S SCARY.
JEEZ, HE'S REALLY $@&# THIS UP.

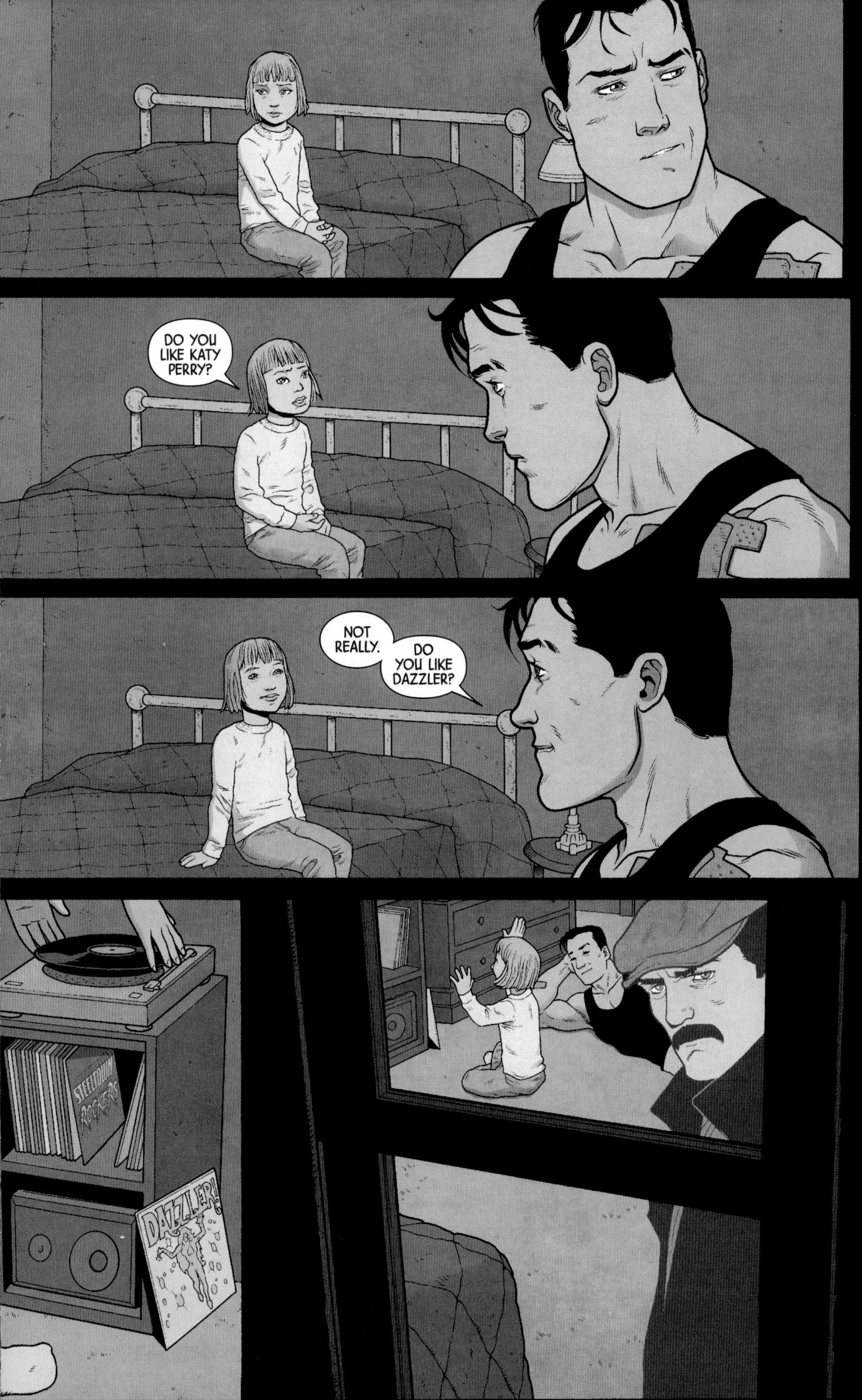
DO YOU LIKE KATY PERRY?
NOT REALLY.
DO YOU LIKE DAZZLER?
STEELTOWN ROCKERS
DAZZLER!

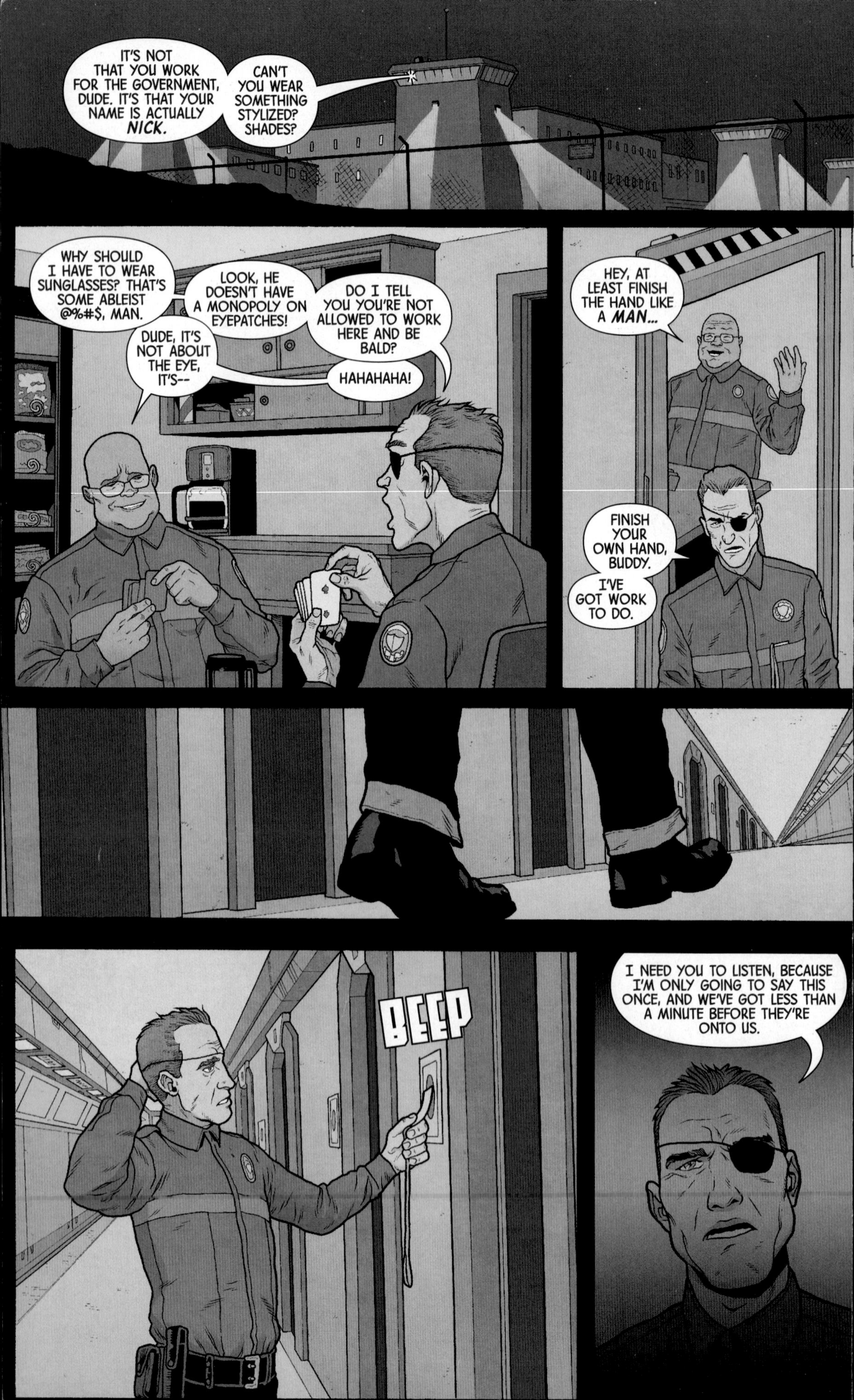
IT'S NOT THAT YOU WORK FOR THE GOVERNMENT, DUDE. IT'S THAT YOUR NAME IS ACTUALLY NICK.
CAN'T YOU WEAR SOMETHING STYLIZED? SHADES?
WHY SHOULD I HAVE TO WEAR SUNGLASSES? THAT'S SOME ABLEIST @%#$, MAN.
LOOK, HE DOESN'T HAVE A MONOPOLY ON EYEPATCHES!
DUDE, IT'S NOT ABOUT THE EYE, IT'S--
DO I TELL YOU YOU'RE NOT ALLOWED TO WORK HERE AND BE BALD?
HAHAHAHA!
HEY, AT LEAST FINISH THE HAND LIKE A MAN...
FINISH YOUR OWN HAND, BUDDY.
I'VE GOT WORK TO DO.
BEEP
I NEED YOU TO LISTEN, BECAUSE I'M ONLY GOING TO SAY THIS ONCE, AND WE'VE GOT LESS THAN A MINUTE BEFORE THEY'RE ONTO US.

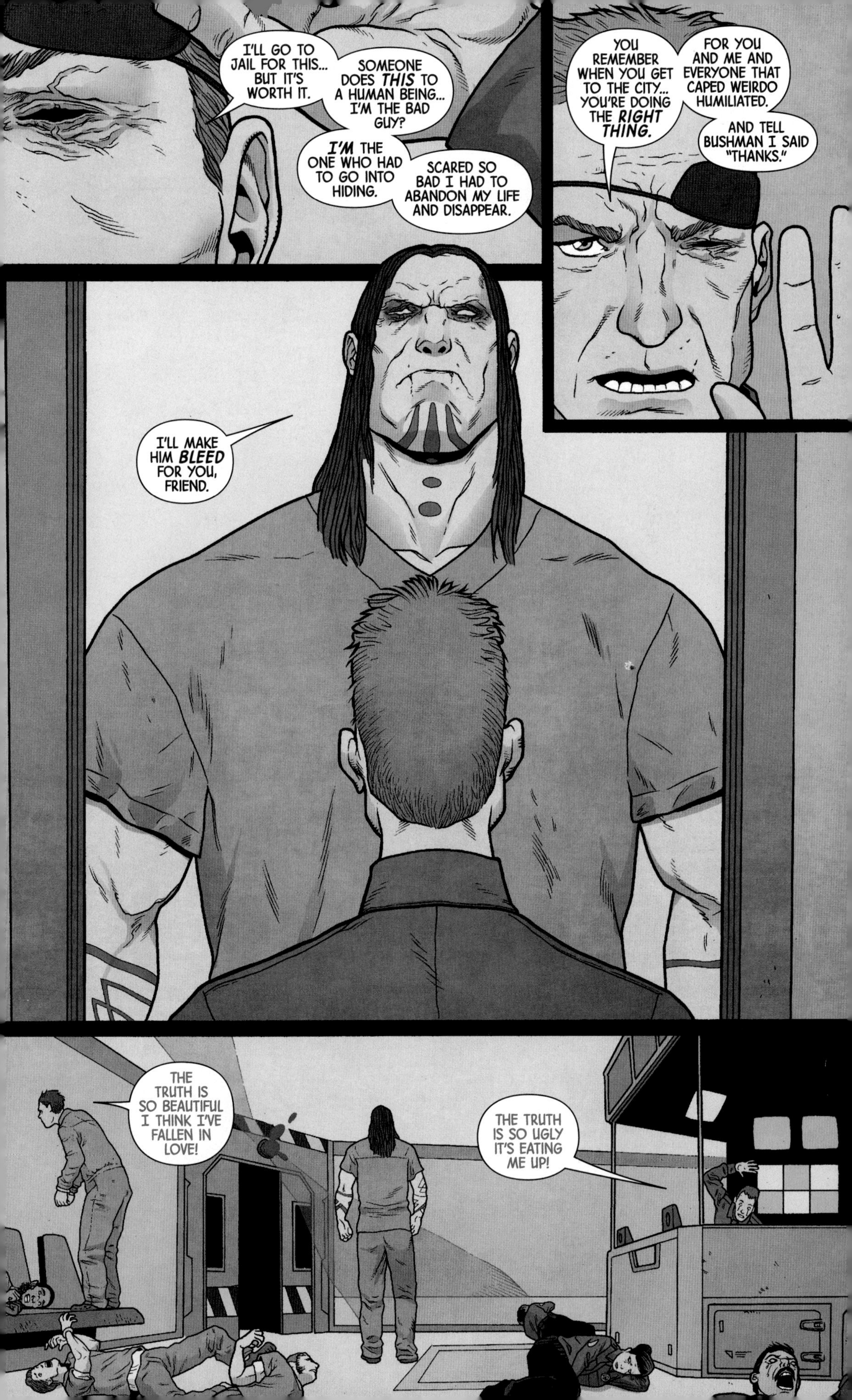
I'LL GO TO JAIL FOR THIS... BUT IT'S WORTH IT.
SOMEONE DOES THIS TO A HUMAN BEING... I'M THE BAD GUY?
I'M THE ONE WHO HAD TO GO INTO HIDING.
SCARED SO BAD I HAD TO ABANDON MY LIFE AND DISAPPEAR.
YOU REMEMBER WHEN YOU GET TO THE CITY... YOU'RE DOING THE RIGHT THING.
FOR YOU AND ME AND EVERYONE THAT CAPED WEIRDO HUMILIATED.
AND TELL BUSHMAN I SAID "THANKS."
I'LL MAKE HIM BLEED FOR YOU, FRIEND.
THE TRUTH IS SO BEAUTIFUL I THINK I'VE FALLEN IN LOVE!
THE TRUTH IS SO UGLY IT'S EATING ME UP!

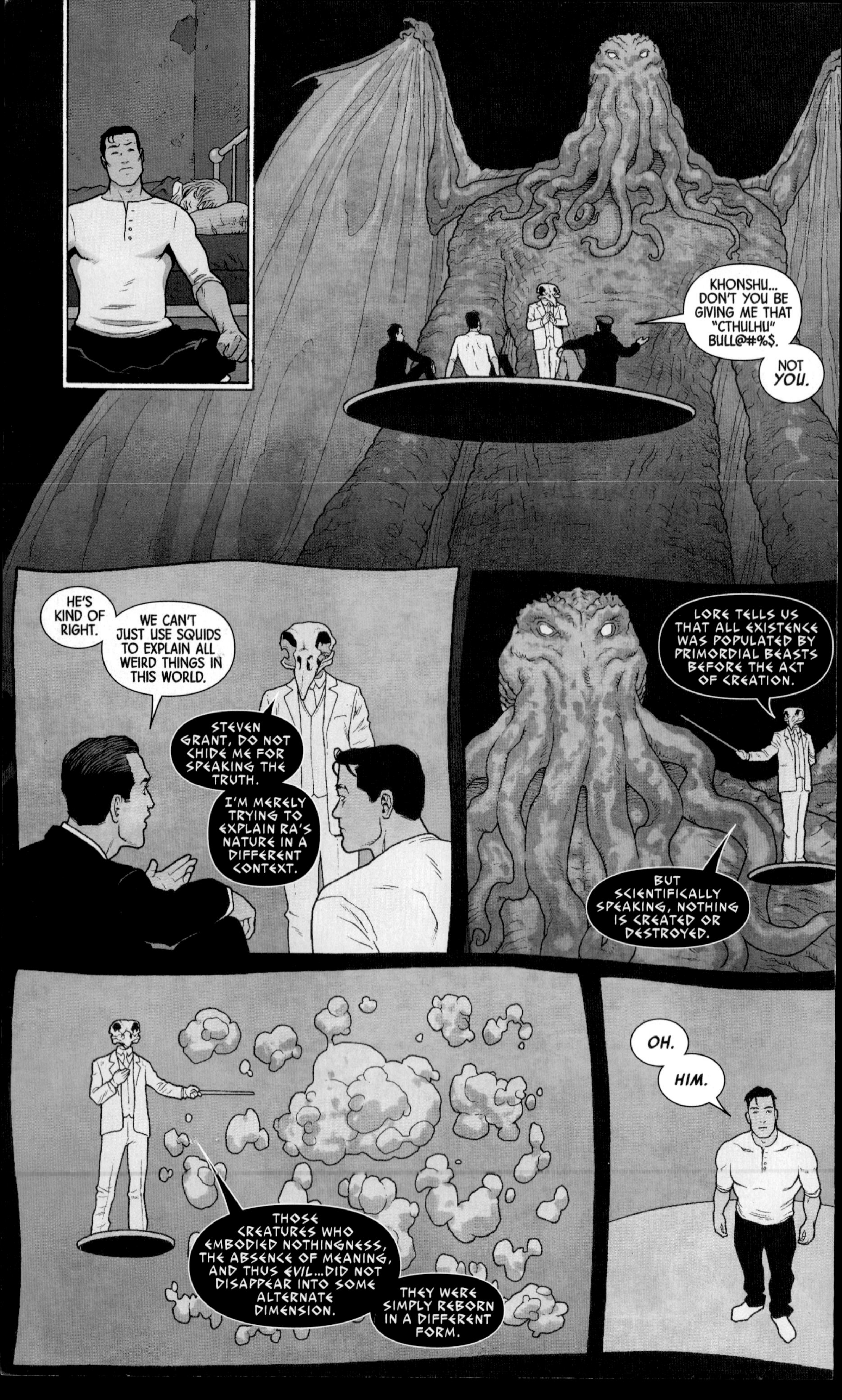
KHONSHU... DON'T YOU BE GIVING ME THAT "CTHULHU" BULL@#%$.
NOT YOU.
HE'S KIND OF RIGHT.
WE CAN'T JUST USE SQUIDS TO EXPLAIN ALL WEIRD THINGS IN THIS WORLD.
STEVEN GRANT, DO NOT CHIDE ME FOR SPEAKING THE TRUTH.
I'M MERELY TRYING TO EXPLAIN RA'S NATURE IN A DIFFERENT CONTEXT.
LORE TELLS US THAT ALL EXISTENCE WAS POPULATED BY PRIMORDIAL BEASTS BEFORE THE ACT OF CREATION.
BUT SCIENTIFICALLY SPEAKING, NOTHING IS CREATED OR DESTROYED.
THOSE CREATURES WHO EMBODIED NOTHINGNESS, THE ABSENCE OF MEANING, AND THUS EVIL...DID NOT DISAPPEAR INTO SOME ALTERNATE DIMENSION.
THEY WERE SIMPLY REBORN IN A DIFFERENT FORM.
OH.
HIM.

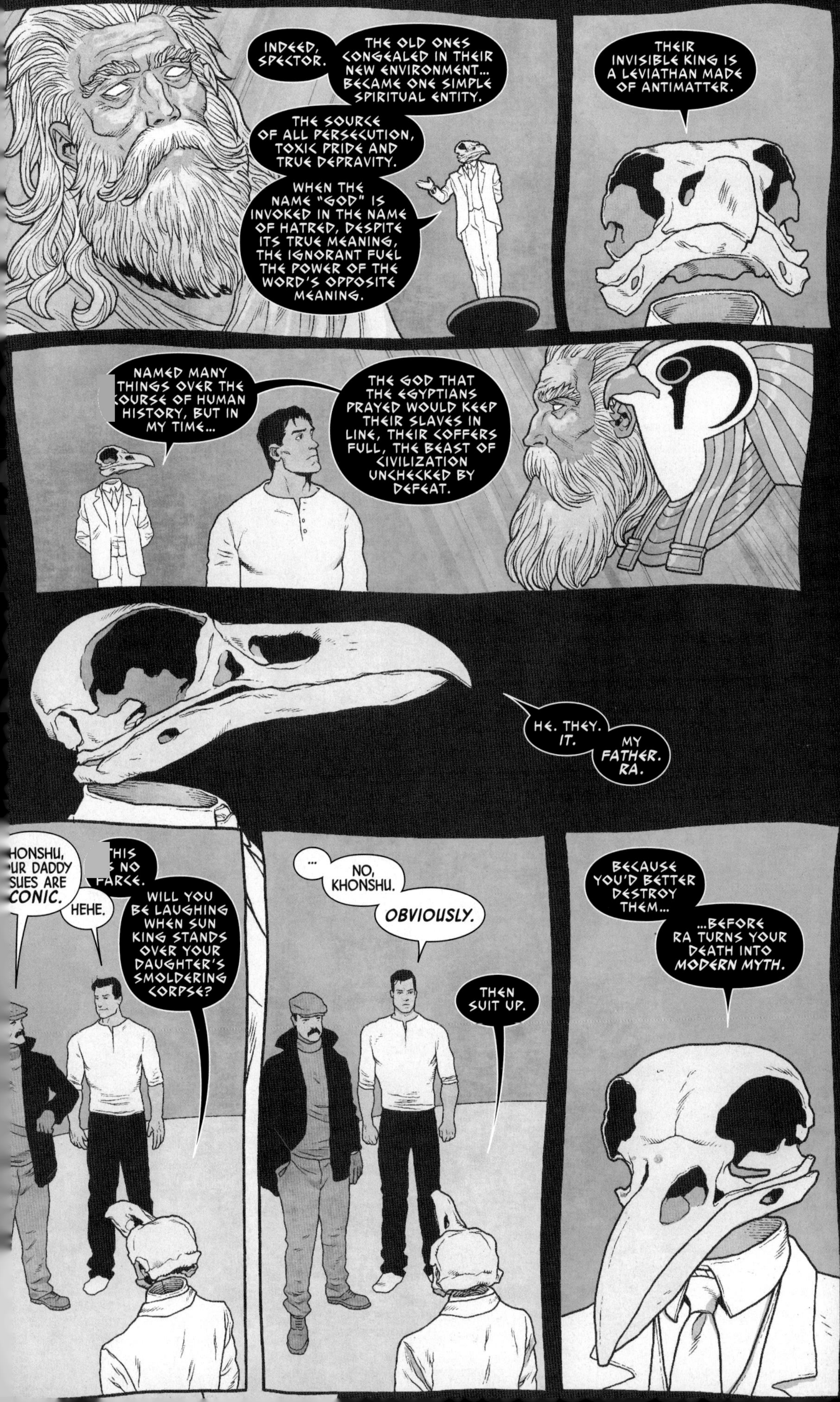
INDEED, SPECTOR.
THE OLD ONES CONGEALED IN THEIR NEW ENVIRONMENT... BECAME ONE SIMPLE SPIRITUAL ENTITY.
THE SOURCE OF ALL PERSECUTION, TOXIC PRIDE AND TRUE DEPRAVITY.
WHEN THE NAME "GOD" IS INVOKED IN THE NAME OF HATRED, DESPITE ITS TRUE MEANING, THE IGNORANT FUEL THE POWER OF THE WORD'S OPPOSITE MEANING.
THEIR INVISIBLE KING IS A LEVIATHAN MADE OF ANTIMATTER.
NAMED MANY THINGS OVER THE OURSE OF HUMAN HISTORY, BUT IN MY TIME...
THE GOD THAT THE EGYPTIANS PRAYED WOULD KEEP THEIR SLAVES IN LINE, THEIR COFFERS FULL, THE BEAST OF CIVILIZATION UNCHECKED BY DEFEAT.
HE. THEY. IT.
MY FATHER. RA.
HONSHU, UR DADDY SUES ARE CONIC.
HEHE.
THIS S NO FARCE.
WILL YOU BE LAUGHING WHEN SUN KING STANDS OVER YOUR DAUGHTER'S SMOLDERING CORPSE?
...
NO, KHONSHU.
OBVIOUSLY.
THEN SUIT UP.
BECAUSE YOU'D BETTER DESTROY THEM...
...BEFORE RA TURNS YOUR DEATH INTO MODERN MYTH.

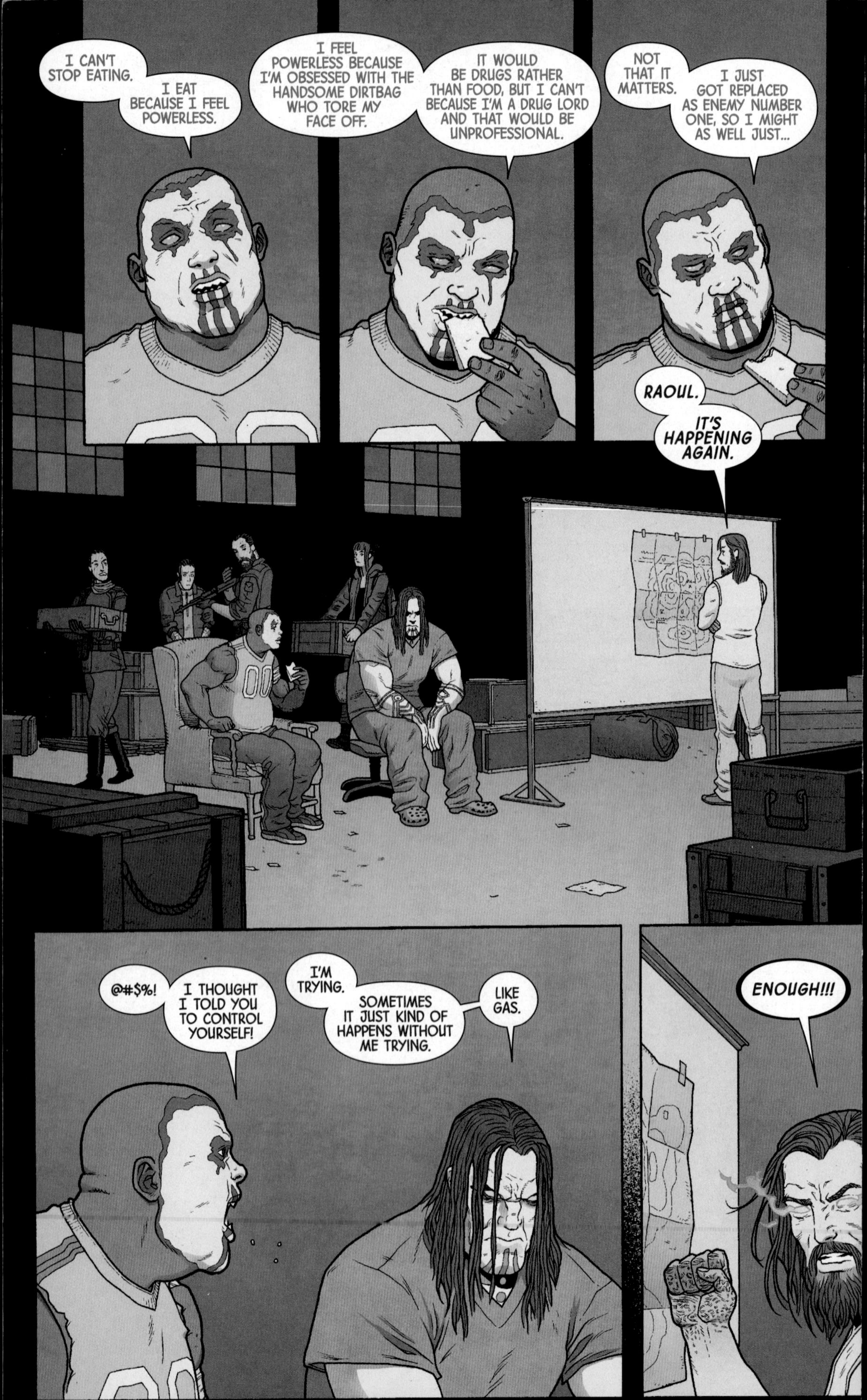

I CAN'T STOP EATING.
I EAT BECAUSE I FEEL POWERLESS.
I FEEL POWERLESS BECAUSE I'M OBSESSED WITH THE HANDSOME DIRTBAG WHO TORE MY FACE OFF.
IT WOULD BE DRUGS RATHER THAN FOOD, BUT I CAN'T BECAUSE I'M A DRUG LORD AND THAT WOULD BE UNPROFESSIONAL.
NOT THAT IT MATTERS.
I JUST GOT REPLACED AS ENEMY NUMBER ONE, SO I MIGHT AS WELL JUST...
RAOUL.
IT'S HAPPENING AGAIN.
@#$%!
I THOUGHT I TOLD YOU TO CONTROL YOURSELF!
I'M TRYING.
SOMETIMES IT JUST KIND OF HAPPENS WITHOUT ME TRYING.
LIKE GAS.
ENOUGH!!!

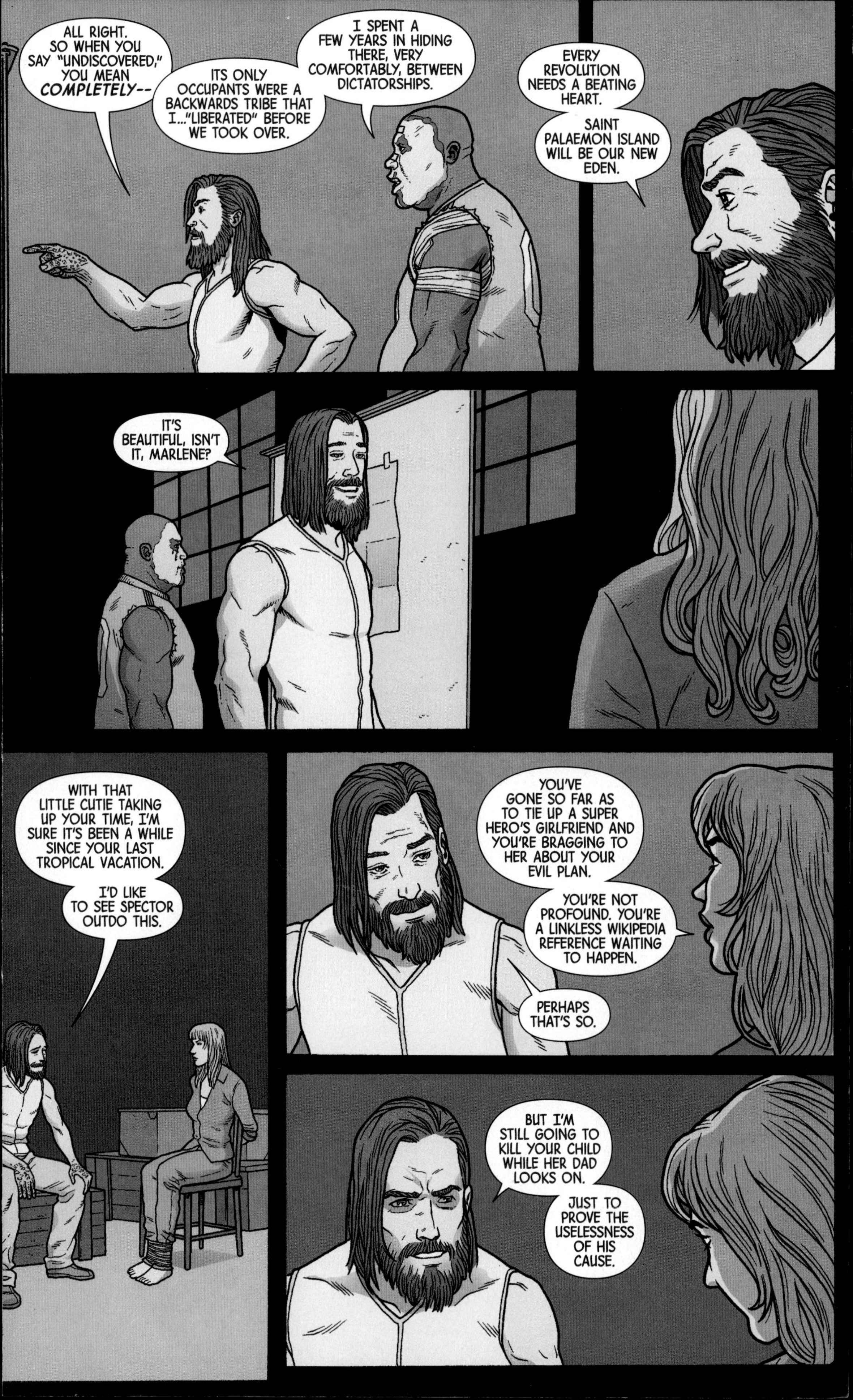
ALL RIGHT. SO WHEN YOU SAY "UNDISCOVERED," YOU MEAN *COMPLETELY*--
ITS ONLY OCCUPANTS WERE A BACKWARDS TRIBE THAT I..."LIBERATED" BEFORE WE TOOK OVER.
I SPENT A FEW YEARS IN HIDING THERE, VERY COMFORTABLY, BETWEEN DICTATORSHIPS.
EVERY REVOLUTION NEEDS A BEATING HEART.
SAINT PALAEMON ISLAND WILL BE OUR NEW EDEN.
IT'S BEAUTIFUL, ISN'T IT, MARLENE?
WITH THAT LITTLE CUTIE TAKING UP YOUR TIME, I'M SURE IT'S BEEN A WHILE SINCE YOUR LAST TROPICAL VACATION.
I'D LIKE TO SEE SPECTOR OUTDO THIS.
YOU'VE GONE SO FAR AS TO TIE UP A SUPER HERO'S GIRLFRIEND AND YOU'RE BRAGGING TO HER ABOUT YOUR EVIL PLAN.
YOU'RE NOT PROFOUND. YOU'RE A LINKLESS WIKIPEDIA REFERENCE WAITING TO HAPPEN.
PERHAPS THAT'S SO.
BUT I'M STILL GOING TO KILL YOUR CHILD WHILE HER DAD LOOKS ON.
JUST TO PROVE THE USELESSNESS OF HIS CAUSE.

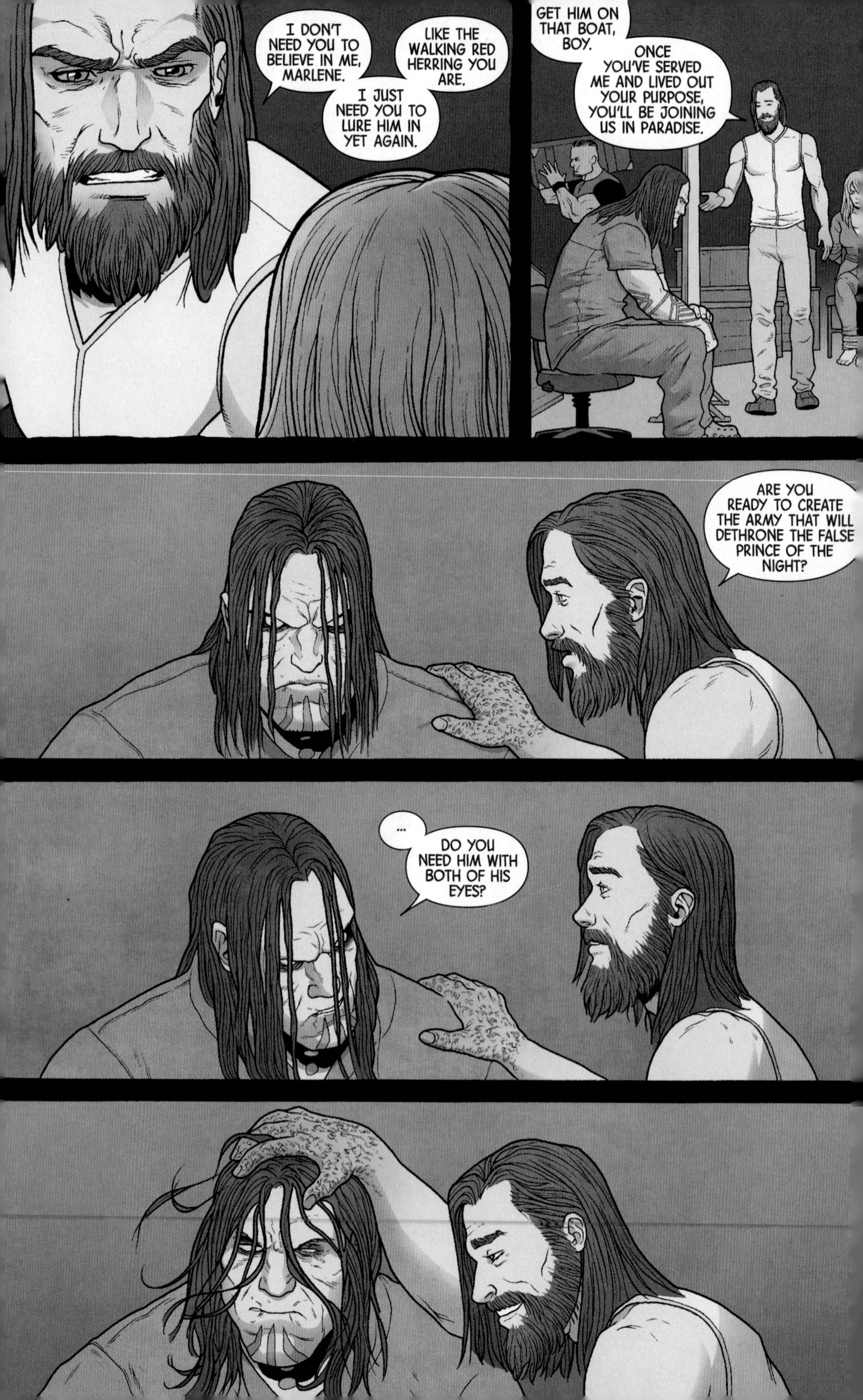
I DON'T NEED YOU TO BELIEVE IN ME, MARLENE.
LIKE THE WALKING RED HERRING YOU ARE.
I JUST NEED YOU TO LURE HIM IN YET AGAIN.
GET HIM ON THAT BOAT, BOY.
ONCE YOU'VE SERVED ME AND LIVED OUT YOUR PURPOSE, YOU'LL BE JOINING US IN PARADISE.
ARE YOU READY TO CREATE THE ARMY THAT WILL DETHRONE THE FALSE PRINCE OF THE NIGHT?
...
DO YOU NEED HIM WITH BOTH OF HIS EYES?

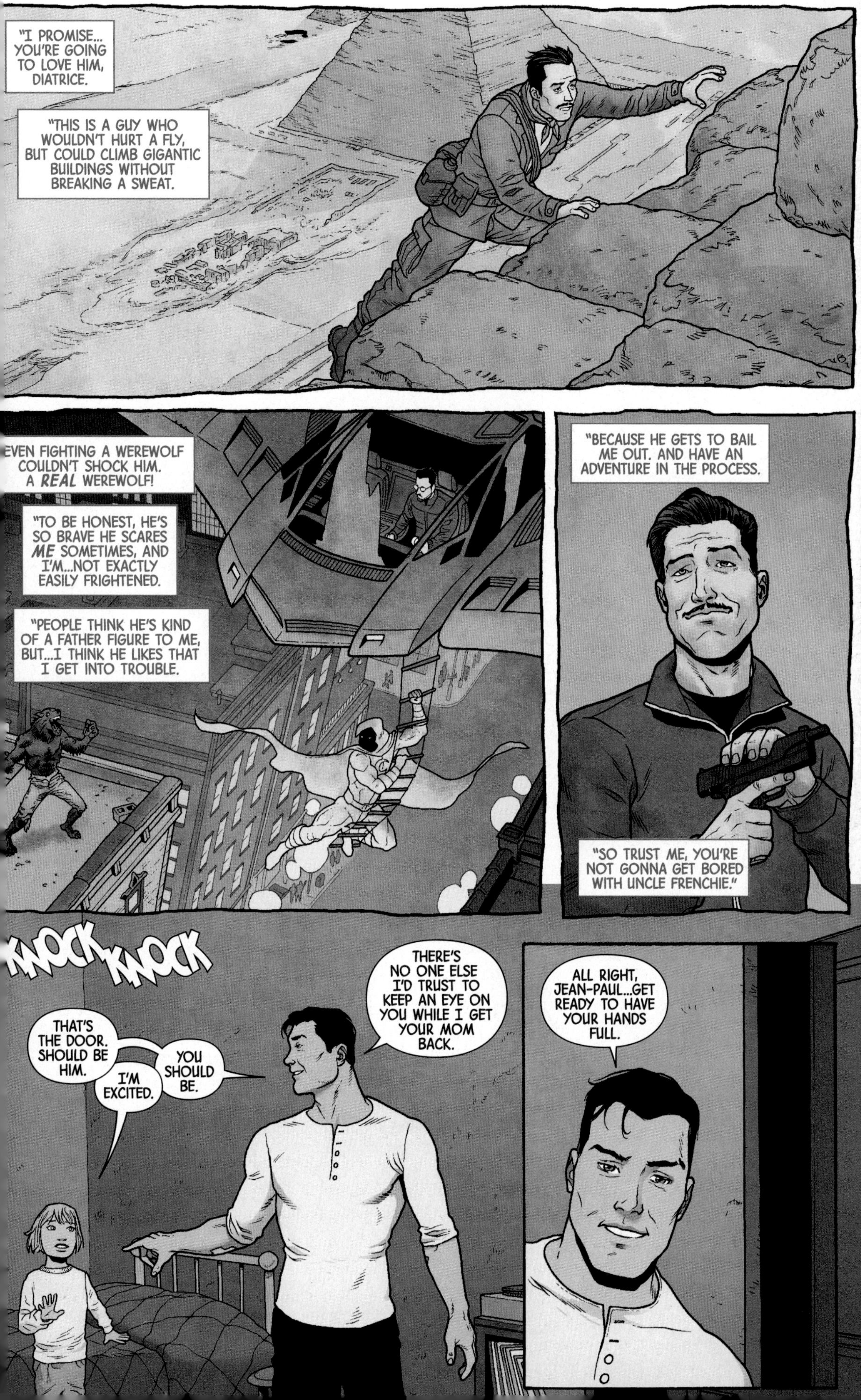
"I PROMISE... YOU'RE GOING TO LOVE HIM, DIATRICE.
"THIS IS A GUY WHO WOULDN'T HURT A FLY, BUT COULD CLIMB GIGANTIC BUILDINGS WITHOUT BREAKING A SWEAT.
EVEN FIGHTING A WEREWOLF COULDN'T SHOCK HIM. A REAL WEREWOLF!
"TO BE HONEST, HE'S SO BRAVE HE SCARES ME SOMETIMES, AND I'M...NOT EXACTLY EASILY FRIGHTENED.
"PEOPLE THINK HE'S KIND OF A FATHER FIGURE TO ME, BUT...I THINK HE LIKES THAT I GET INTO TROUBLE.
"BECAUSE HE GETS TO BAIL ME OUT. AND HAVE AN ADVENTURE IN THE PROCESS.
"SO TRUST ME, YOU'RE NOT GONNA GET BORED WITH UNCLE FRENCHIE."
KNOCK KNOCK
THAT'S THE DOOR. SHOULD BE HIM.
I'M EXCITED.
YOU SHOULD BE.
THERE'S NO ONE ELSE I'D TRUST TO KEEP AN EYE ON YOU WHILE I GET YOUR MOM BACK.
ALL RIGHT, JEAN-PAUL...GET READY TO HAVE YOUR HANDS FULL.

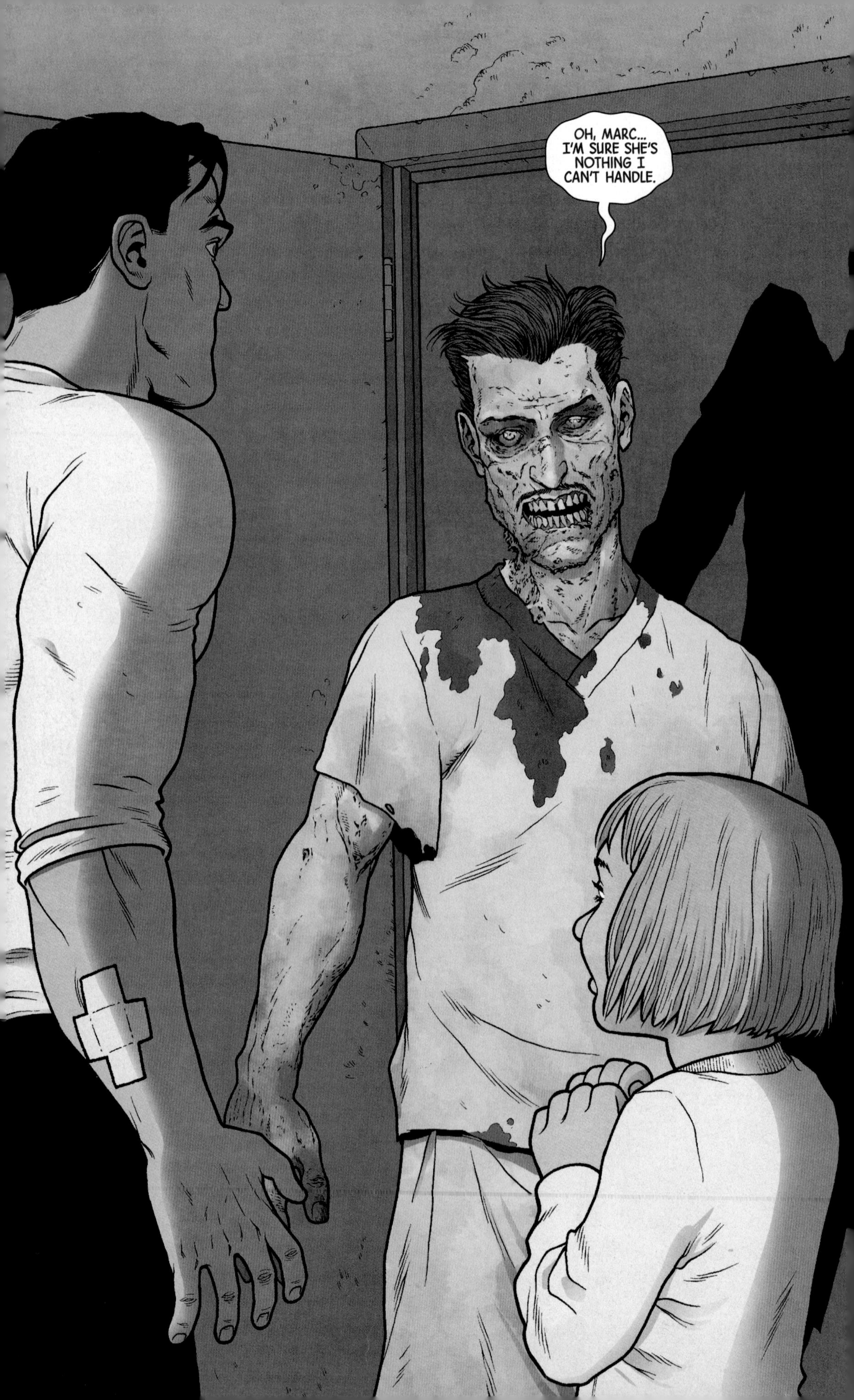
OH, MARC... I'M SURE SHE'S NOTHING I CAN'T HANDLE.

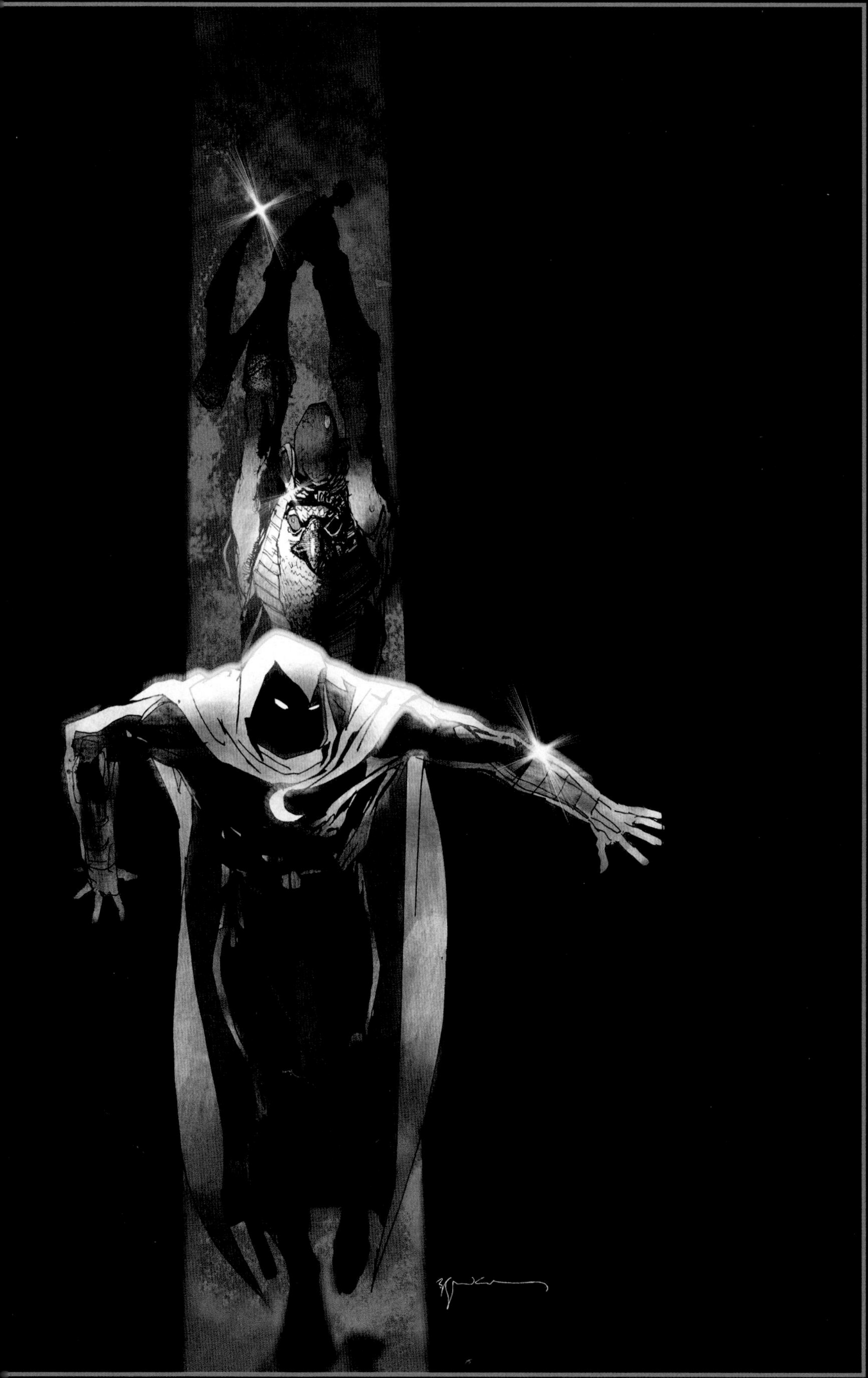

188 HOMAGE VARIANT BY **BILL SIENKIEWICZ**

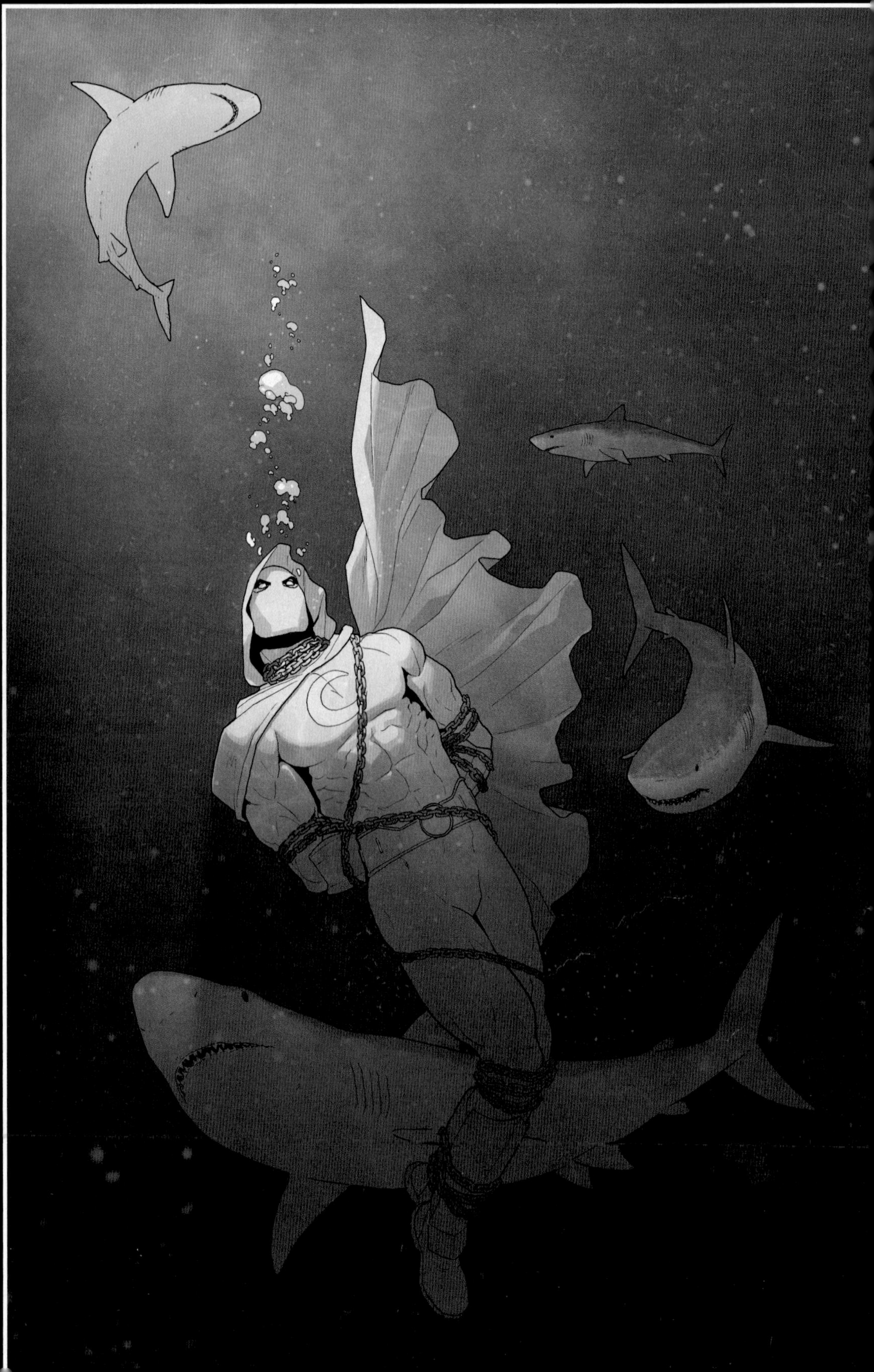

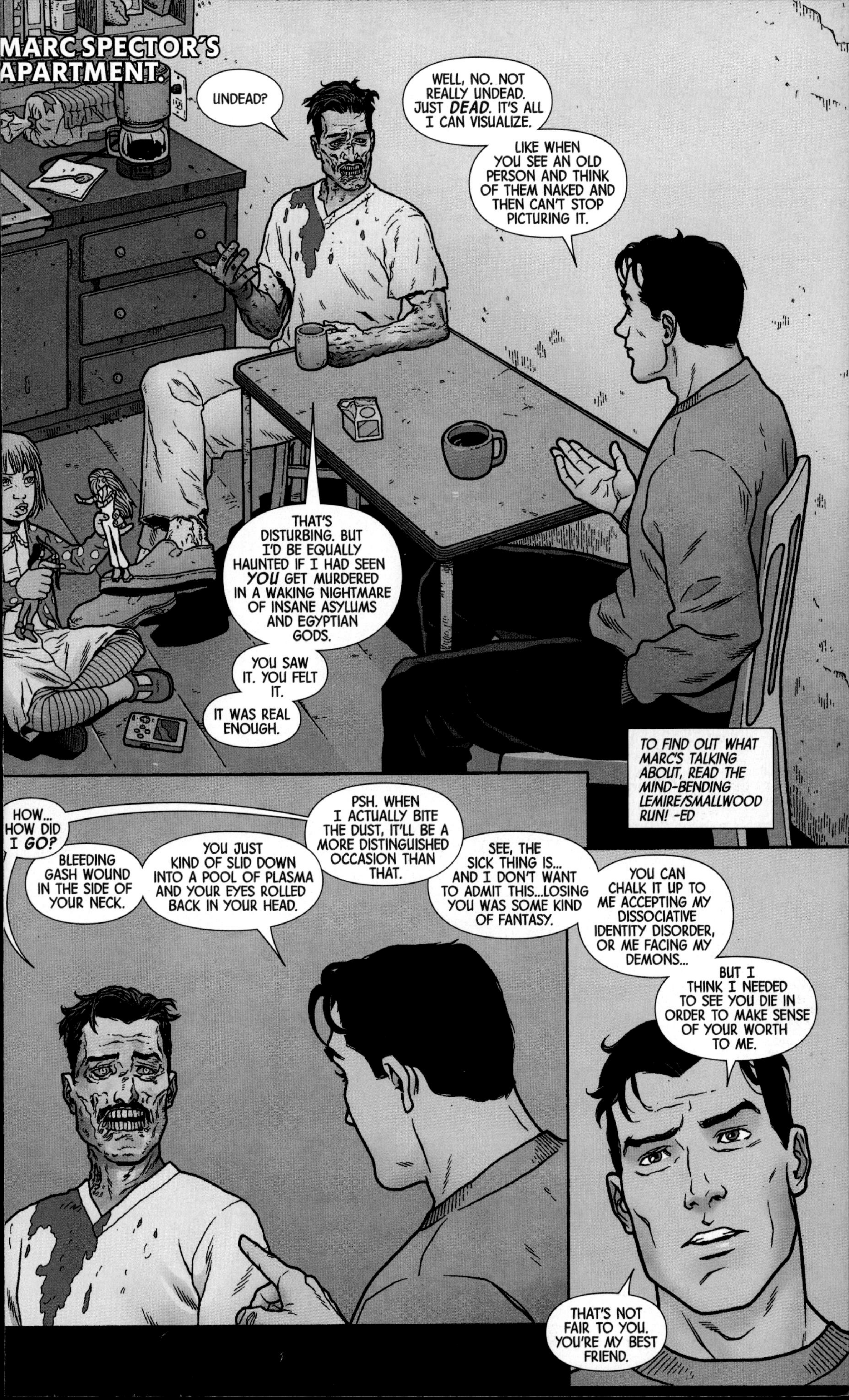
MARC SPECTOR'S APARTMENT.
UNDEAD?
WELL, NO. NOT REALLY UNDEAD. JUST DEAD. IT'S ALL I CAN VISUALIZE.
LIKE WHEN YOU SEE AN OLD PERSON AND THINK OF THEM NAKED AND THEN CAN'T STOP PICTURING IT.
THAT'S DISTURBING. BUT I'D BE EQUALLY HAUNTED IF I HAD SEEN YOU GET MURDERED IN A WAKING NIGHTMARE OF INSANE ASYLUMS AND EGYPTIAN GODS.
YOU SAW IT. YOU FELT IT.
IT WAS REAL ENOUGH.
TO FIND OUT WHAT MARC'S TALKING ABOUT, READ THE MIND-BENDING LEMIRE/SMALLWOOD RUN! -ED
HOW... HOW DID I GO?
BLEEDING GASH WOUND IN THE SIDE OF YOUR NECK.
YOU JUST KIND OF SLID DOWN INTO A POOL OF PLASMA AND YOUR EYES ROLLED BACK IN YOUR HEAD.
PSH. WHEN I ACTUALLY BITE THE DUST, IT'LL BE A MORE DISTINGUISHED OCCASION THAN THAT.
SEE, THE SICK THING IS... AND I DON'T WANT TO ADMIT THIS...LOSING YOU WAS SOME KIND OF FANTASY.
YOU CAN CHALK IT UP TO ME ACCEPTING MY DISSOCIATIVE IDENTITY DISORDER, OR ME FACING MY DEMONS...
BUT I THINK I NEEDED TO SEE YOU DIE IN ORDER TO MAKE SENSE OF YOUR WORTH TO ME.
THAT'S NOT FAIR TO YOU. YOU'RE MY BEST FRIEND.

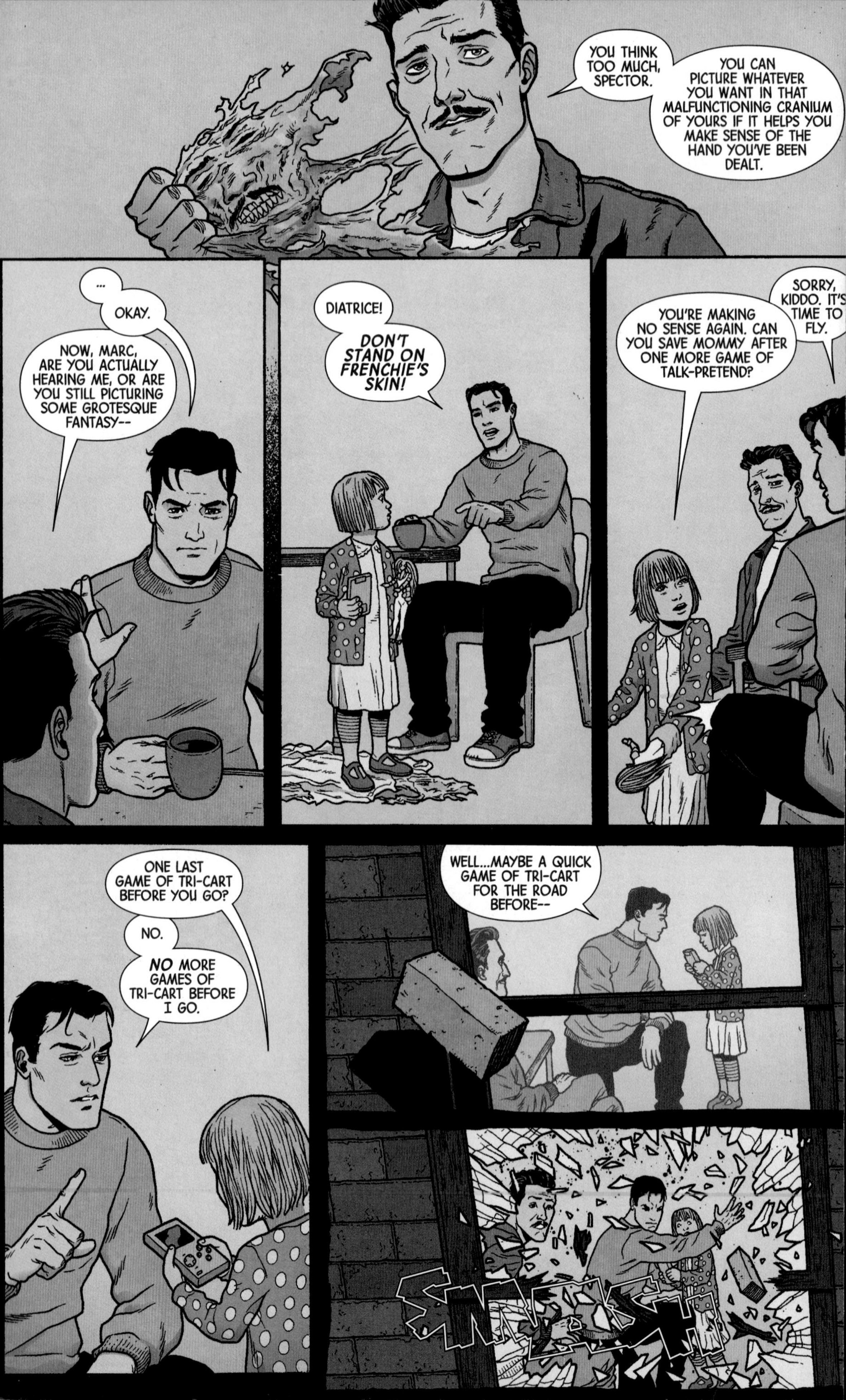

YOU THINK TOO MUCH, SPECTOR.
YOU CAN PICTURE WHATEVER YOU WANT IN THAT MALFUNCTIONING CRANIUM OF YOURS IF IT HELPS YOU MAKE SENSE OF THE HAND YOU'VE BEEN DEALT.
...
OKAY.
NOW, MARC, ARE YOU ACTUALLY HEARING ME, OR ARE YOU STILL PICTURING SOME GROTESQUE FANTASY--
DIATRICE!
DON'T STAND ON FRENCHIE'S SKIN!
SORRY, KIDDO. IT'S TIME TO FLY.
YOU'RE MAKING NO SENSE AGAIN. CAN YOU SAVE MOMMY AFTER ONE MORE GAME OF TALK-PRETEND?
ONE LAST GAME OF TRI-CART BEFORE YOU GO?
NO.
NO MORE GAMES OF TRI-CART BEFORE I GO.
WELL...MAYBE A QUICK GAME OF TRI-CART FOR THE ROAD BEFORE--
SMASH!

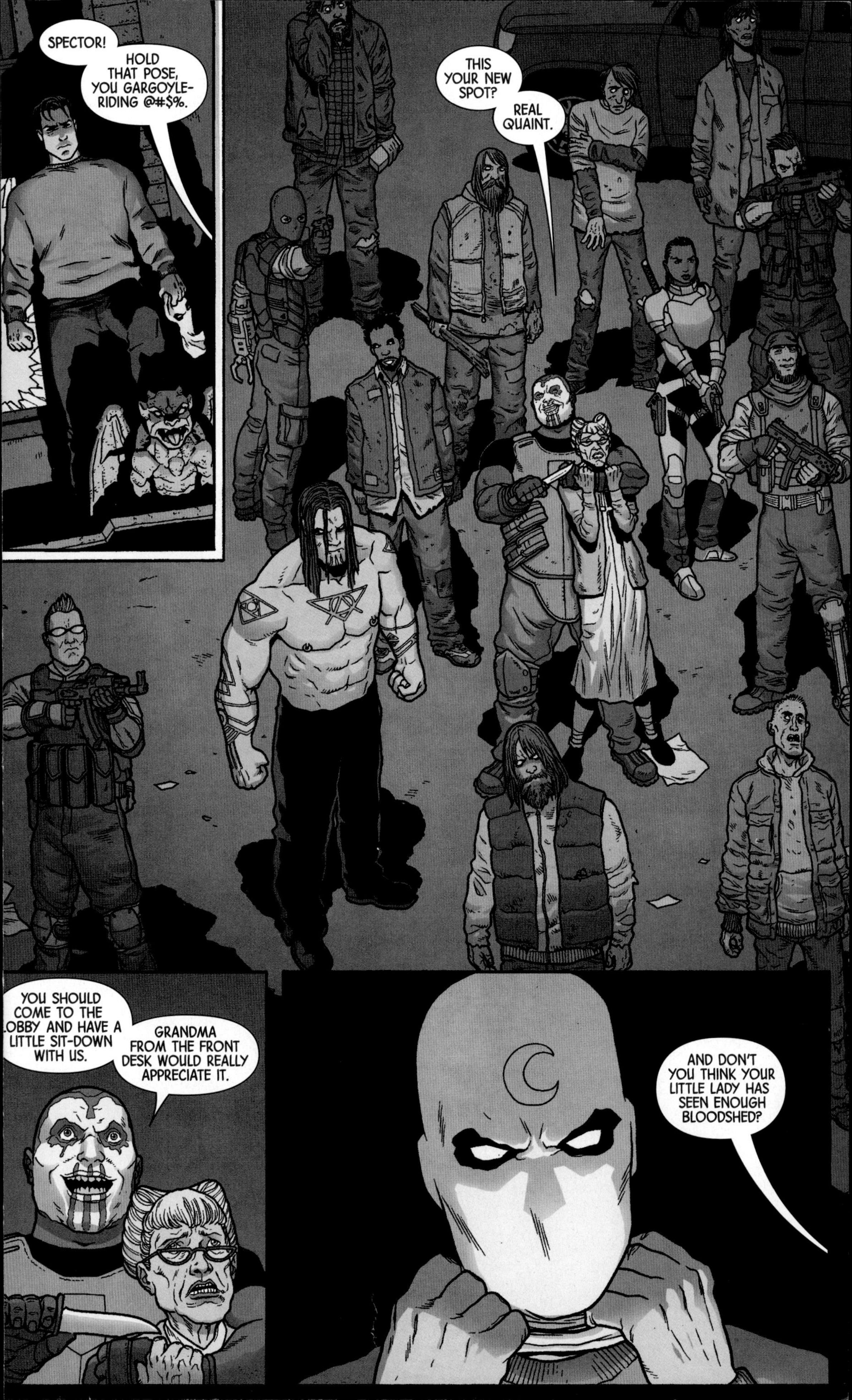
SPECTOR!
HOLD THAT POSE, YOU GARGOYLE-RIDING @#$%.
THIS YOUR NEW SPOT?
REAL QUAINT.
YOU SHOULD COME TO THE LOBBY AND HAVE A LITTLE SIT-DOWN WITH US.
GRANDMA FROM THE FRONT DESK WOULD REALLY APPRECIATE IT.
AND DON'T YOU THINK YOUR LITTLE LADY HAS SEEN ENOUGH BLOODSHED?

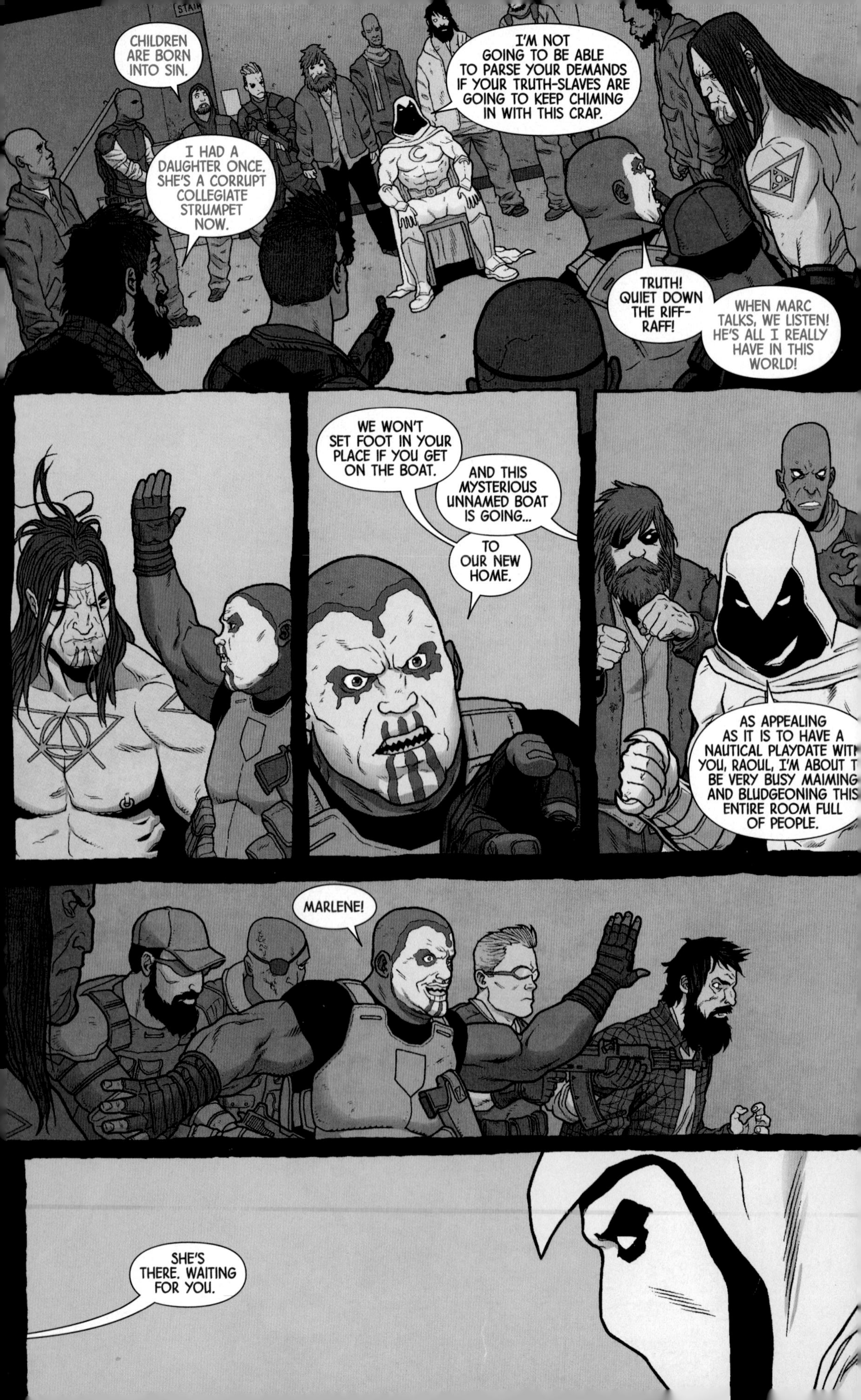
CHILDREN ARE BORN INTO SIN.
I'M NOT GOING TO BE ABLE TO PARSE YOUR DEMANDS IF YOUR TRUTH-SLAVES ARE GOING TO KEEP CHIMING IN WITH THIS CRAP.
I HAD A DAUGHTER ONCE. SHE'S A CORRUPT COLLEGIATE STRUMPET NOW.
TRUTH! QUIET DOWN THE RIFF-RAFF!
WHEN MARC TALKS, WE LISTEN! HE'S ALL I REALLY HAVE IN THIS WORLD!
WE WON'T SET FOOT IN YOUR PLACE IF YOU GET ON THE BOAT.
AND THIS MYSTERIOUS UNNAMED BOAT IS GOING...
TO OUR NEW HOME.
AS APPEALING AS IT IS TO HAVE A NAUTICAL PLAYDATE WITH YOU, RAOUL, I'M ABOUT TO BE VERY BUSY MAIMING AND BLUDGEONING THIS ENTIRE ROOM FULL OF PEOPLE.
MARLENE!
SHE'S THERE. WAITING FOR YOU.

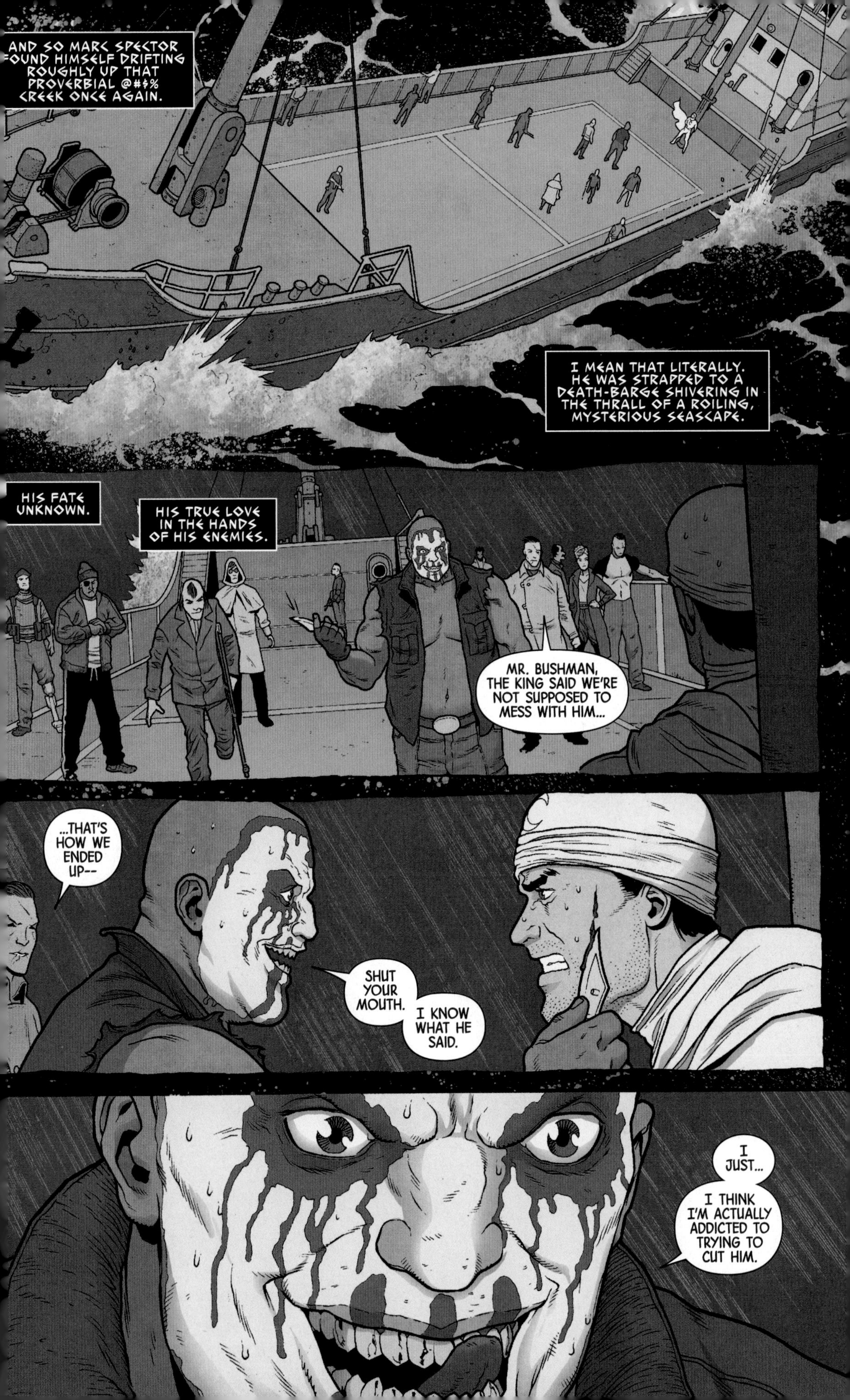
AND SO MARC SPECTOR FOUND HIMSELF DRIFTING ROUGHLY UP THAT PROVERBIAL @#$% CREEK ONCE AGAIN.
I MEAN THAT LITERALLY. HE WAS STRAPPED TO A DEATH-BARGE SHIVERING IN THE THRALL OF A ROILING, MYSTERIOUS SEASCAPE.
HIS FATE UNKNOWN.
HIS TRUE LOVE IN THE HANDS OF HIS ENEMIES.
MR. BUSHMAN, THE KING SAID WE'RE NOT SUPPOSED TO MESS WITH HIM...
...THAT'S HOW WE ENDED UP--
SHUT YOUR MOUTH.
I KNOW WHAT HE SAID.
I JUST...
I THINK I'M ACTUALLY ADDICTED TO TRYING TO CUT HIM.

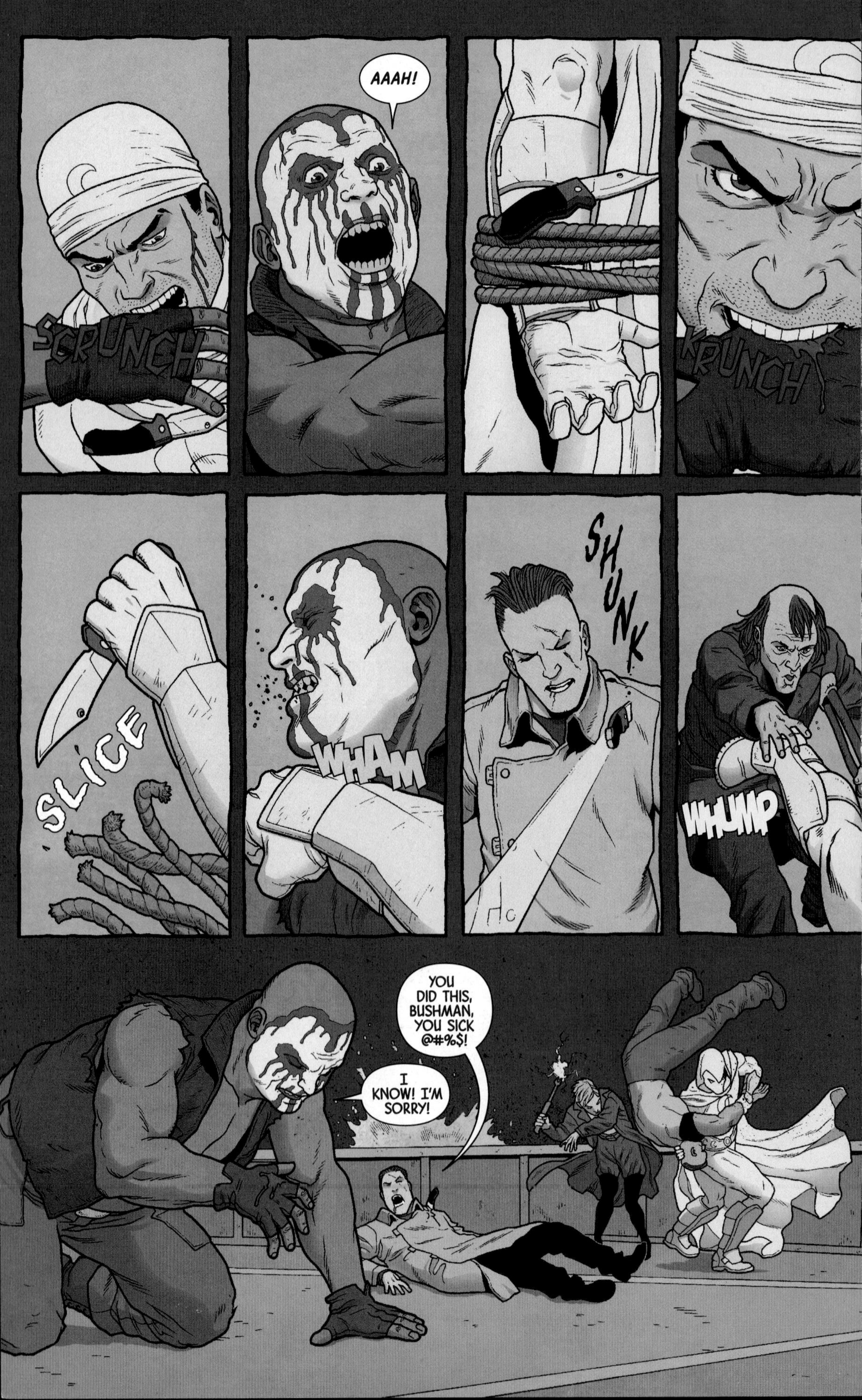
SCRUNCH
AAAH!
KRUNCH
SLICE
WHAM
SHUNK
WHUMP
YOU DID THIS, BUSHMAN, YOU SICK @#%$!
I KNOW! I'M SORRY!

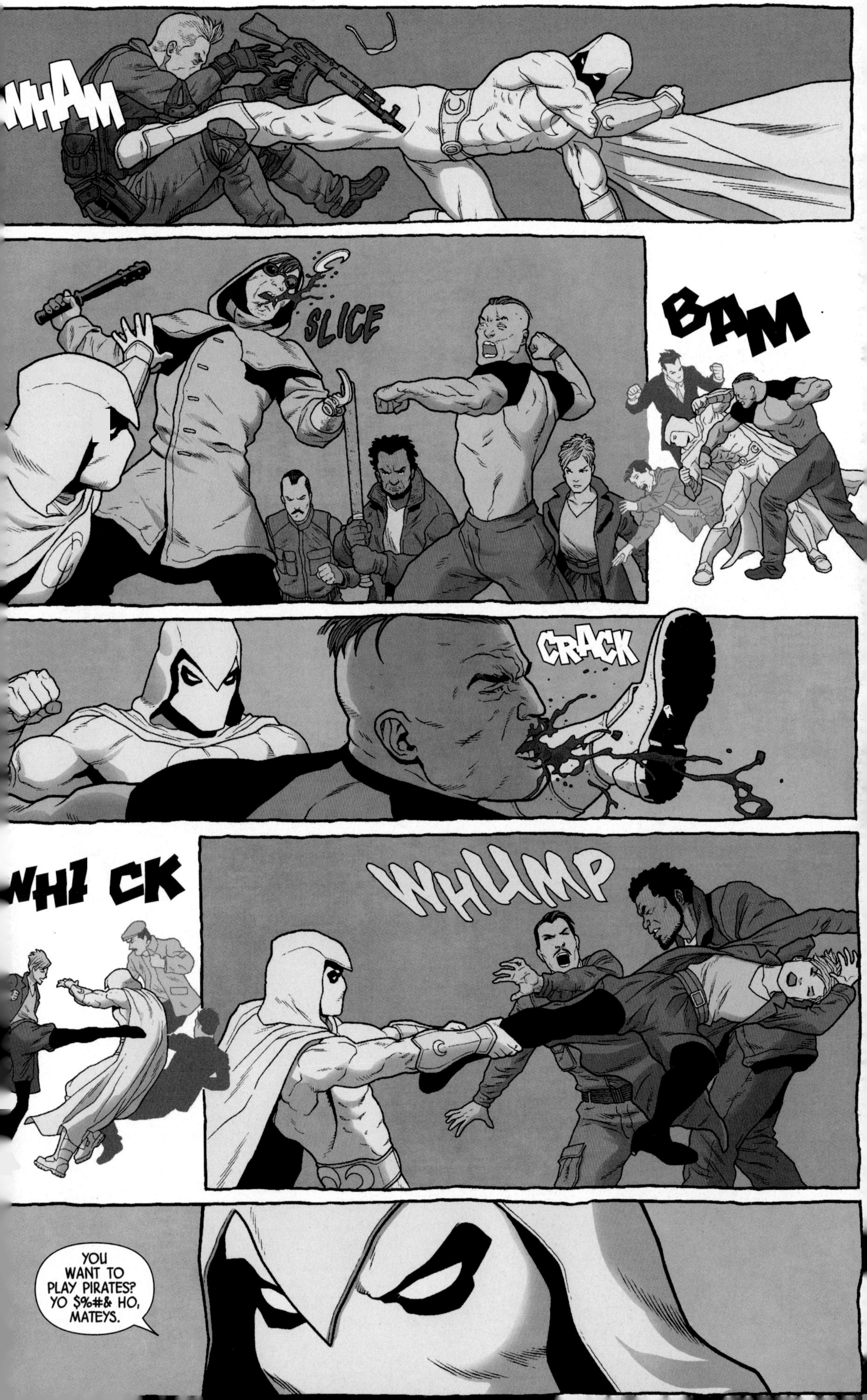
WHAM
SLICE
BAM
CRACK
WHUMP
YOU WANT TO PLAY PIRATES? YO $%#& HO, MATEYS.

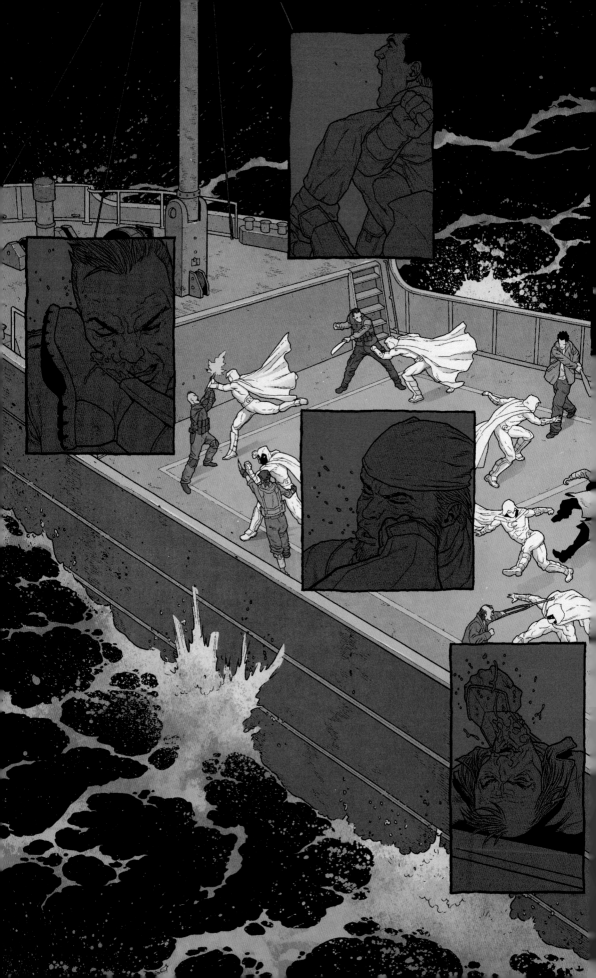

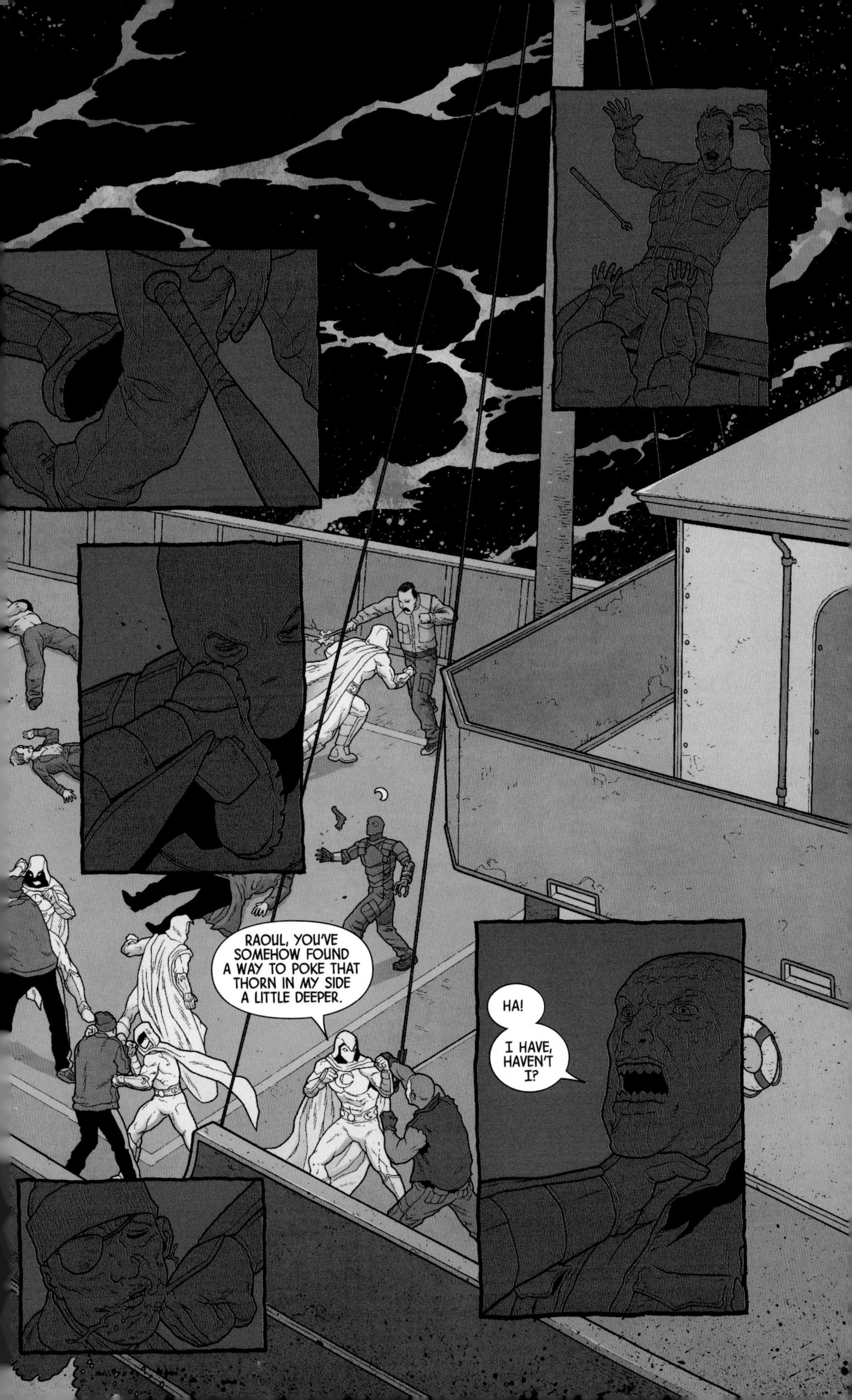
RAOUL, YOU'VE SOMEHOW FOUND A WAY TO POKE THAT THORN IN MY SIDE A LITTLE DEEPER.
HA!
I HAVE, HAVEN'T I?

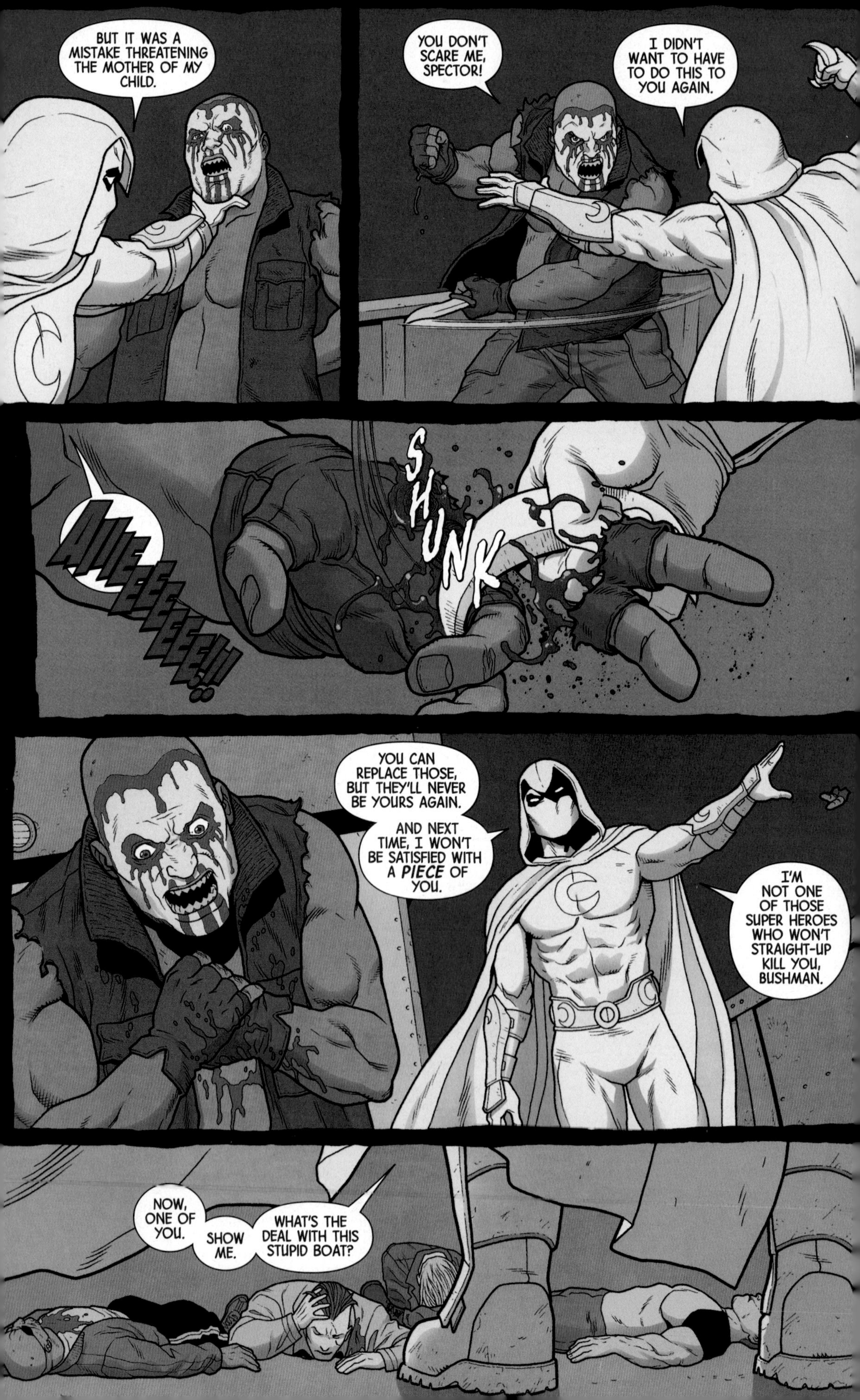
BUT IT WAS A MISTAKE THREATENING THE MOTHER OF MY CHILD.
YOU DON'T SCARE ME, SPECTOR!
I DIDN'T WANT TO HAVE TO DO THIS TO YOU AGAIN.
SHUNK
AIIEEEEEEEE!!!
YOU CAN REPLACE THOSE, BUT THEY'LL NEVER BE YOURS AGAIN.
AND NEXT TIME, I WON'T BE SATISFIED WITH A PIECE OF YOU.
I'M NOT ONE OF THOSE SUPER HEROES WHO WON'T STRAIGHT-UP KILL YOU, BUSHMAN.
NOW, ONE OF YOU.
SHOW ME.
WHAT'S THE DEAL WITH THIS STUPID BOAT?

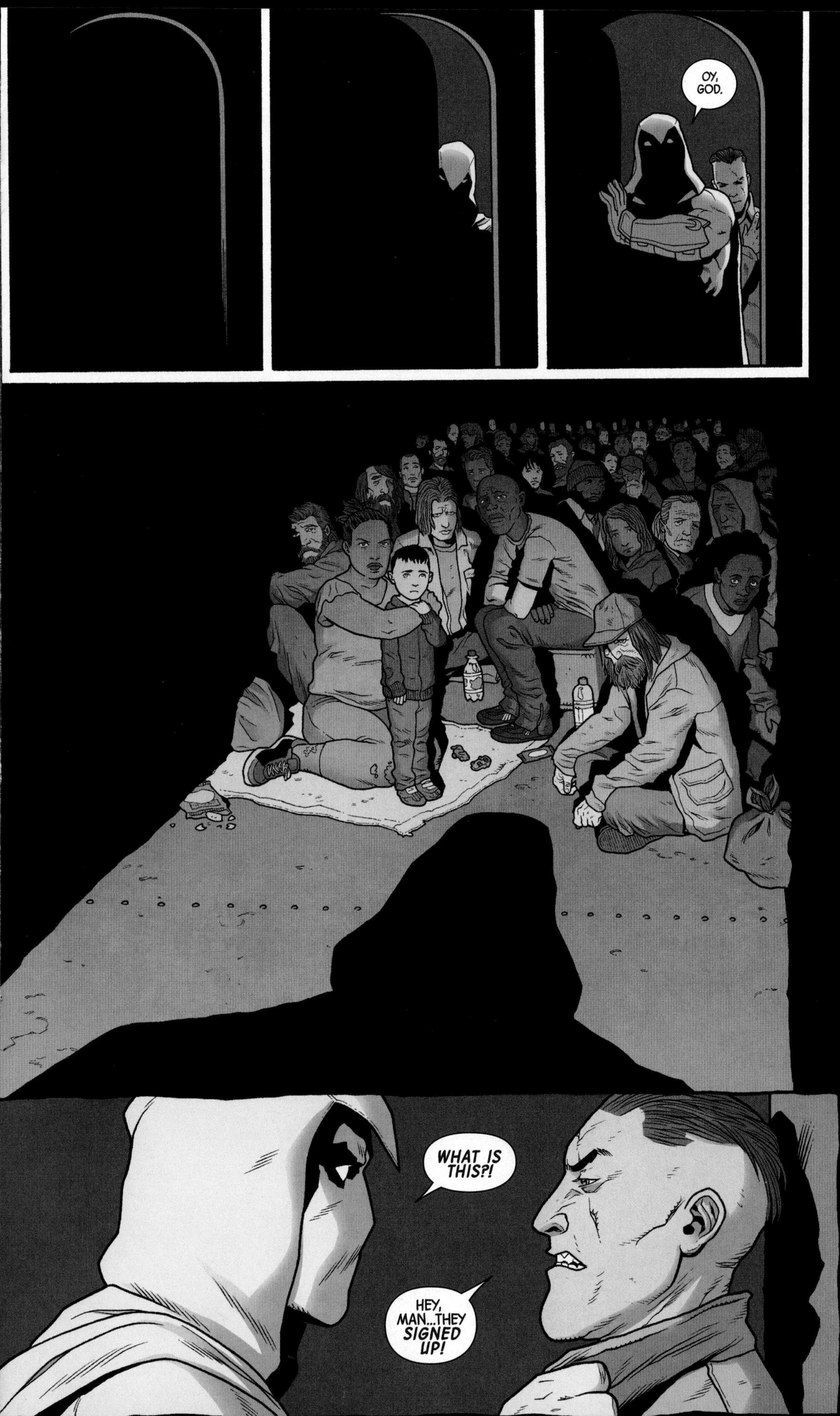
OY, GOD.
WHAT IS THIS?!
HEY, MAN...THEY SIGNED UP!

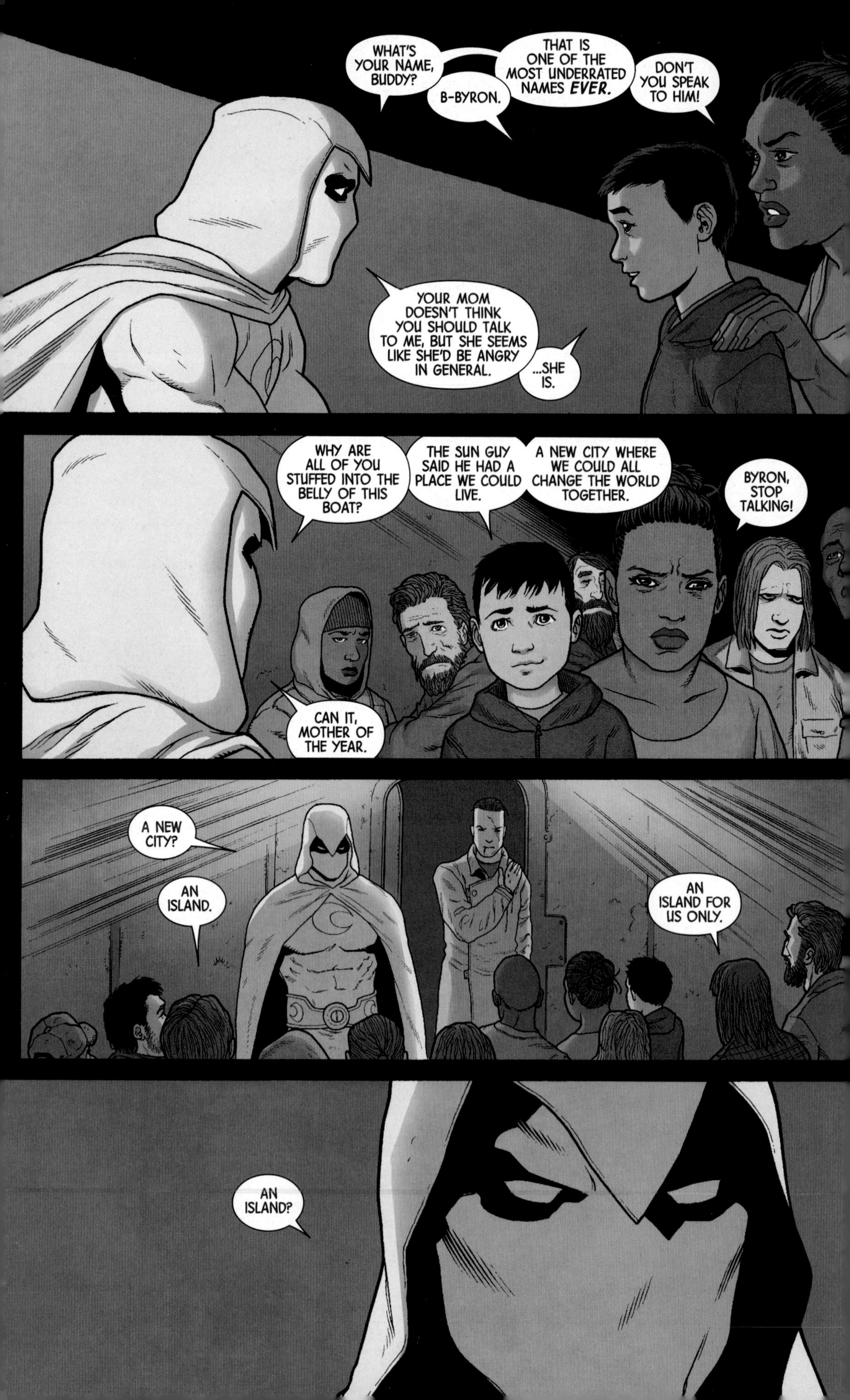
WHAT'S YOUR NAME, BUDDY?
B-BYRON.
THAT IS ONE OF THE MOST UNDERRATED NAMES *EVER.*
DON'T YOU SPEAK TO HIM!
YOUR MOM DOESN'T THINK YOU SHOULD TALK TO ME, BUT SHE SEEMS LIKE SHE'D BE ANGRY IN GENERAL.
...SHE IS.
WHY ARE ALL OF YOU STUFFED INTO THE BELLY OF THIS BOAT?
THE SUN GUY SAID HE HAD A PLACE WE COULD LIVE.
A NEW CITY WHERE WE COULD ALL CHANGE THE WORLD TOGETHER.
BYRON, STOP TALKING!
CAN IT, MOTHER OF THE YEAR.
A NEW CITY?
AN ISLAND.
AN ISLAND FOR US ONLY.
AN ISLAND?

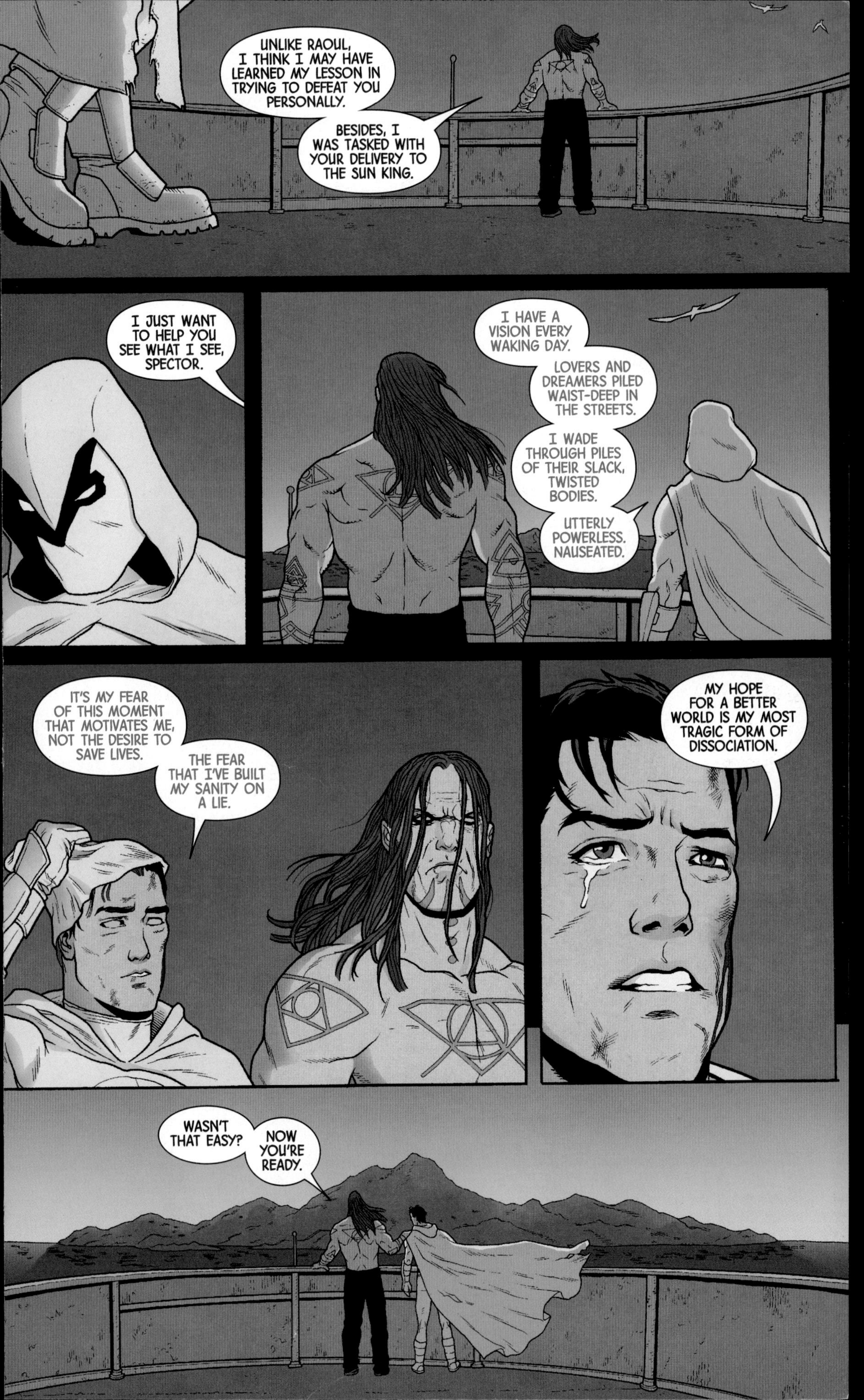
UNLIKE RAOUL, I THINK I MAY HAVE LEARNED MY LESSON IN TRYING TO DEFEAT YOU PERSONALLY.
BESIDES, I WAS TASKED WITH YOUR DELIVERY TO THE SUN KING.
I JUST WANT TO HELP YOU SEE WHAT I SEE, SPECTOR.
I HAVE A VISION EVERY WAKING DAY.
LOVERS AND DREAMERS PILED WAIST-DEEP IN THE STREETS.
I WADE THROUGH PILES OF THEIR SLACK, TWISTED BODIES.
UTTERLY POWERLESS. NAUSEATED.
IT'S MY FEAR OF THIS MOMENT THAT MOTIVATES ME, NOT THE DESIRE TO SAVE LIVES.
THE FEAR THAT I'VE BUILT MY SANITY ON A LIE.
MY HOPE FOR A BETTER WORLD IS MY MOST TRAGIC FORM OF DISSOCIATION.
WASN'T THAT EASY?
NOW YOU'RE READY.

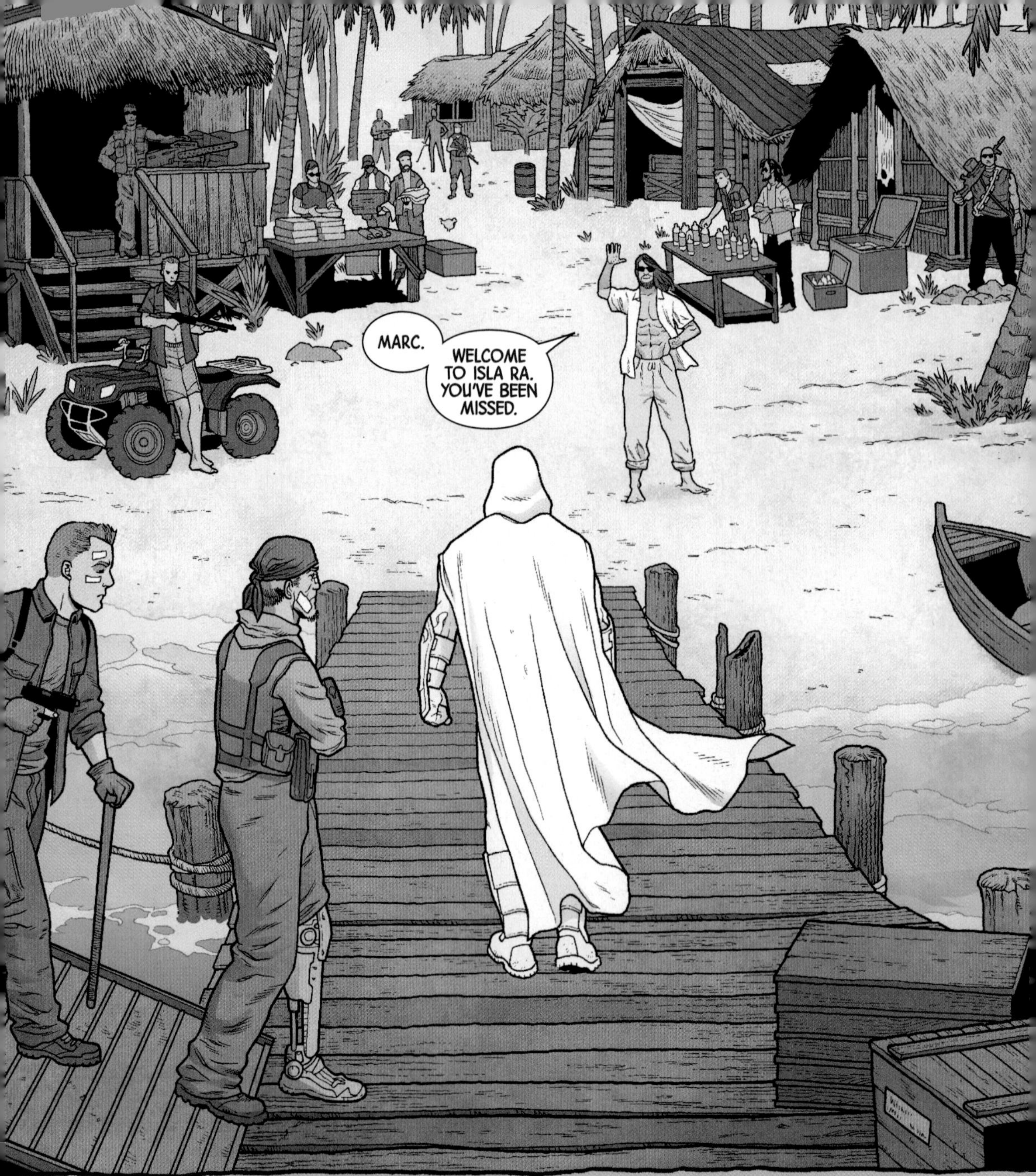
MARC.
WELCOME TO ISLA RA. YOU'VE BEEN MISSED.

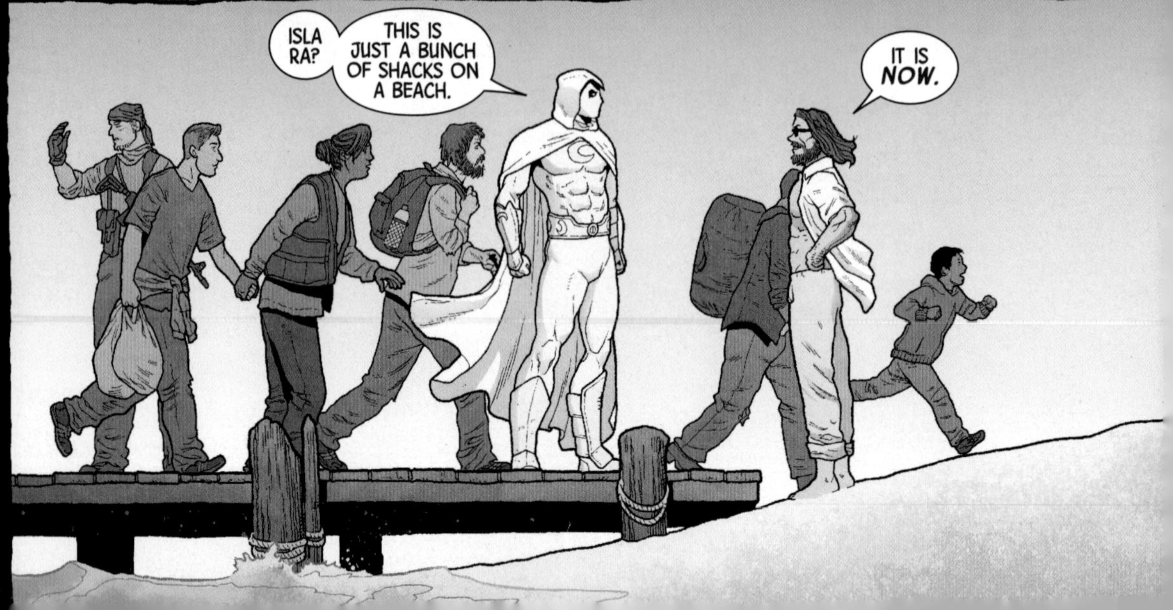
ISLA RA?
THIS IS JUST A BUNCH OF SHACKS ON A BEACH.
IT IS *NOW.*

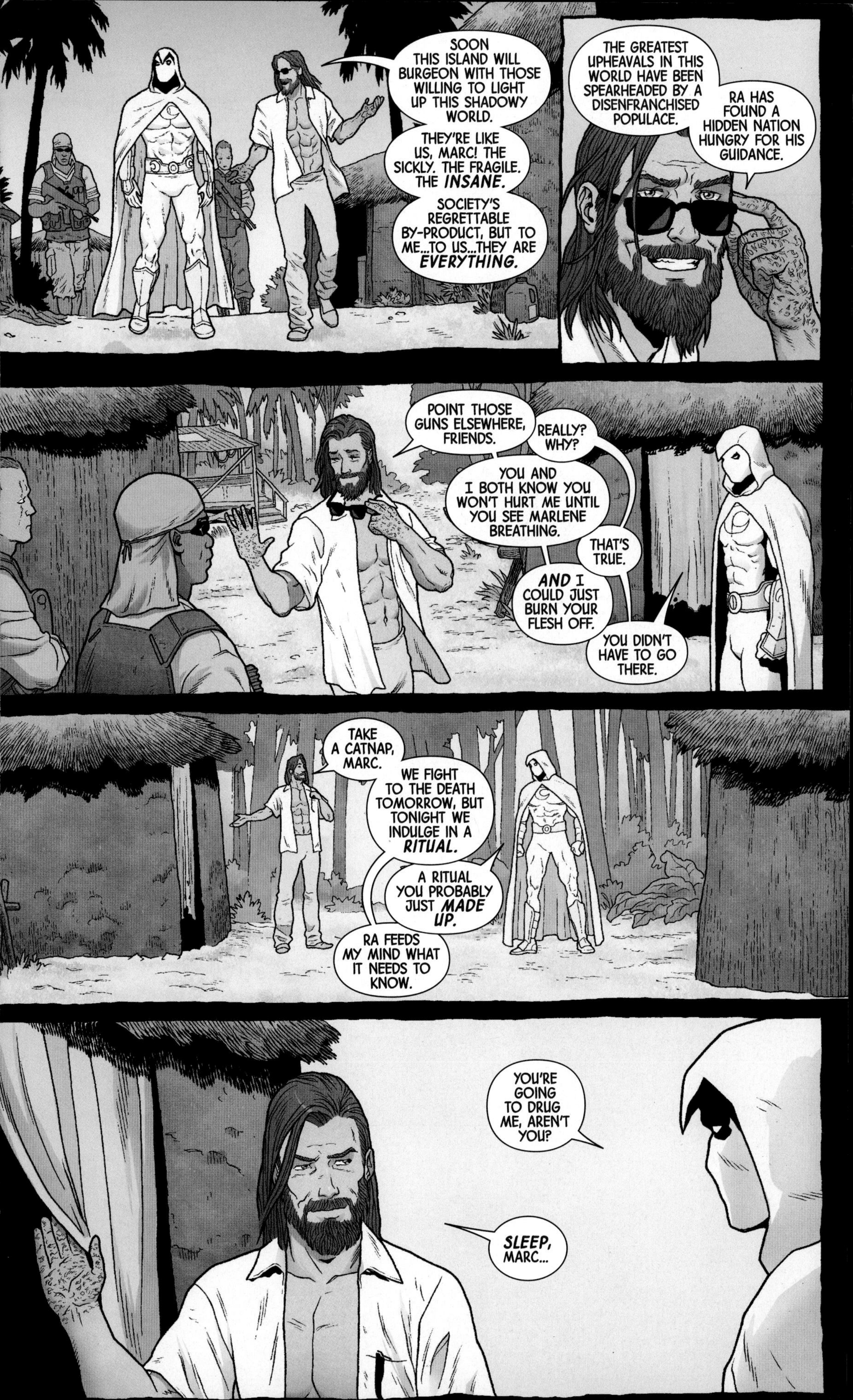
SOON THIS ISLAND WILL BURGEON WITH THOSE WILLING TO LIGHT UP THIS SHADOWY WORLD.
THEY'RE LIKE US, MARC! THE SICKLY. THE FRAGILE. THE INSANE.
SOCIETY'S REGRETTABLE BY-PRODUCT, BUT TO ME...TO US...THEY ARE EVERYTHING.
THE GREATEST UPHEAVALS IN THIS WORLD HAVE BEEN SPEARHEADED BY A DISENFRANCHISED POPULACE.
RA HAS FOUND A HIDDEN NATION HUNGRY FOR HIS GUIDANCE.
POINT THOSE GUNS ELSEWHERE, FRIENDS.
REALLY? WHY?
YOU AND I BOTH KNOW YOU WON'T HURT ME UNTIL YOU SEE MARLENE BREATHING.
THAT'S TRUE.
AND I COULD JUST BURN YOUR FLESH OFF.
YOU DIDN'T HAVE TO GO THERE.
TAKE A CATNAP, MARC.
WE FIGHT TO THE DEATH TOMORROW, BUT TONIGHT WE INDULGE IN A RITUAL.
A RITUAL YOU PROBABLY JUST MADE UP.
RA FEEDS MY MIND WHAT IT NEEDS TO KNOW.
YOU'RE GOING TO DRUG ME, AREN'T YOU?
SLEEP, MARC...

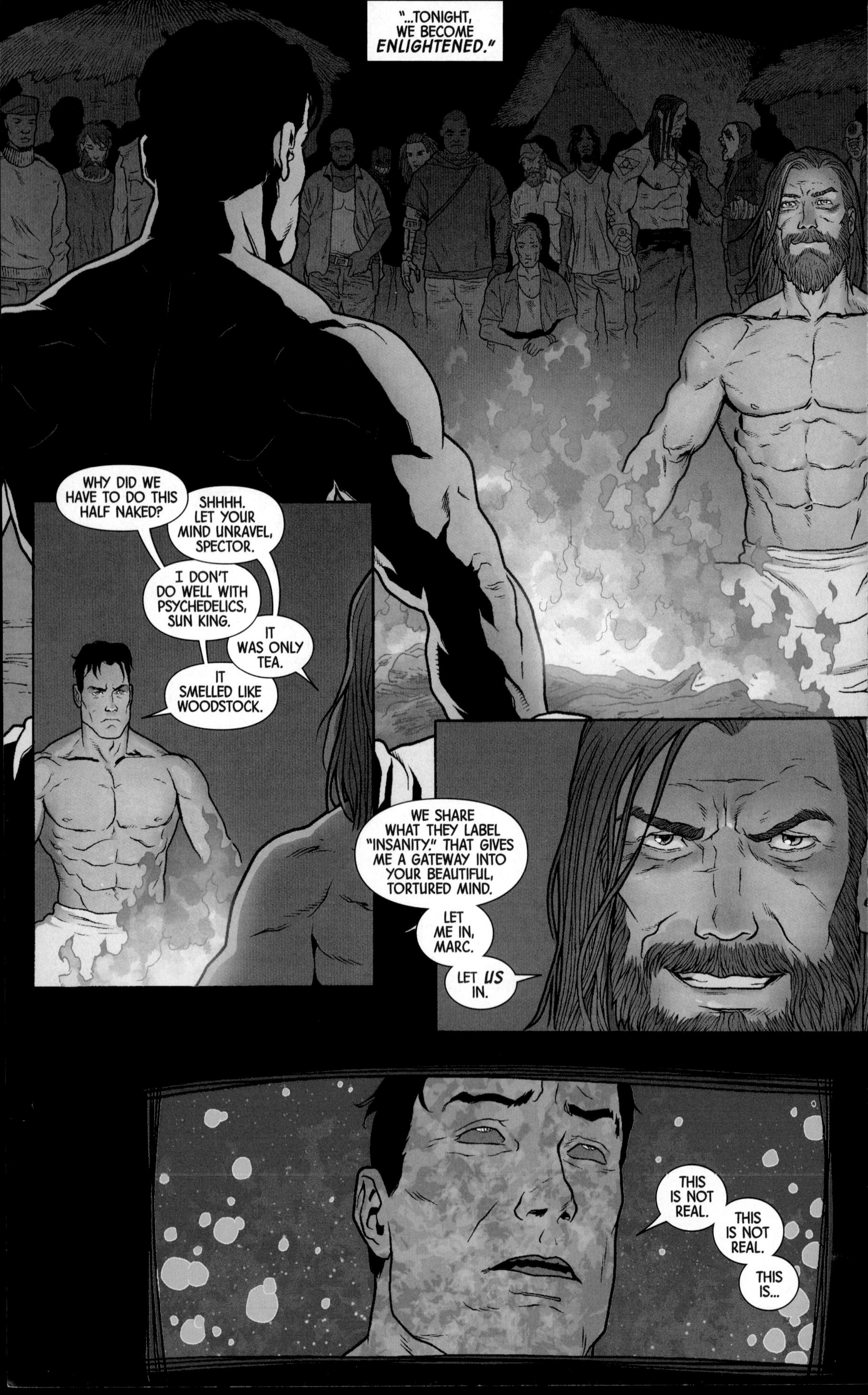
"...TONIGHT, WE BECOME ENLIGHTENED."
WHY DID WE HAVE TO DO THIS HALF NAKED?
SHHHH. LET YOUR MIND UNRAVEL, SPECTOR.
I DON'T DO WELL WITH PSYCHEDELICS, SUN KING.
IT WAS ONLY TEA.
IT SMELLED LIKE WOODSTOCK.
WE SHARE WHAT THEY LABEL "INSANITY." THAT GIVES ME A GATEWAY INTO YOUR BEAUTIFUL, TORTURED MIND.
LET ME IN, MARC.
LET US IN.
THIS IS NOT REAL.
THIS IS NOT REAL.
THIS IS...

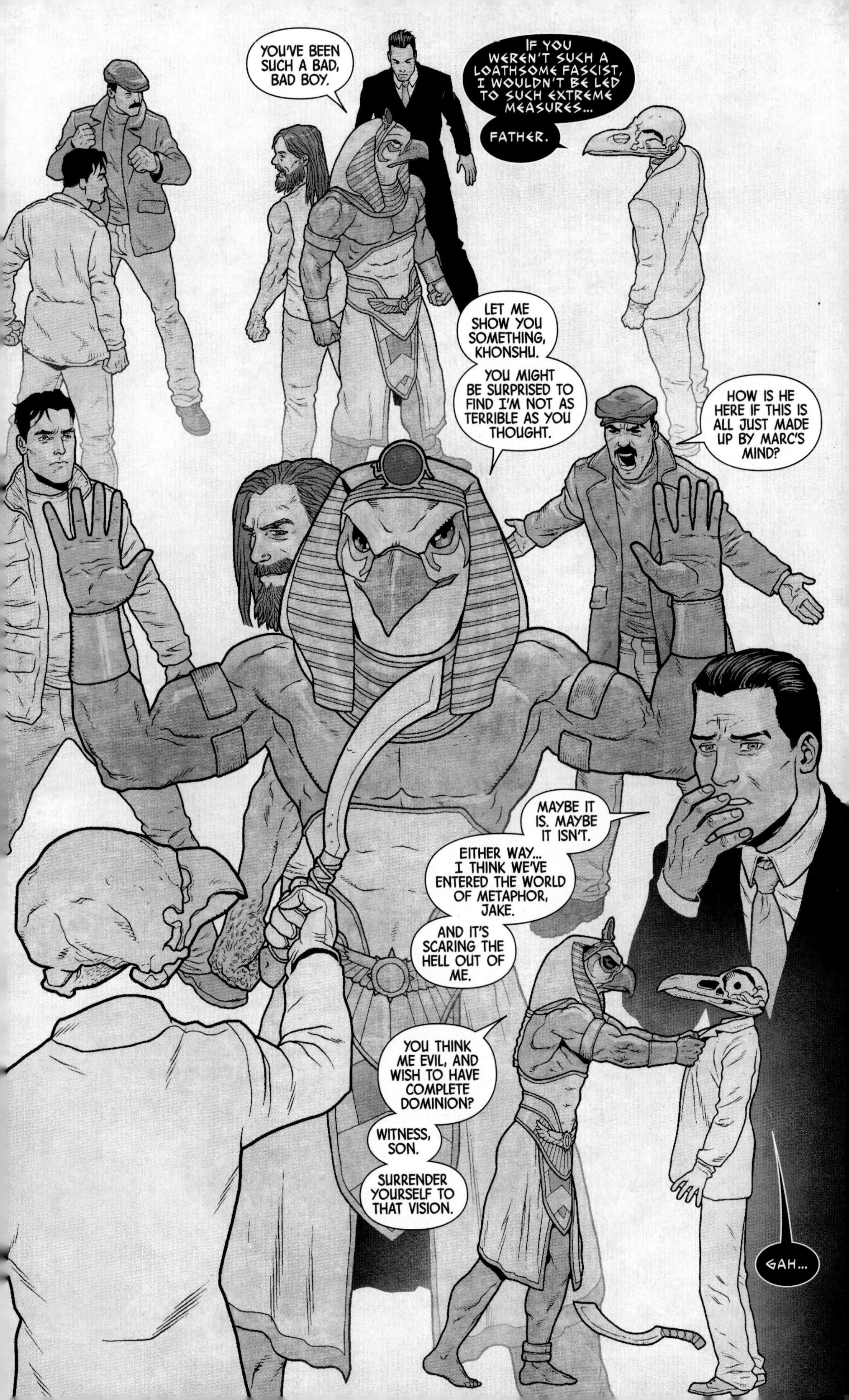
YOU'VE BEEN SUCH A BAD, BAD BOY.
IF YOU WEREN'T SUCH A LOATHSOME FASCIST, I WOULDN'T BE LED TO SUCH EXTREME MEASURES...
FATHER.
LET ME SHOW YOU SOMETHING, KHONSHU.
YOU MIGHT BE SURPRISED TO FIND I'M NOT AS TERRIBLE AS YOU THOUGHT.
HOW IS HE HERE IF THIS IS ALL JUST MADE UP BY MARC'S MIND?
MAYBE IT IS. MAYBE IT ISN'T.
EITHER WAY... I THINK WE'VE ENTERED THE WORLD OF METAPHOR, JAKE.
AND IT'S SCARING THE HELL OUT OF ME.
YOU THINK ME EVIL, AND WISH TO HAVE COMPLETE DOMINION?
WITNESS, SON.
SURRENDER YOURSELF TO THAT VISION.
GAH...

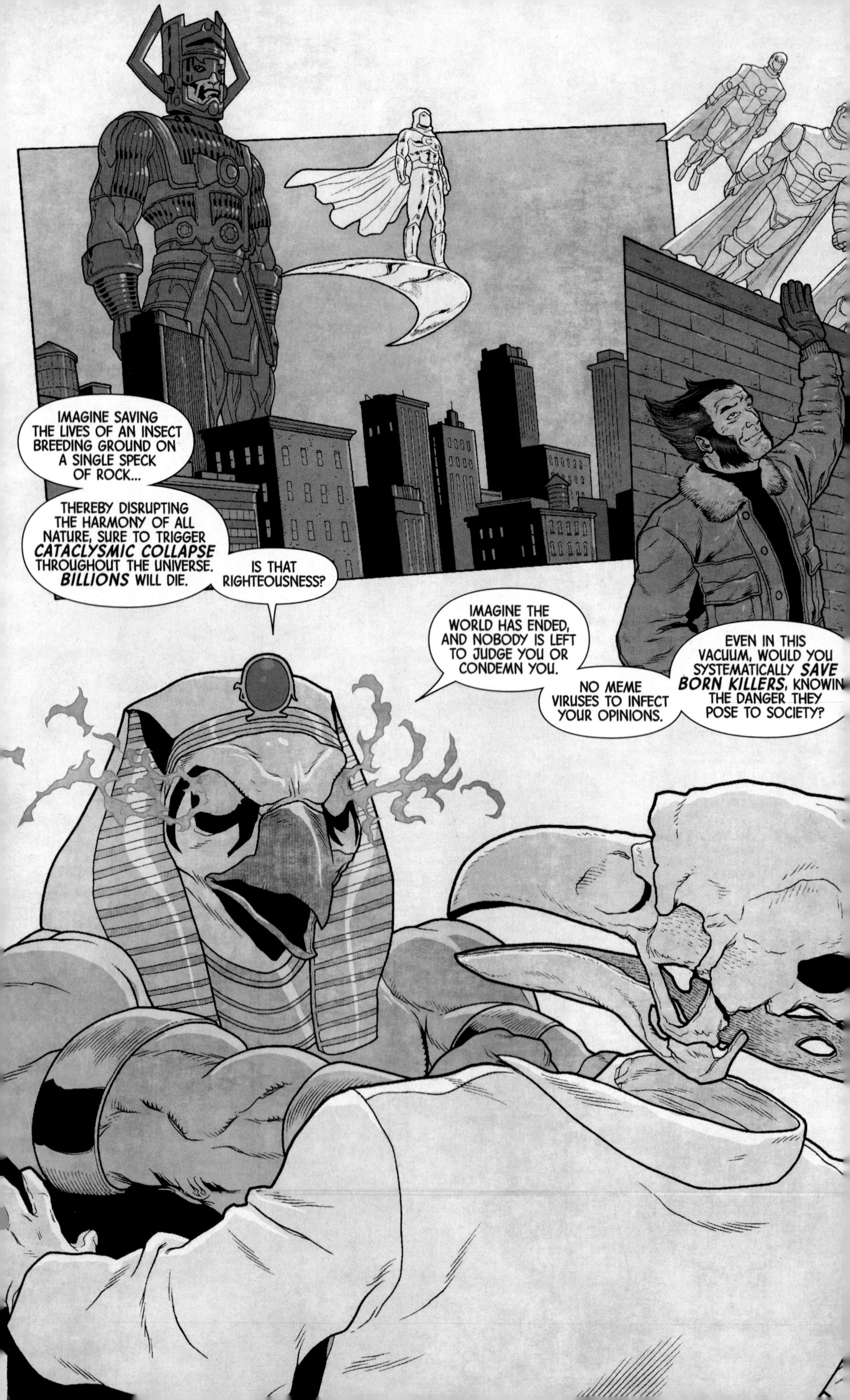
IMAGINE SAVING THE LIVES OF AN INSECT BREEDING GROUND ON A SINGLE SPECK OF ROCK...
THEREBY DISRUPTING THE HARMONY OF ALL NATURE, SURE TO TRIGGER ***CATACLYSMIC COLLAPSE*** THROUGHOUT THE UNIVERSE. ***BILLIONS*** WILL DIE.
IS THAT RIGHTEOUSNESS?
IMAGINE THE WORLD HAS ENDED, AND NOBODY IS LEFT TO JUDGE YOU OR CONDEMN YOU.
NO MEME VIRUSES TO INFECT YOUR OPINIONS.
EVEN IN THIS VACUUM, WOULD YOU SYSTEMATICALLY ***SAVE BORN KILLERS***, KNOWIN THE DANGER THEY POSE TO SOCIETY?

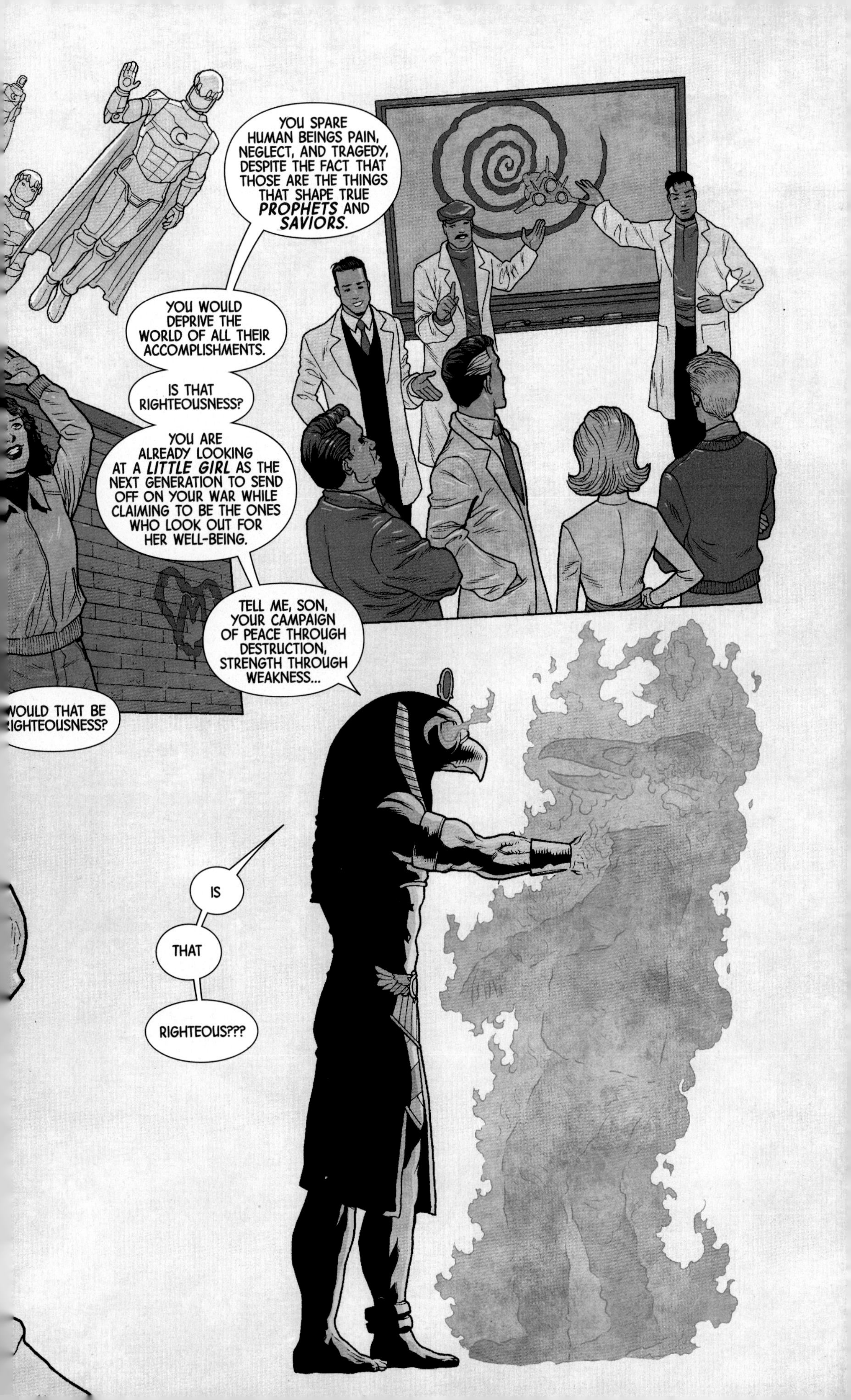

YOU SPARE HUMAN BEINGS PAIN, NEGLECT, AND TRAGEDY, DESPITE THE FACT THAT THOSE ARE THE THINGS THAT SHAPE TRUE PROPHETS AND SAVIORS.
YOU WOULD DEPRIVE THE WORLD OF ALL THEIR ACCOMPLISHMENTS.
IS THAT RIGHTEOUSNESS?
YOU ARE ALREADY LOOKING AT A LITTLE GIRL AS THE NEXT GENERATION TO SEND OFF ON YOUR WAR WHILE CLAIMING TO BE THE ONES WHO LOOK OUT FOR HER WELL-BEING.
TELL ME, SON, YOUR CAMPAIGN OF PEACE THROUGH DESTRUCTION, STRENGTH THROUGH WEAKNESS...
WOULD THAT BE RIGHTEOUSNESS?
IS
THAT
RIGHTEOUS???

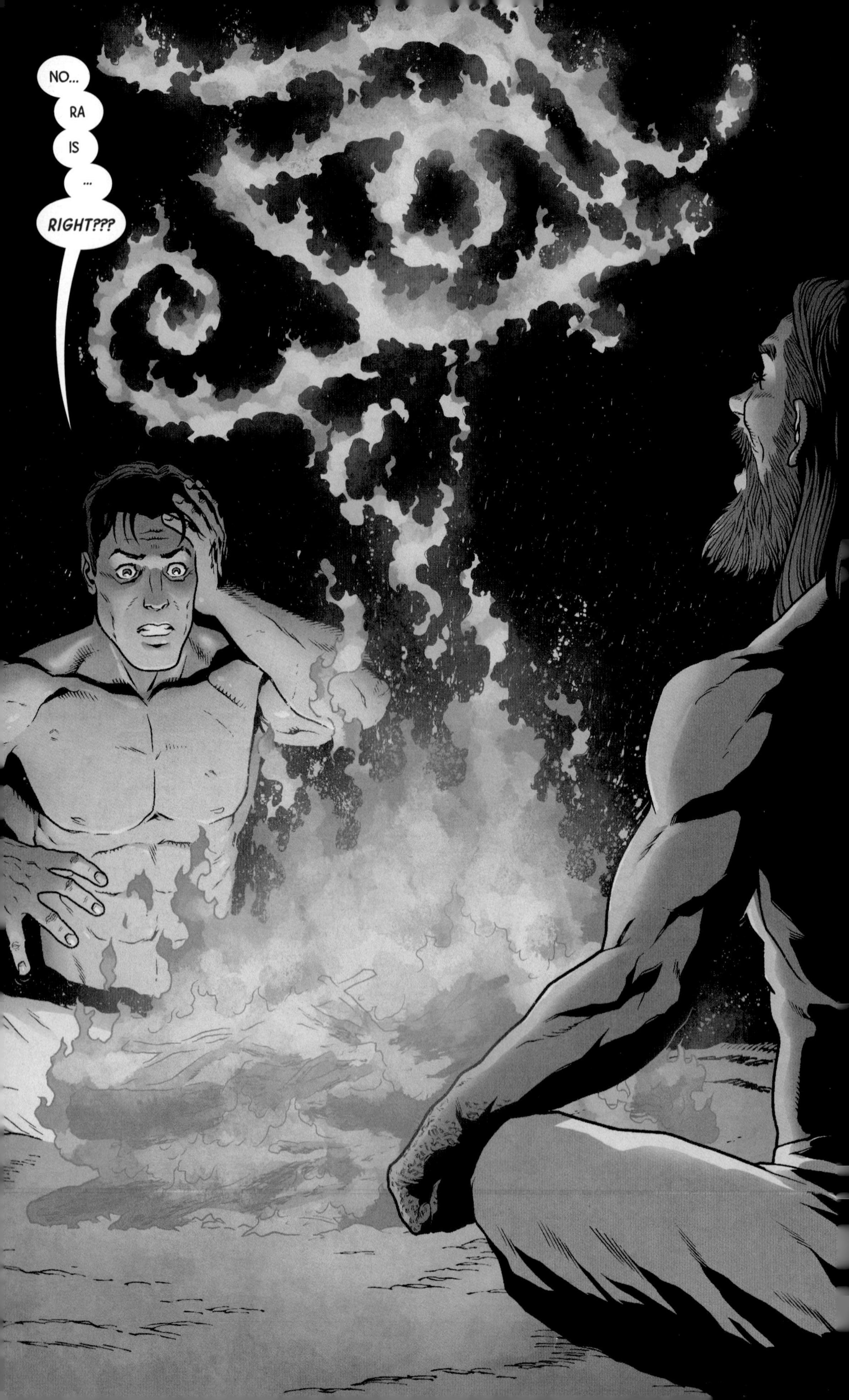
NO...
RA
IS
...
RIGHT???

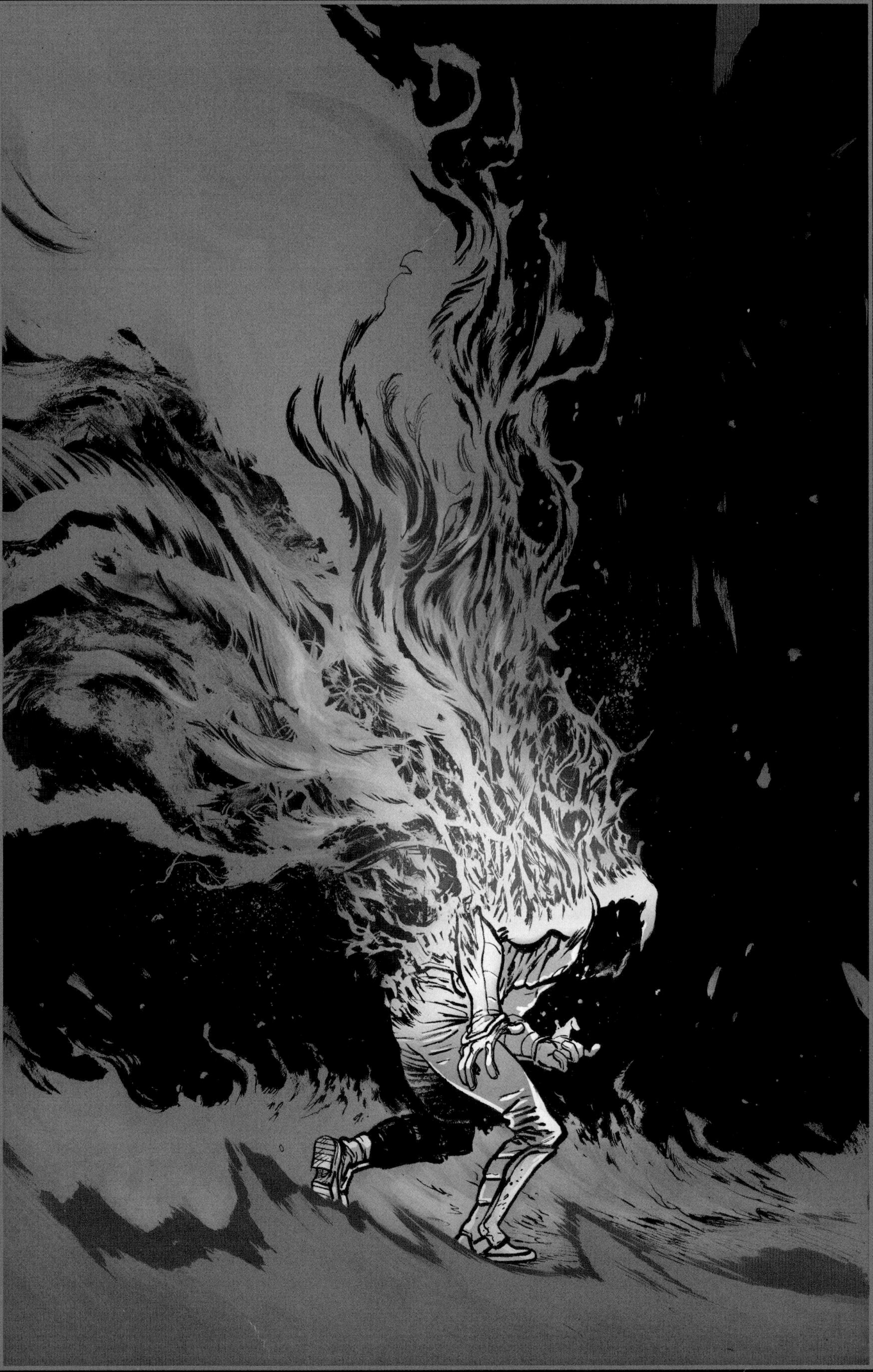

188 PHOENIX VARIANT BY **DANIEL WARREN JOHNSON** & **MIKE SPICER**

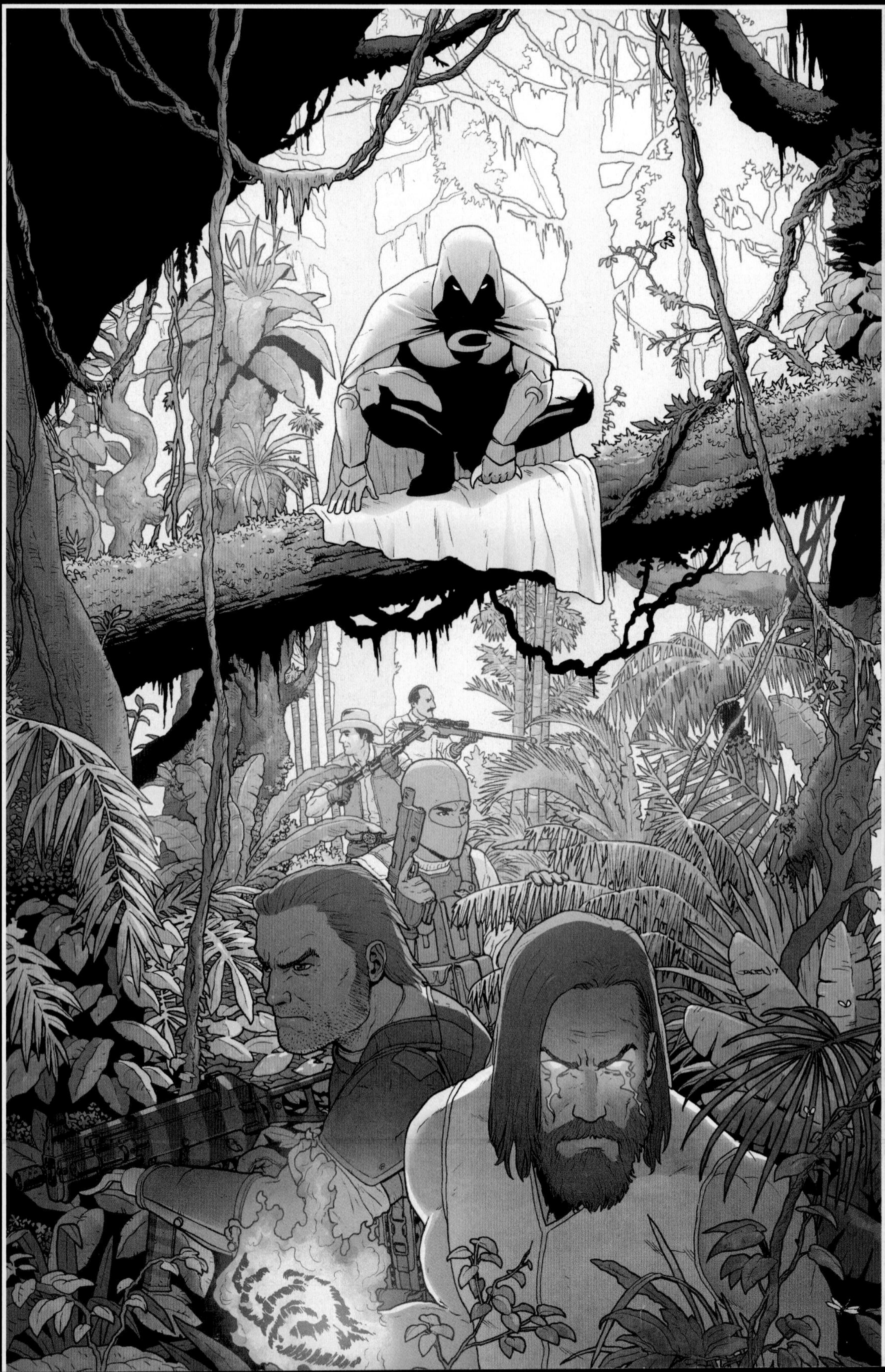

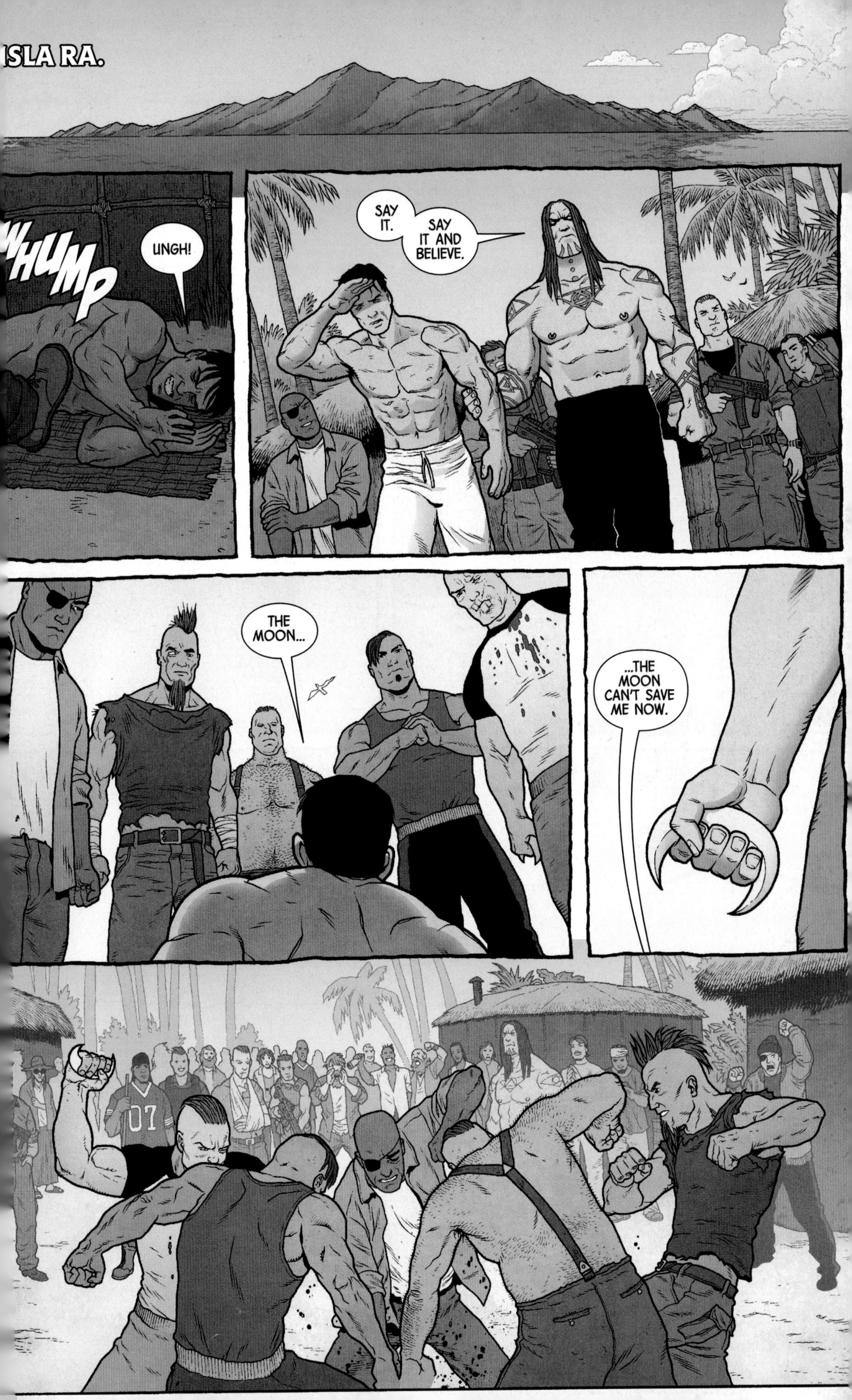
ISLA RA.
WHUMP
UNGH!
SAY IT.
SAY IT AND BELIEVE.
THE MOON...
...THE MOON CAN'T SAVE ME NOW.
07

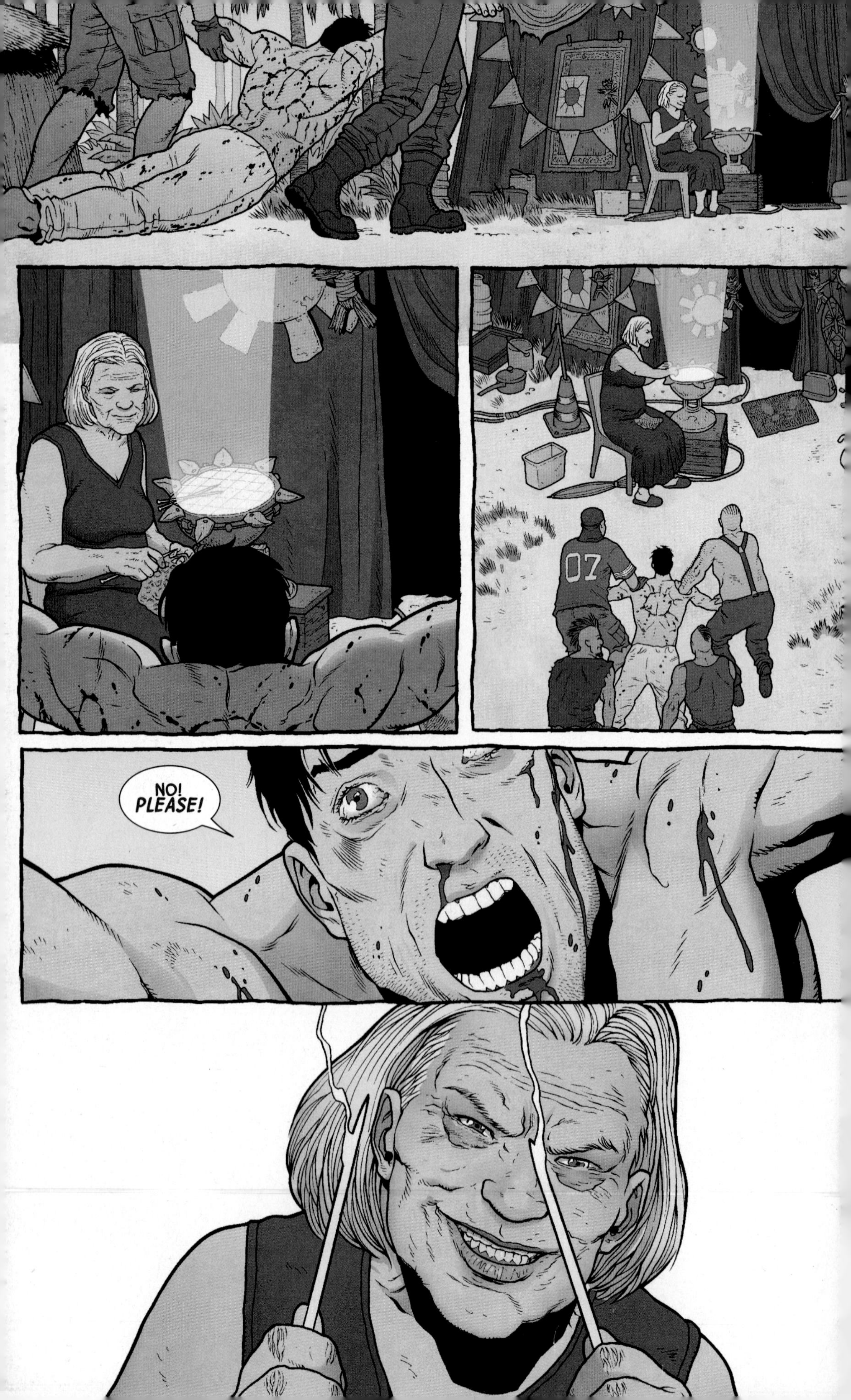
07
NO!
PLEASE!

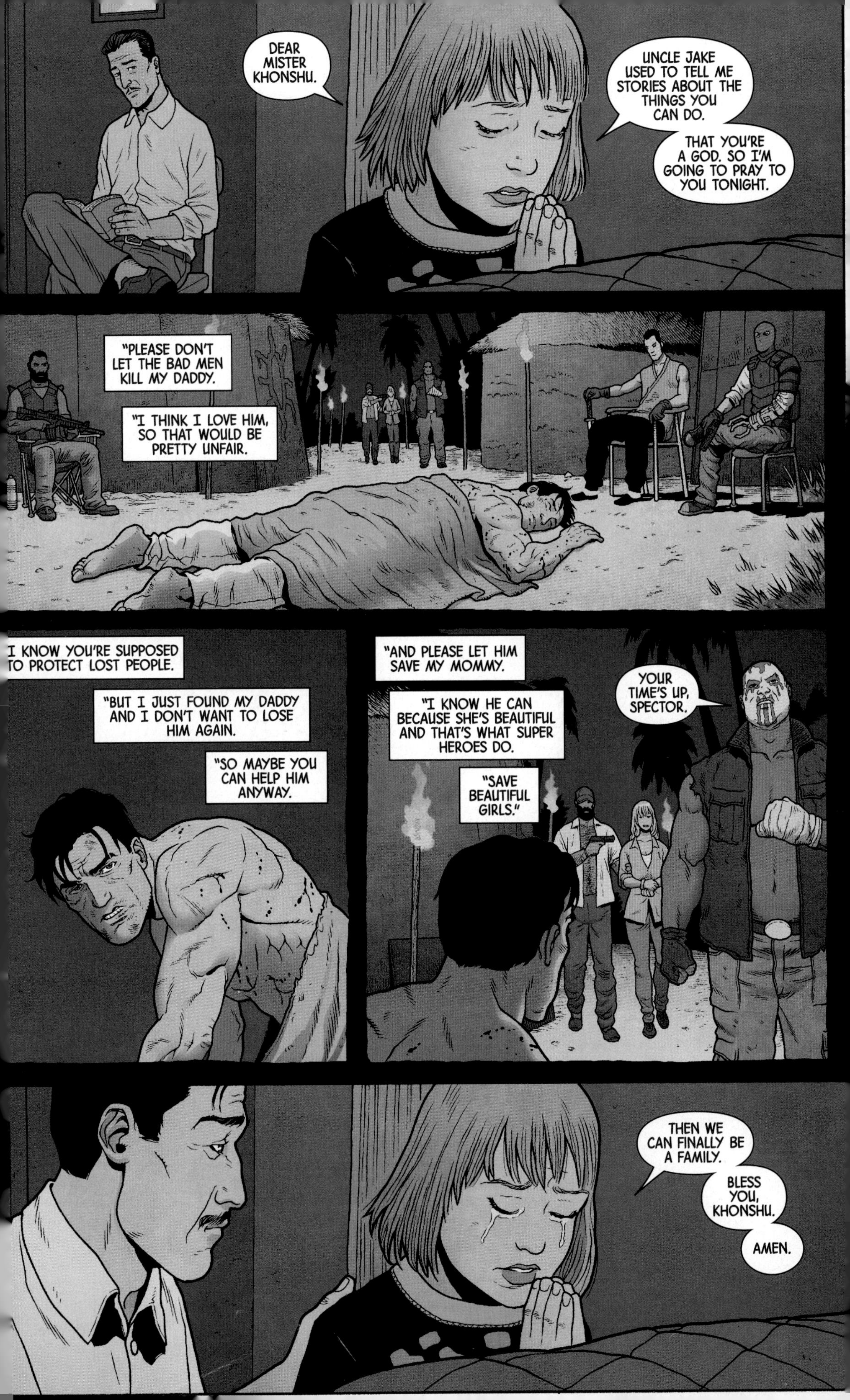
DEAR MISTER KHONSHU.
UNCLE JAKE USED TO TELL ME STORIES ABOUT THE THINGS YOU CAN DO.
THAT YOU'RE A GOD. SO I'M GOING TO PRAY TO YOU TONIGHT.
"PLEASE DON'T LET THE BAD MEN KILL MY DADDY.
"I THINK I LOVE HIM, SO THAT WOULD BE PRETTY UNFAIR.
I KNOW YOU'RE SUPPOSED TO PROTECT LOST PEOPLE.
"BUT I JUST FOUND MY DADDY AND I DON'T WANT TO LOSE HIM AGAIN.
"SO MAYBE YOU CAN HELP HIM ANYWAY.
"AND PLEASE LET HIM SAVE MY MOMMY.
"I KNOW HE CAN BECAUSE SHE'S BEAUTIFUL AND THAT'S WHAT SUPER HEROES DO.
"SAVE BEAUTIFUL GIRLS."
YOUR TIME'S UP, SPECTOR.
THEN WE CAN FINALLY BE A FAMILY.
BLESS YOU, KHONSHU.
AMEN.

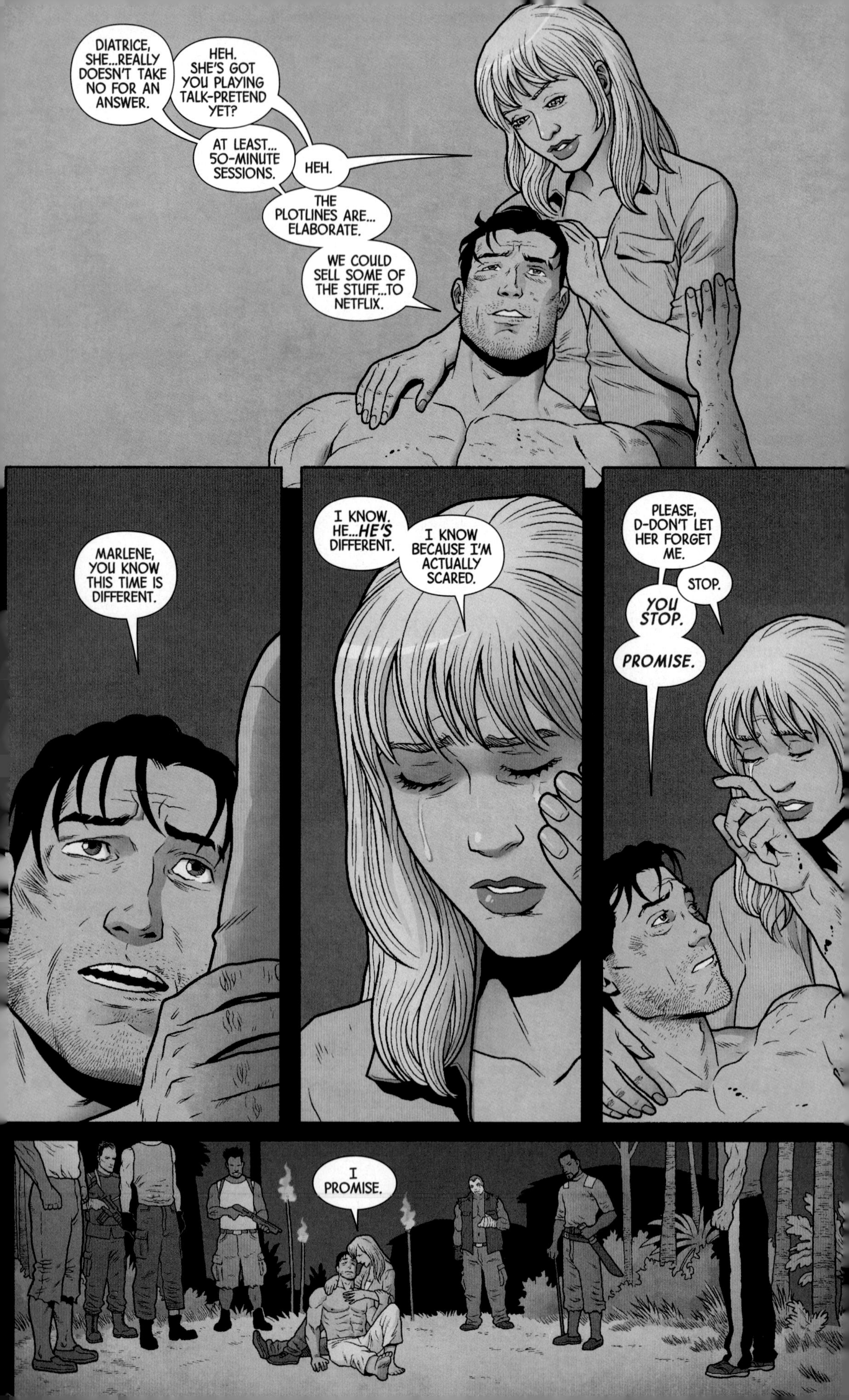
DIATRICE, SHE...REALLY DOESN'T TAKE NO FOR AN ANSWER.
HEH. SHE'S GOT YOU PLAYING TALK-PRETEND YET?
AT LEAST... 50-MINUTE SESSIONS.
HEH.
THE PLOTLINES ARE... ELABORATE.
WE COULD SELL SOME OF THE STUFF...TO NETFLIX.
MARLENE, YOU KNOW THIS TIME IS DIFFERENT.
I KNOW. HE...HE'S DIFFERENT.
I KNOW BECAUSE I'M ACTUALLY SCARED.
PLEASE, D-DON'T LET HER FORGET ME.
STOP.
YOU STOP.
PROMISE.
I PROMISE.

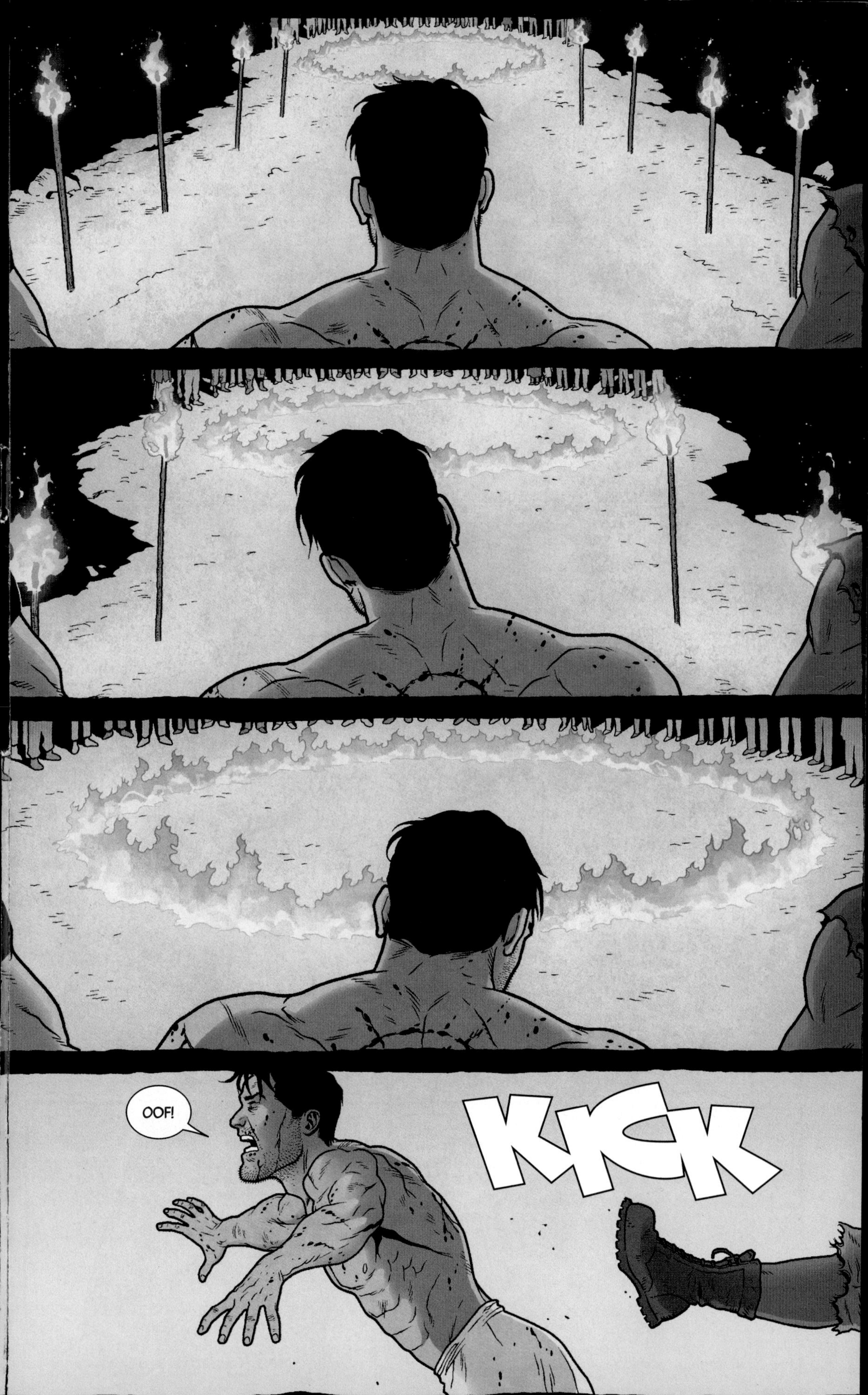
OOF!
KICK

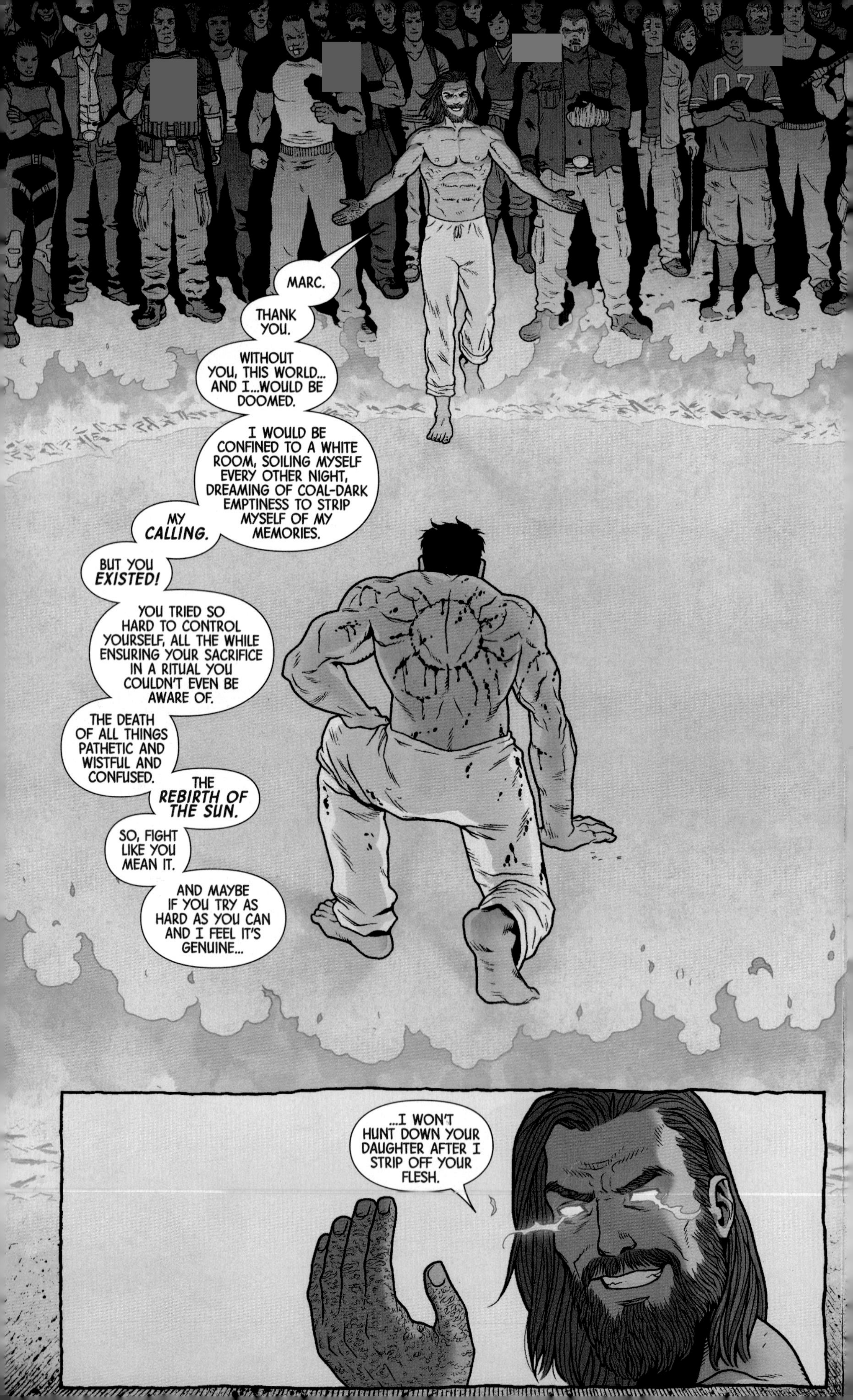
MARC.
THANK YOU.
WITHOUT YOU, THIS WORLD... AND I...WOULD BE DOOMED.
I WOULD BE CONFINED TO A WHITE ROOM, SOILING MYSELF EVERY OTHER NIGHT, DREAMING OF COAL-DARK EMPTINESS TO STRIP MYSELF OF MY MEMORIES.
MY CALLING.
BUT YOU EXISTED!
YOU TRIED SO HARD TO CONTROL YOURSELF, ALL THE WHILE ENSURING YOUR SACRIFICE IN A RITUAL YOU COULDN'T EVEN BE AWARE OF.
THE DEATH OF ALL THINGS PATHETIC AND WISTFUL AND CONFUSED.
THE REBIRTH OF THE SUN.
SO, FIGHT LIKE YOU MEAN IT.
AND MAYBE IF YOU TRY AS HARD AS YOU CAN AND I FEEL IT'S GENUINE...
...I WON'T HUNT DOWN YOUR DAUGHTER AFTER I STRIP OFF YOUR FLESH.

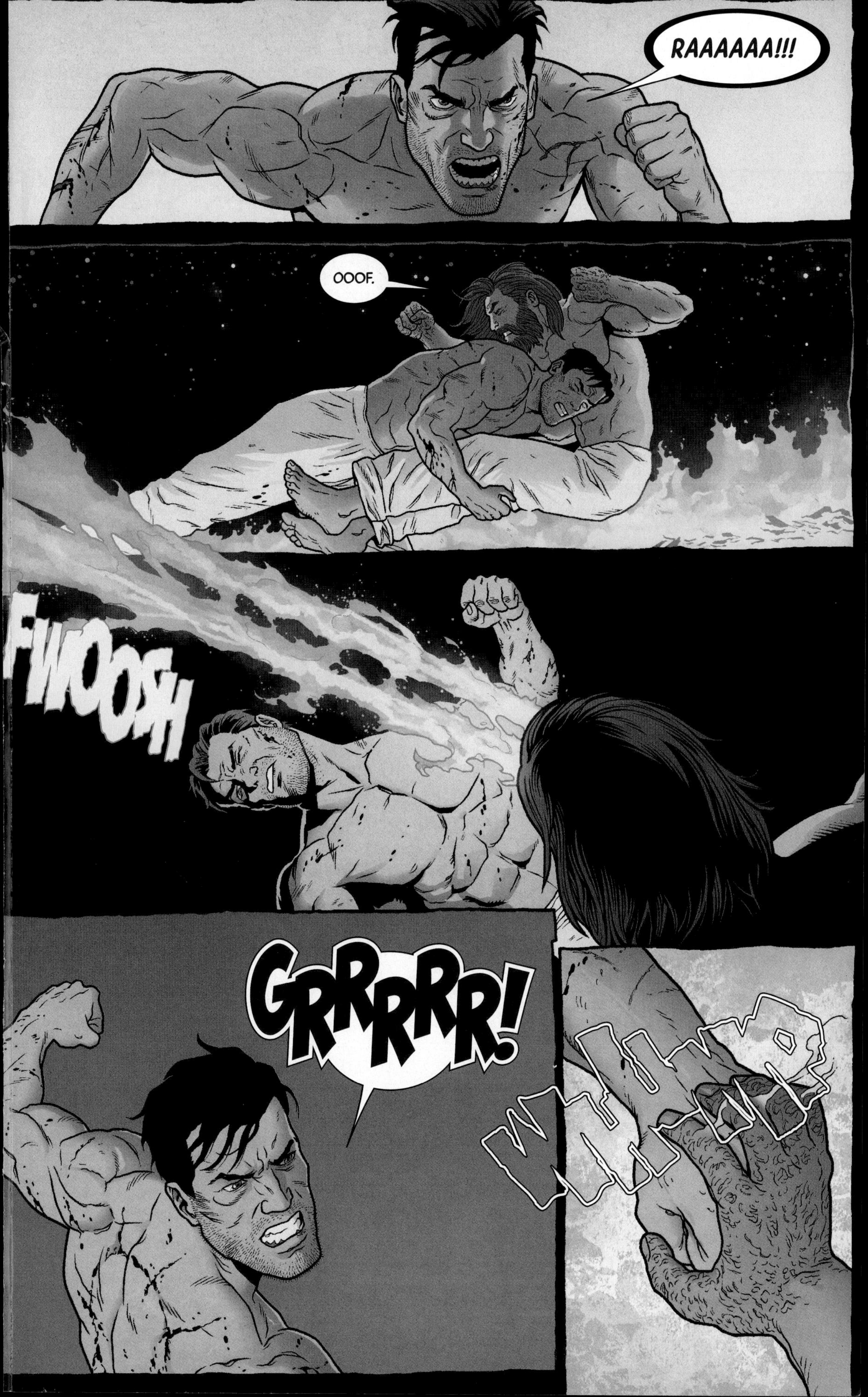
RAAAAAA!!!
OOOF.
FWOOSH
GRRRRR!
WHUMP

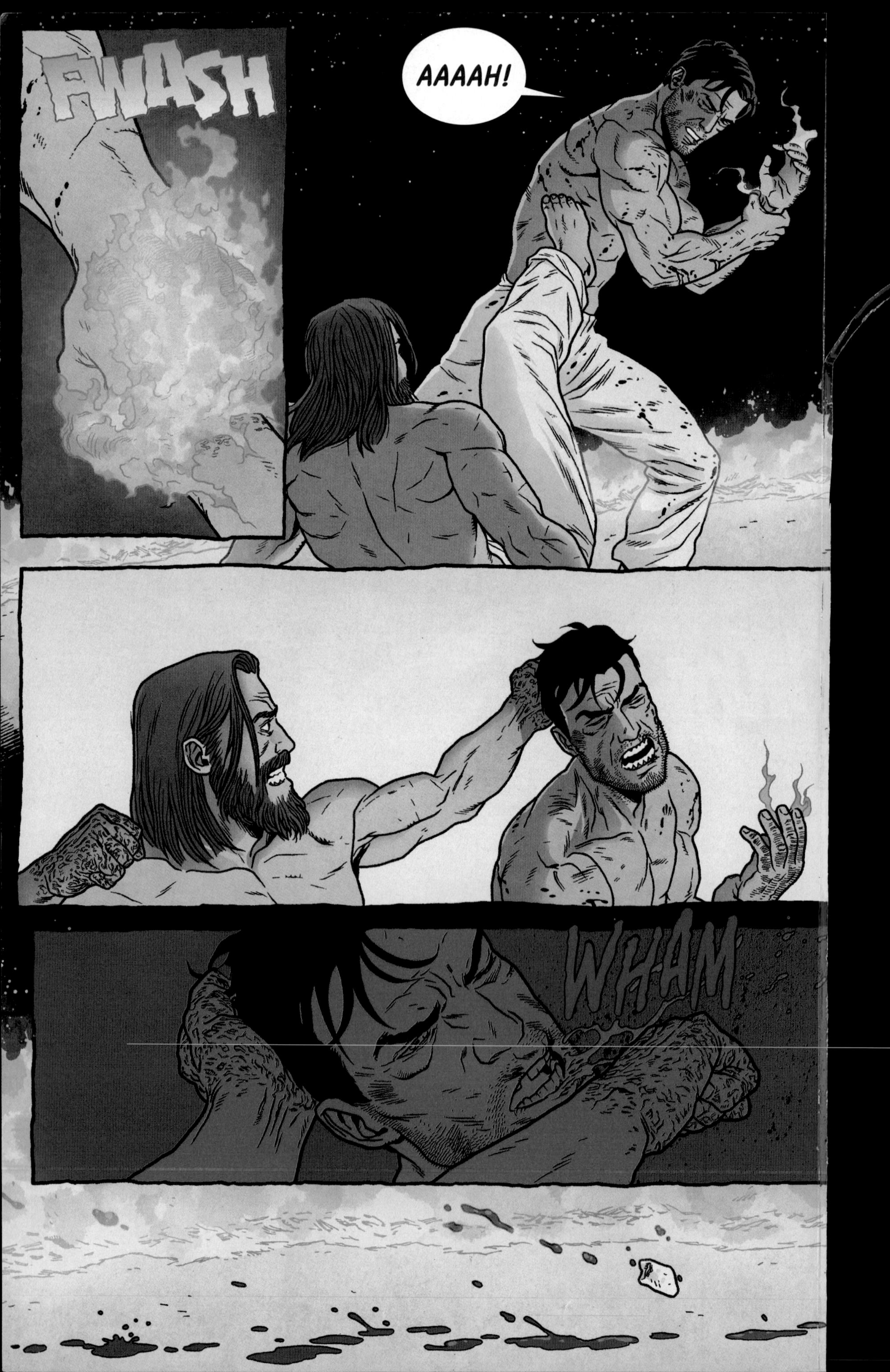
FWASH
AAAAH!
WHAM

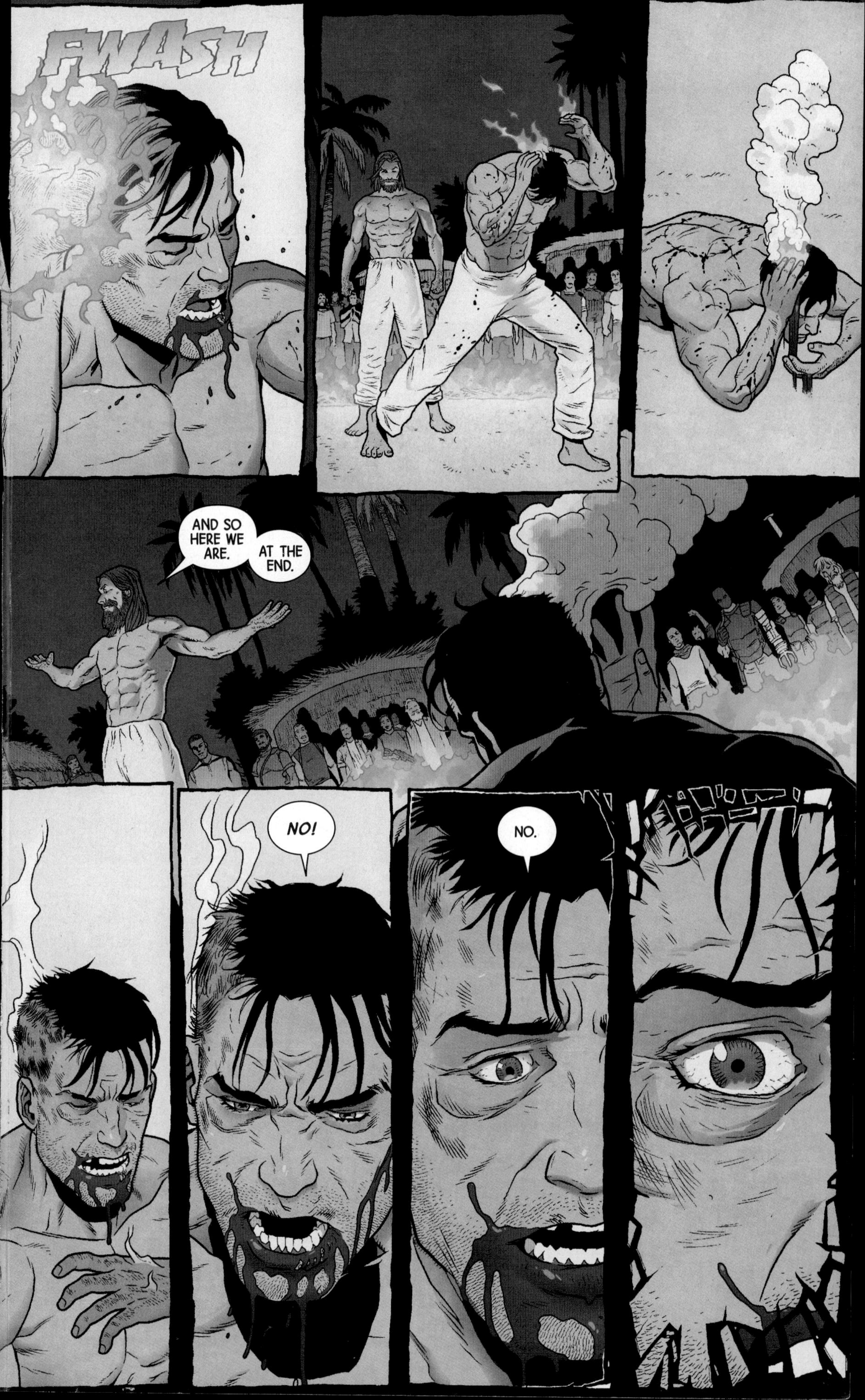
FWASH
AND SO HERE WE ARE.
AT THE END.
NO!
NO.

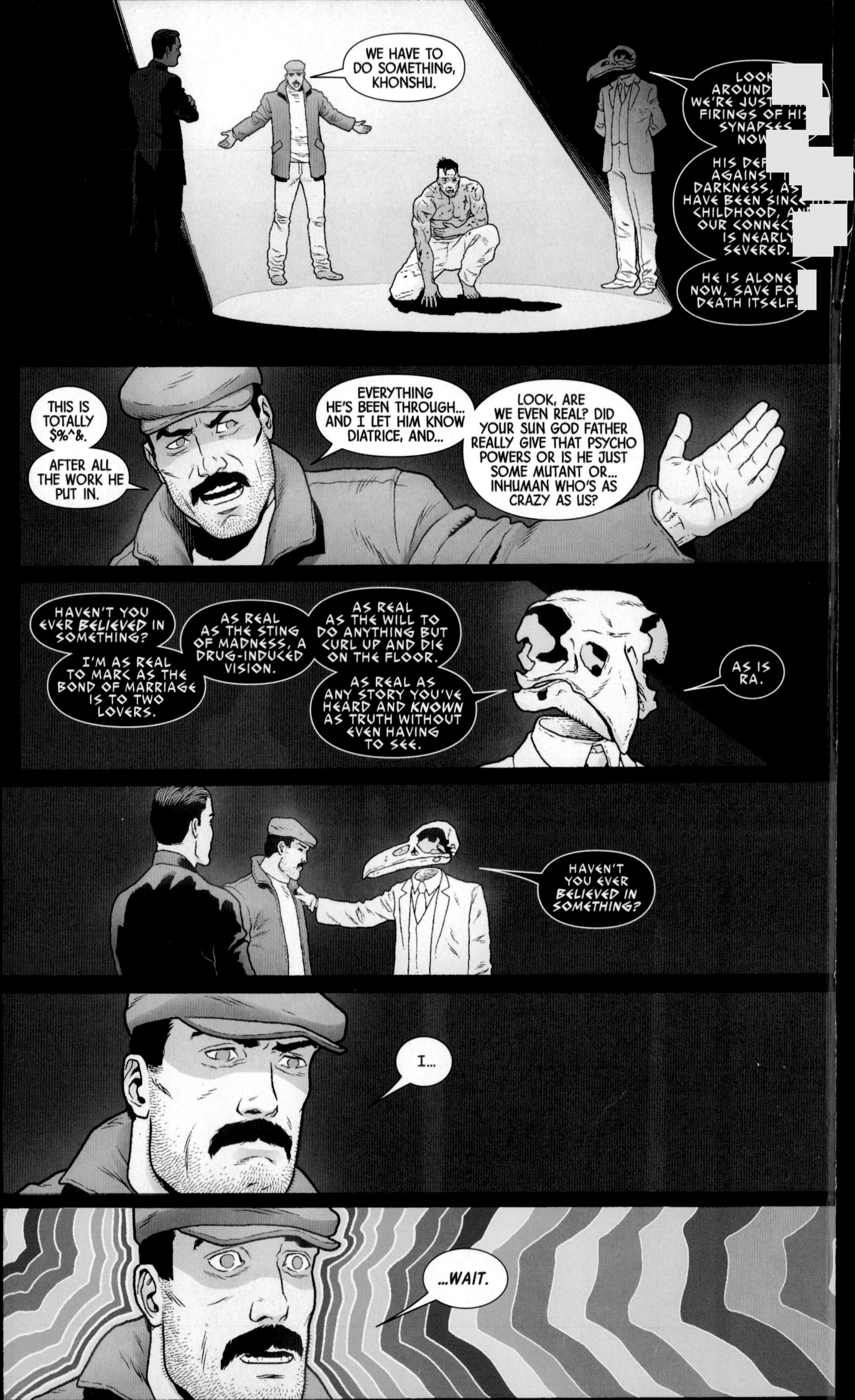

WE HAVE TO DO SOMETHING, KHONSHU.
LOOK AROUND WE'RE JUST FIRINGS OF HI SYNAPSES NOW
HIS DEF AGAINST DARKNESS, AS HAVE BEEN SINC CHILDHOOD, AN OUR CONNECT IS NEARLY SEVERED.
HE IS ALONE NOW, SAVE FO DEATH ITSELF.
THIS IS TOTALLY $%^&.
AFTER ALL THE WORK HE PUT IN.
EVERYTHING HE'S BEEN THROUGH... AND I LET HIM KNOW DIATRICE, AND...
LOOK, ARE WE EVEN REAL? DID YOUR SUN GOD FATHER REALLY GIVE THAT PSYCHO POWERS OR IS HE JUST SOME MUTANT OR... INHUMAN WHO'S AS CRAZY AS US?
HAVEN'T YOU EVER BELIEVED IN SOMETHING?
I'M AS REAL TO MARC AS THE BOND OF MARRIAGE IS TO TWO LOVERS.
AS REAL AS THE STING OF MADNESS, A DRUG-INDUCED VISION.
AS REAL AS THE WILL TO DO ANYTHING BUT CURL UP AND DIE ON THE FLOOR.
AS REAL AS ANY STORY YOU'VE HEARD AND KNOWN AS TRUTH WITHOUT EVEN HAVING TO SEE.
AS IS RA.
HAVEN'T YOU EVER BELIEVED IN SOMETHING?
I...
...WAIT.

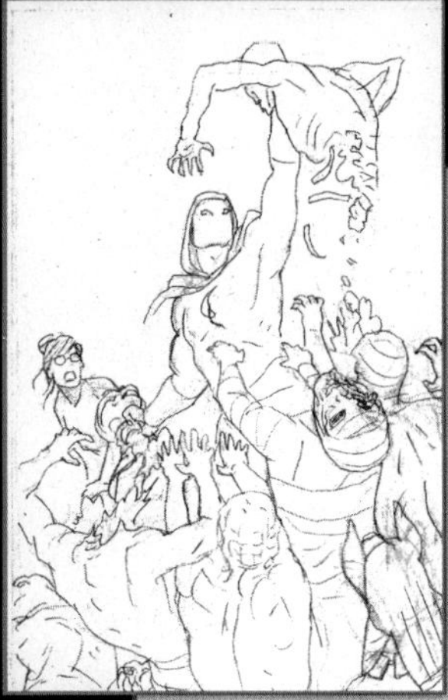

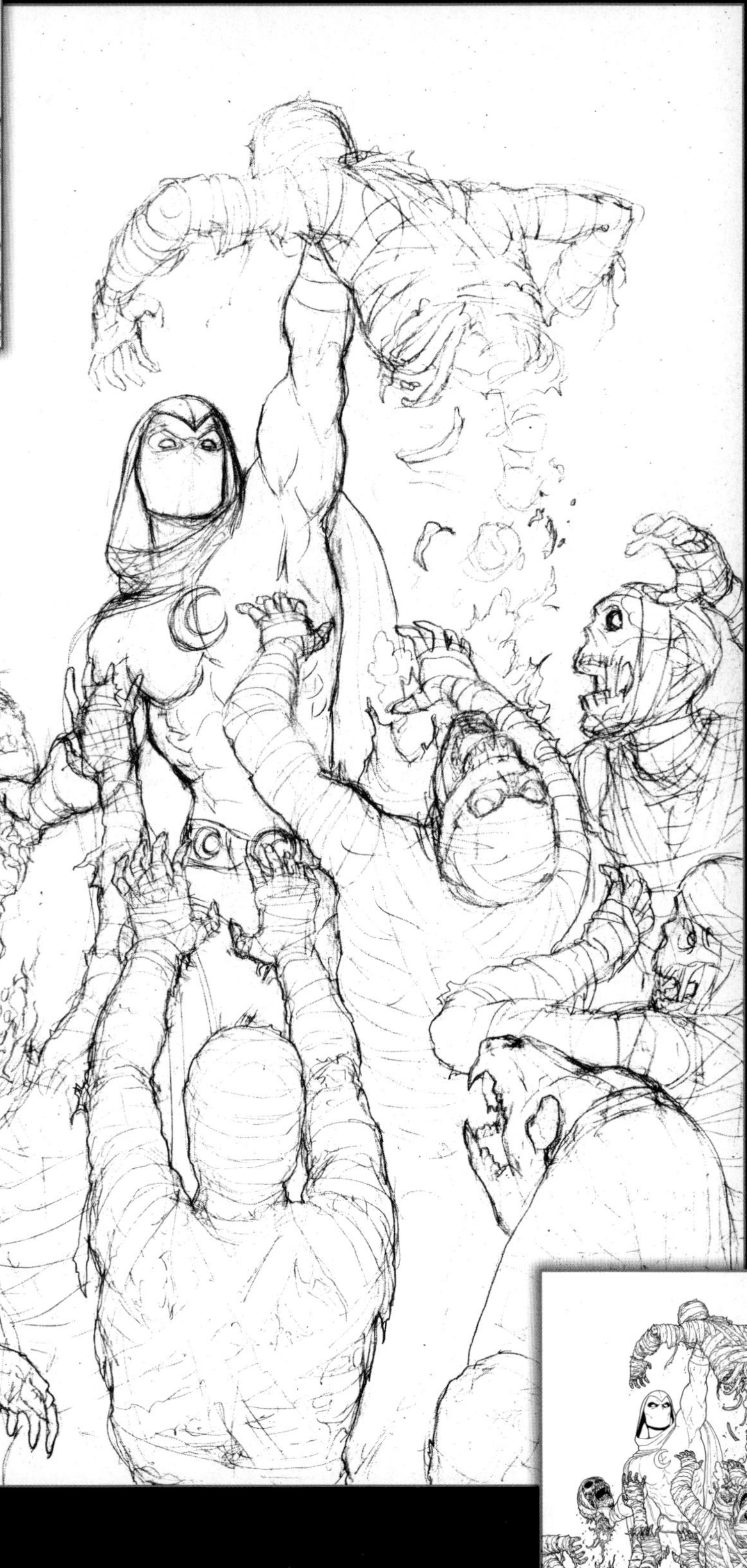

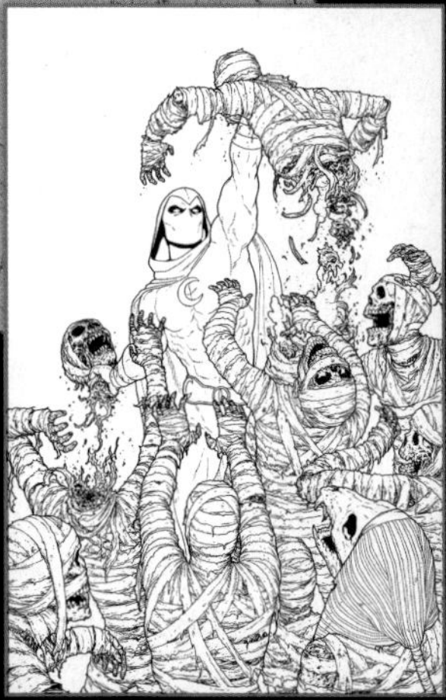

188, PAGE 15 ART PROCESS BY **JACEN BURROWS**

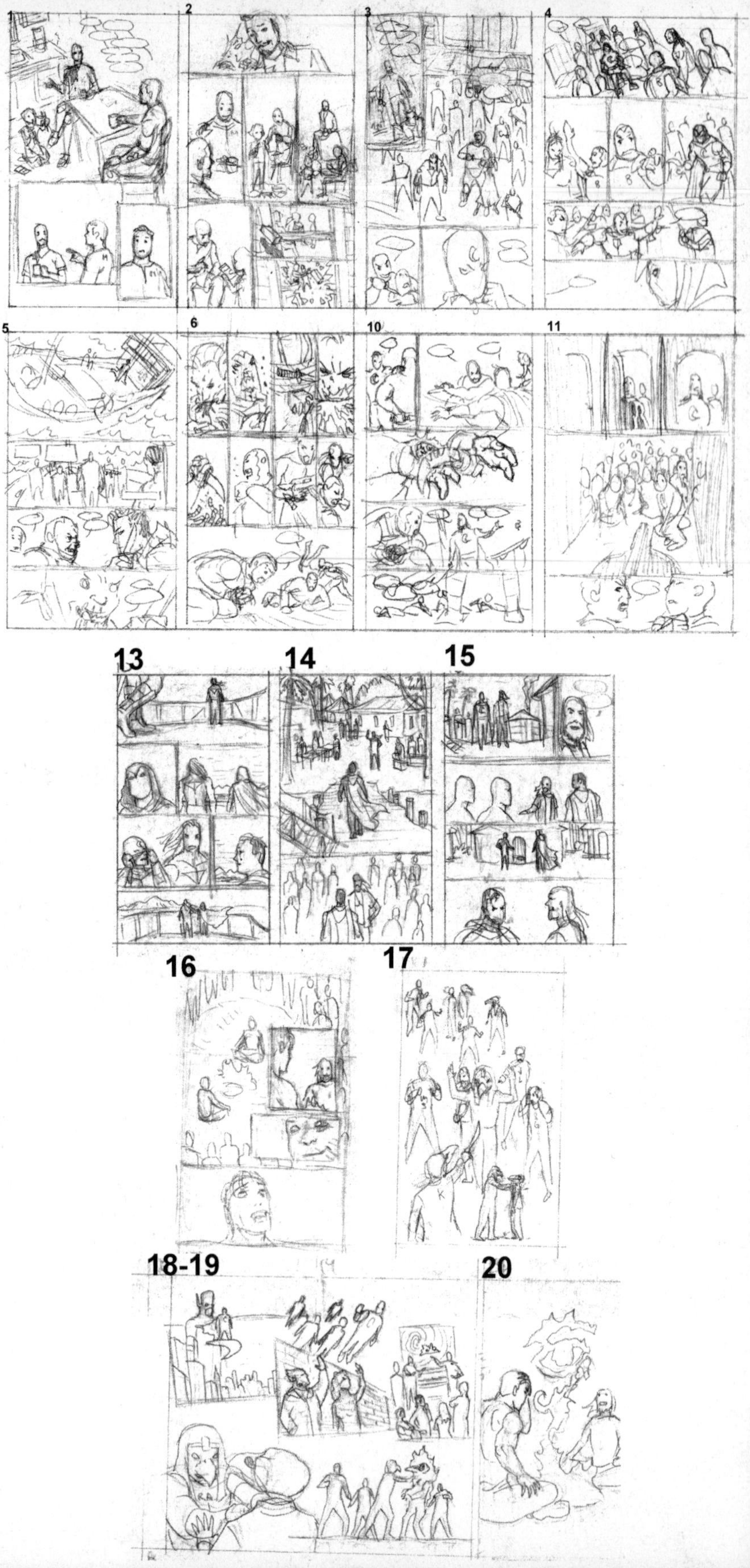
1
2
3
4
5
6
10
11
13
14
15
16
17
18-19
20

192, THUMBNAILS BY JACEN BURROWS

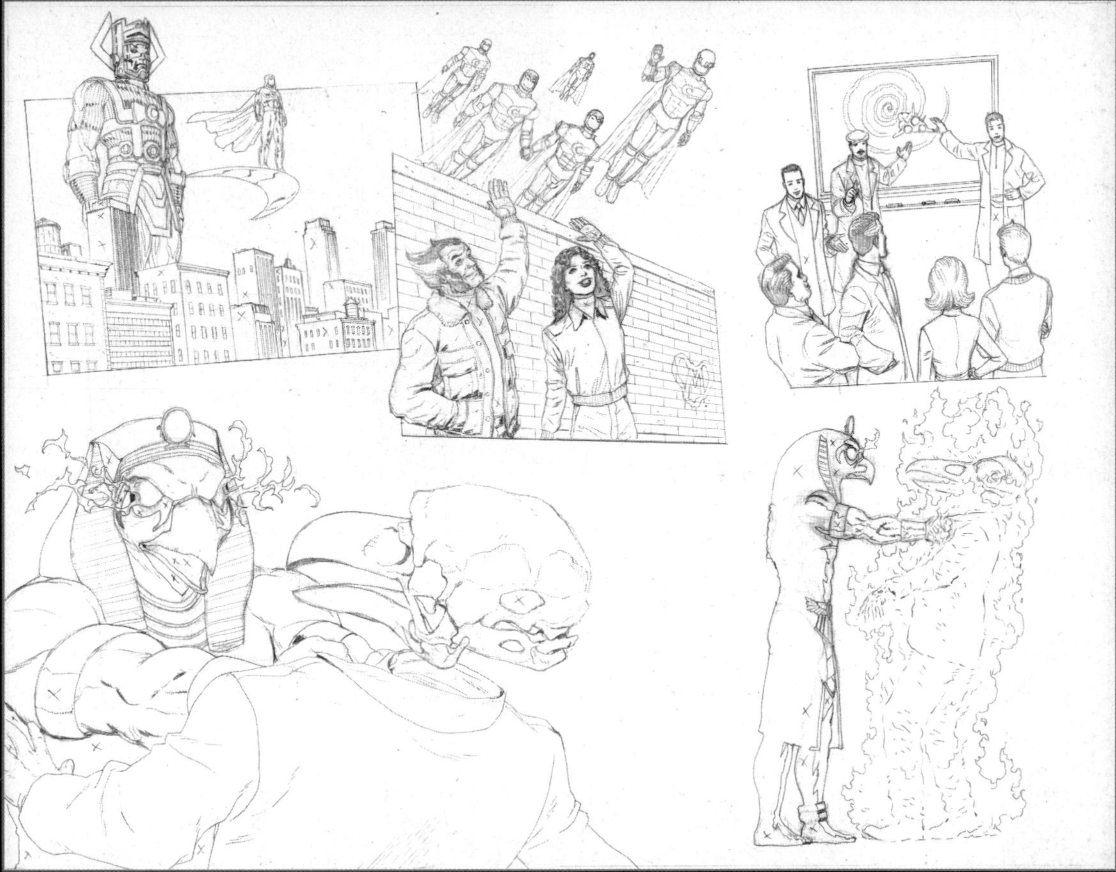

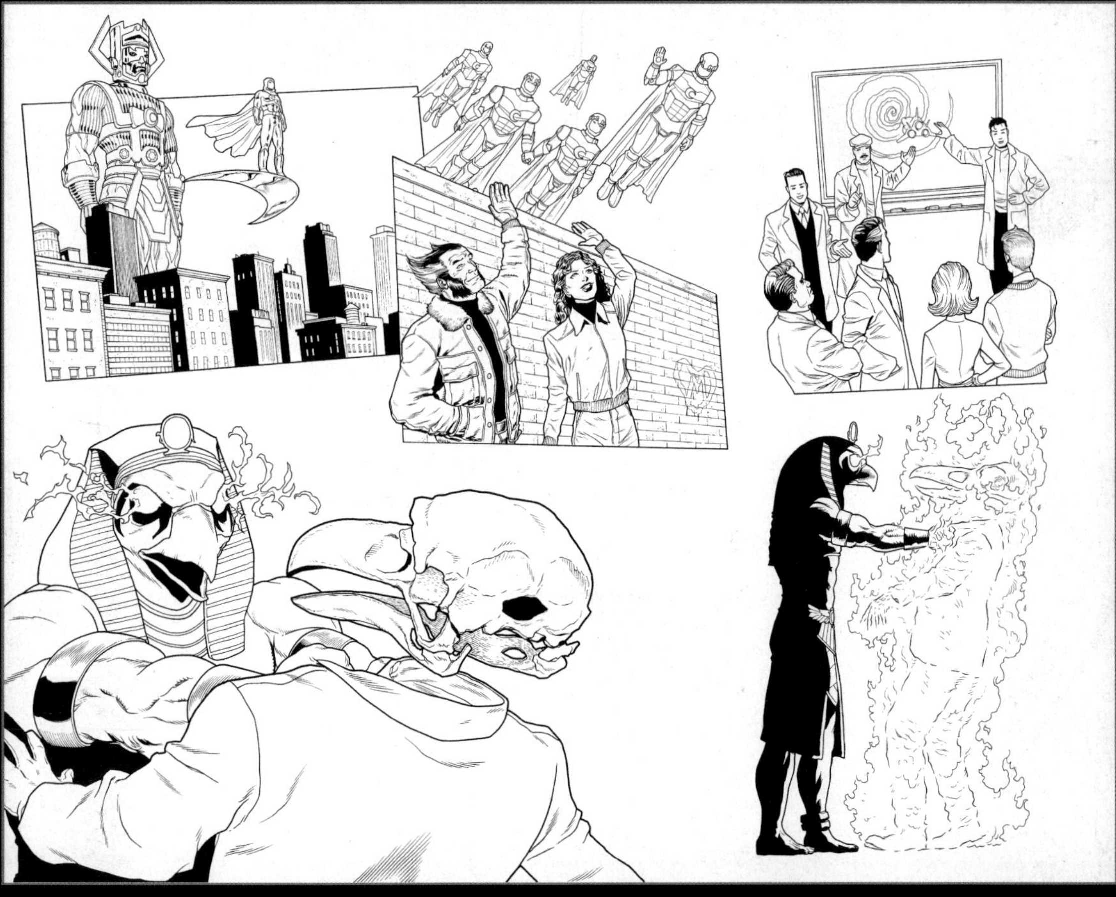

192, PAGES 18-19 ART PROCESS BY **JACEN BURROWS** & **GUILLERMO ORTEGO**

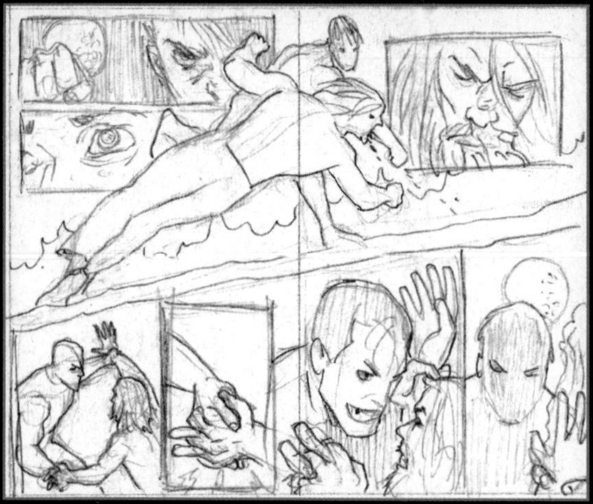

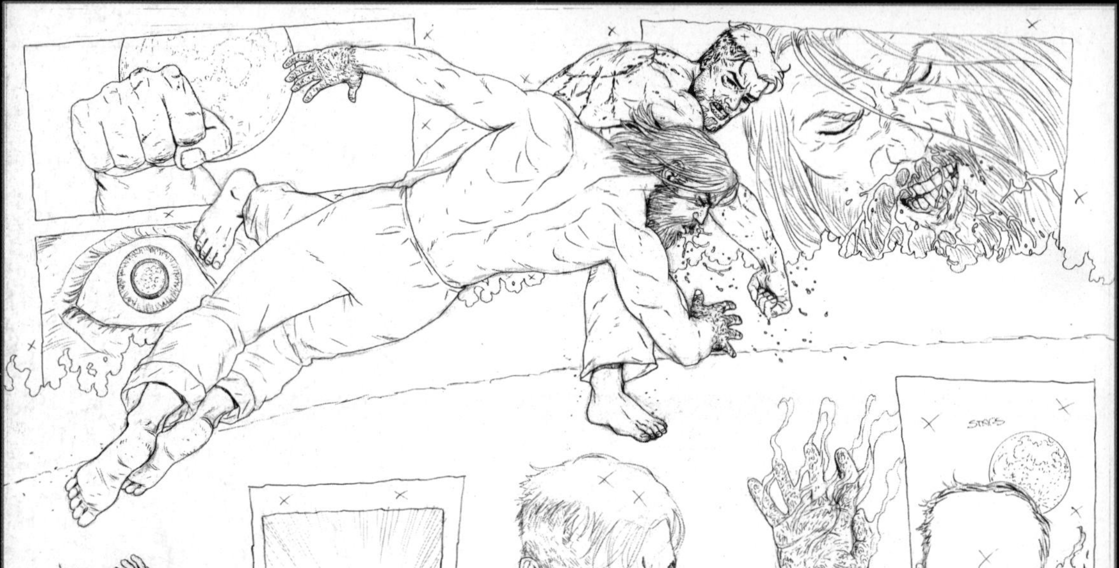

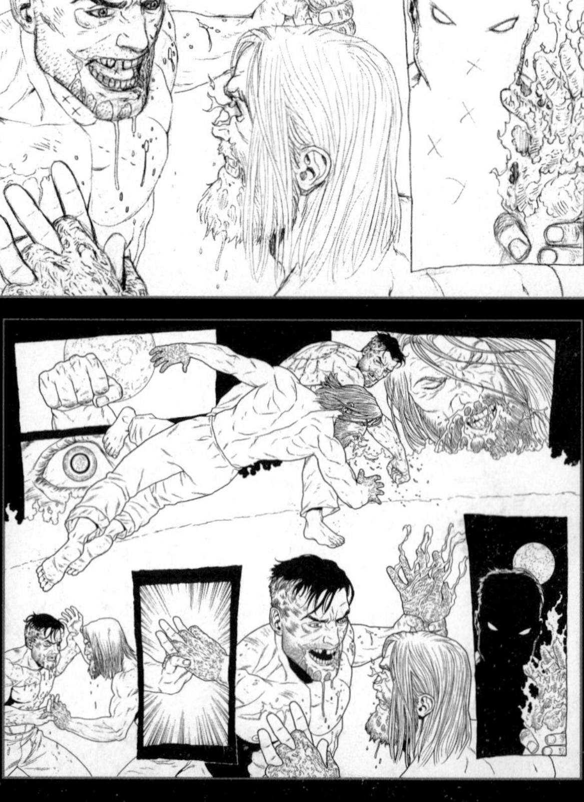

193, PAGES 14-15 ART PROCESS BY
JACEN BURROWS & GUILLERMO ORTEGO

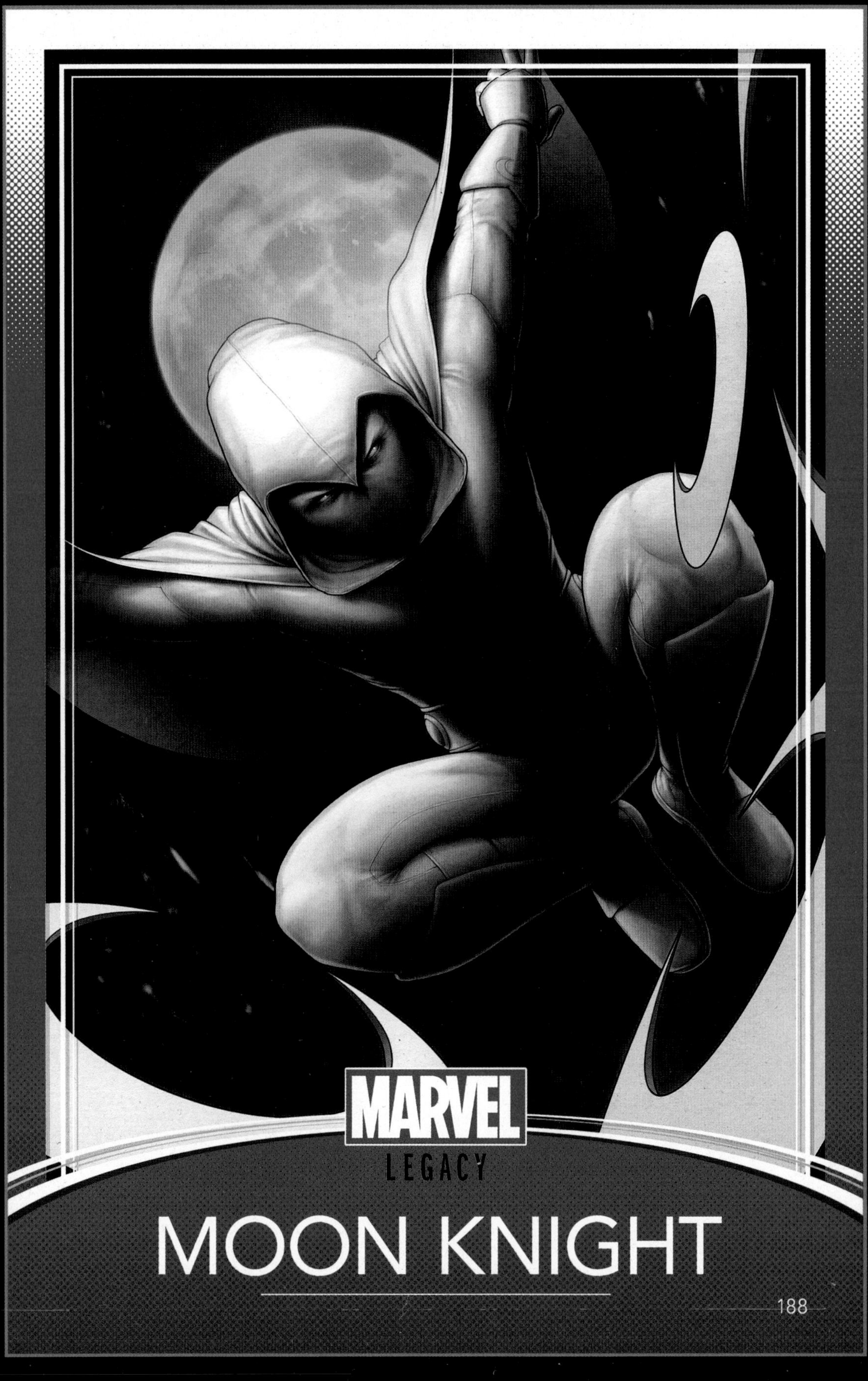
MARVEL
LEGACY
MOON KNIGHT
188

188 TRADING CARD VARIANT BY JOHN TYLER CHRISTOPHER

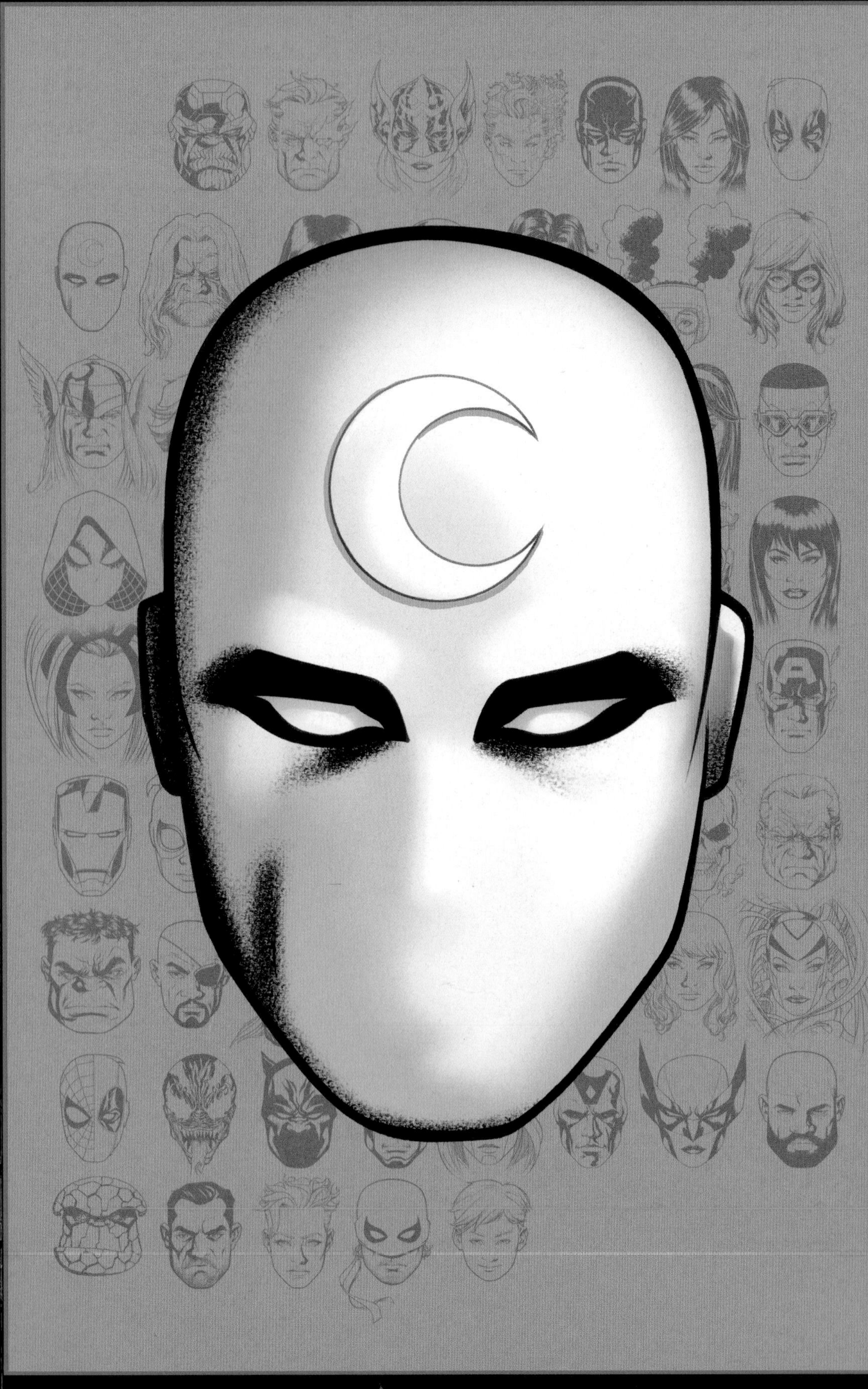

188 LEGACY HEADSHOT VARIANT BY MIKE McKONE & RACHELLE ROSENBERG

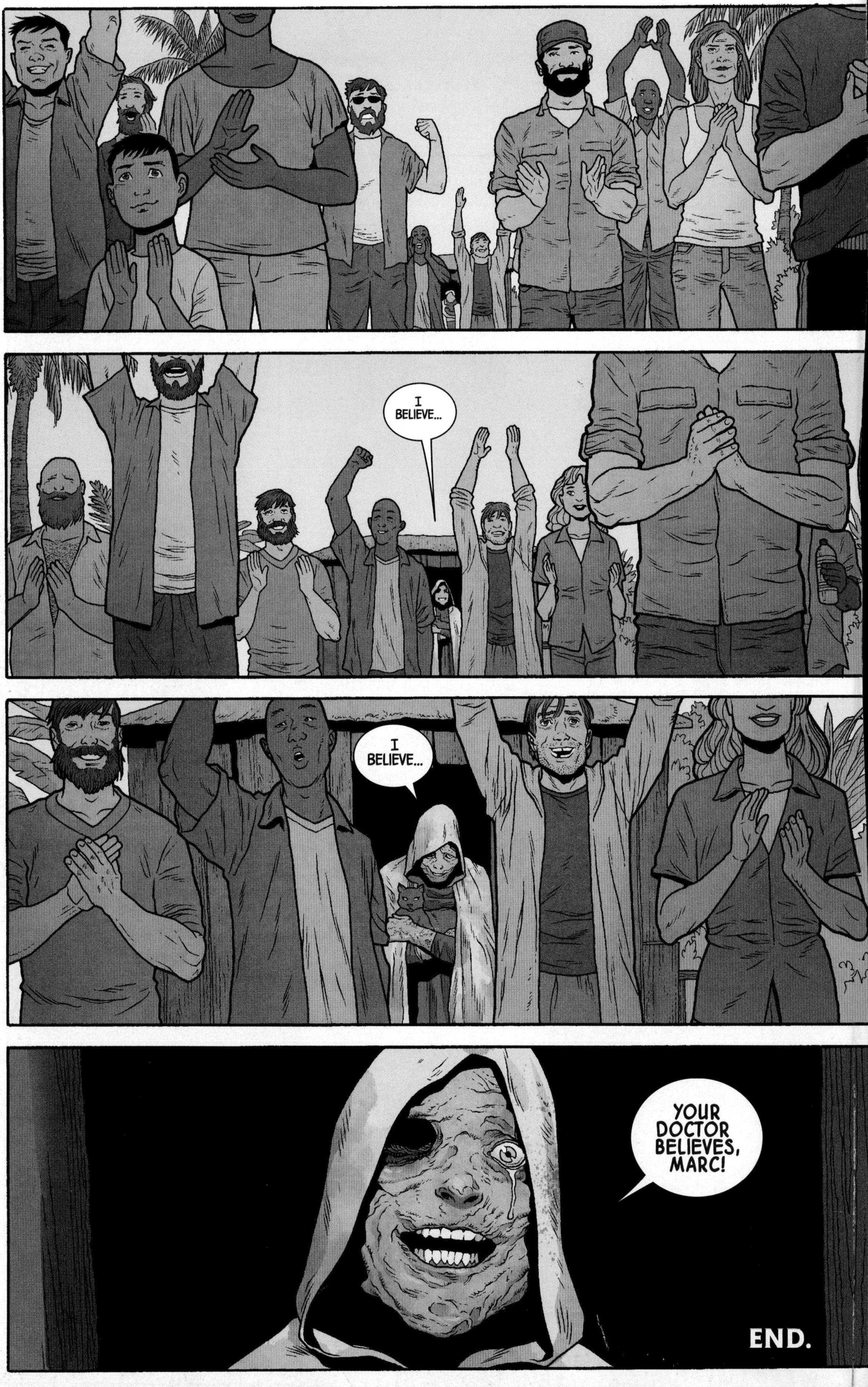
I BELIEVE...
I BELIEVE...
YOUR DOCTOR BELIEVES, MARC!
END.

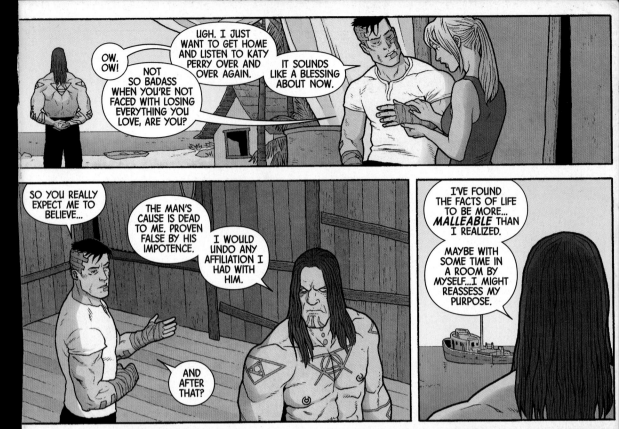

OW. OW!

NOT SO BADASS WHEN YOU'RE NOT FACED WITH LOSING EVERYTHING YOU LOVE, ARE YOU?

UGH. I JUST WANT TO GET HOME AND LISTEN TO KATY PERRY OVER AND OVER AGAIN.

IT SOUNDS LIKE A BLESSING ABOUT NOW.

SO YOU REALLY EXPECT ME TO BELIEVE...

THE MAN'S CAUSE IS DEAD TO ME. PROVEN FALSE BY HIS IMPOTENCE.

I WOULD UNDO ANY AFFILIATION I HAD WITH HIM.

AND AFTER THAT?

I'VE FOUND THE FACTS OF LIFE TO BE MORE... *MALLEABLE* THAN I REALIZED.

MAYBE WITH SOME TIME IN A ROOM BY MYSELF...I MIGHT REASSESS MY PURPOSE.

WELL, I'M NOT GOING TO SUDDENLY BECOME CHARLES XAVIER AND PRETEND I HAVE SOME GRAND PLAN FOR EVERYTHING NOW.

ALL OF YOU JUST GOT STUCK ON A DESERT ISLAND BECAUSE YOU LET YOURSELF GET CONVINCED OF A BUNCH OF CRAP BY A COMPLETELY MAD SUPER VILLAIN.

UNLIKE THE SO-CALLED SUN KING, I DON'T CLAIM TO HAVE ANY ANSWERS. IN FACT, I MOST DEFINITELY *LACK* THEM.

SUN KING CONVINCED ME OF ONE THING...

EVERY KNIGHT NEEDS A FEW WILLING WARRIORS TO AID HIM IN BATTLE.

I'M WILLING TO SERVE AS AN ADVISOR. TO HELP YOU FIGHT BACK AGAINST BEING TAKEN ADVANTAGE OF LIKE THIS AGAIN.

SO I HAVE TO ASK...

...ANYONE HERE LOOK GOOD IN WHITE?

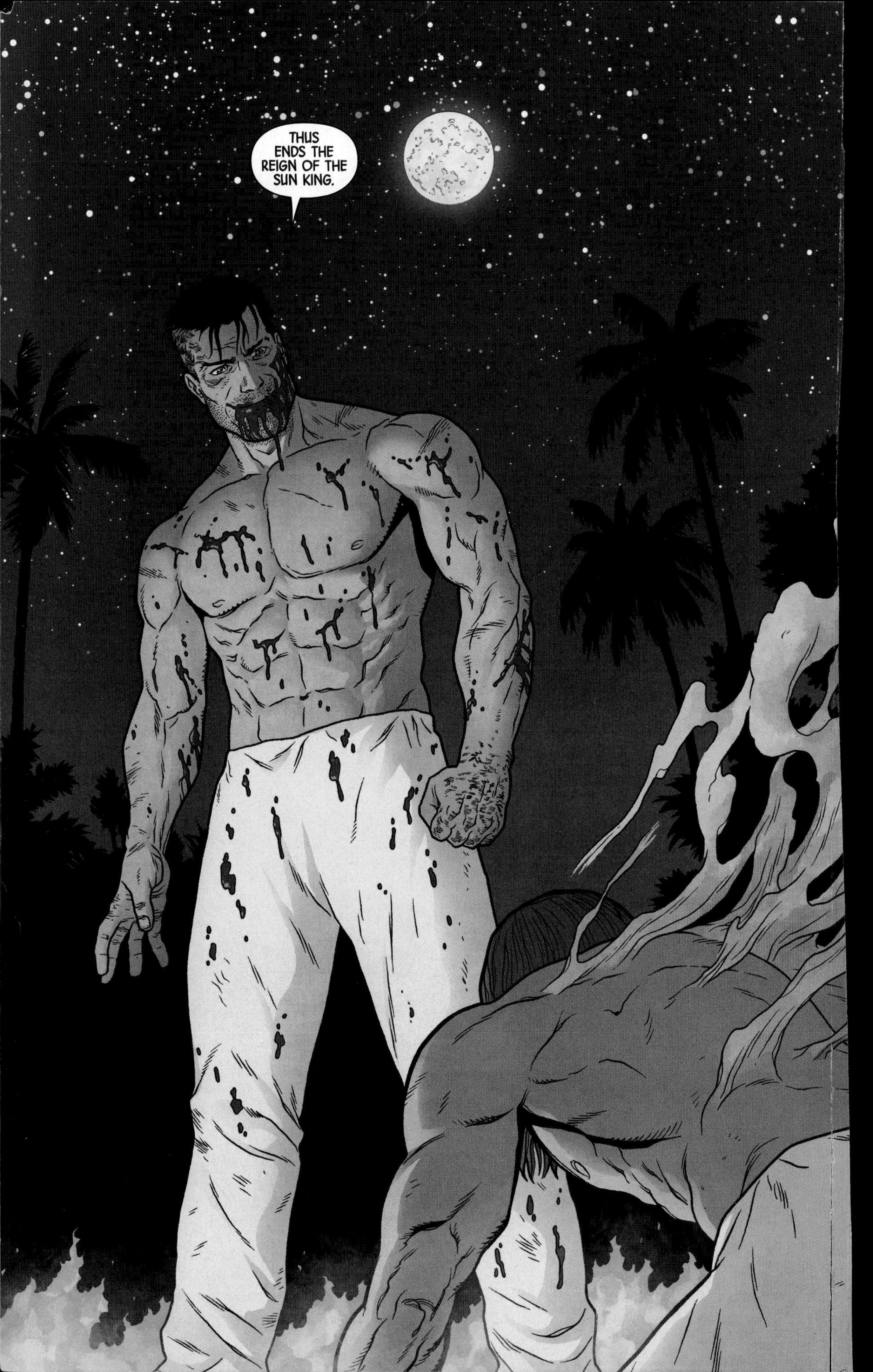
THUS ENDS THE REIGN OF THE SUN KING.

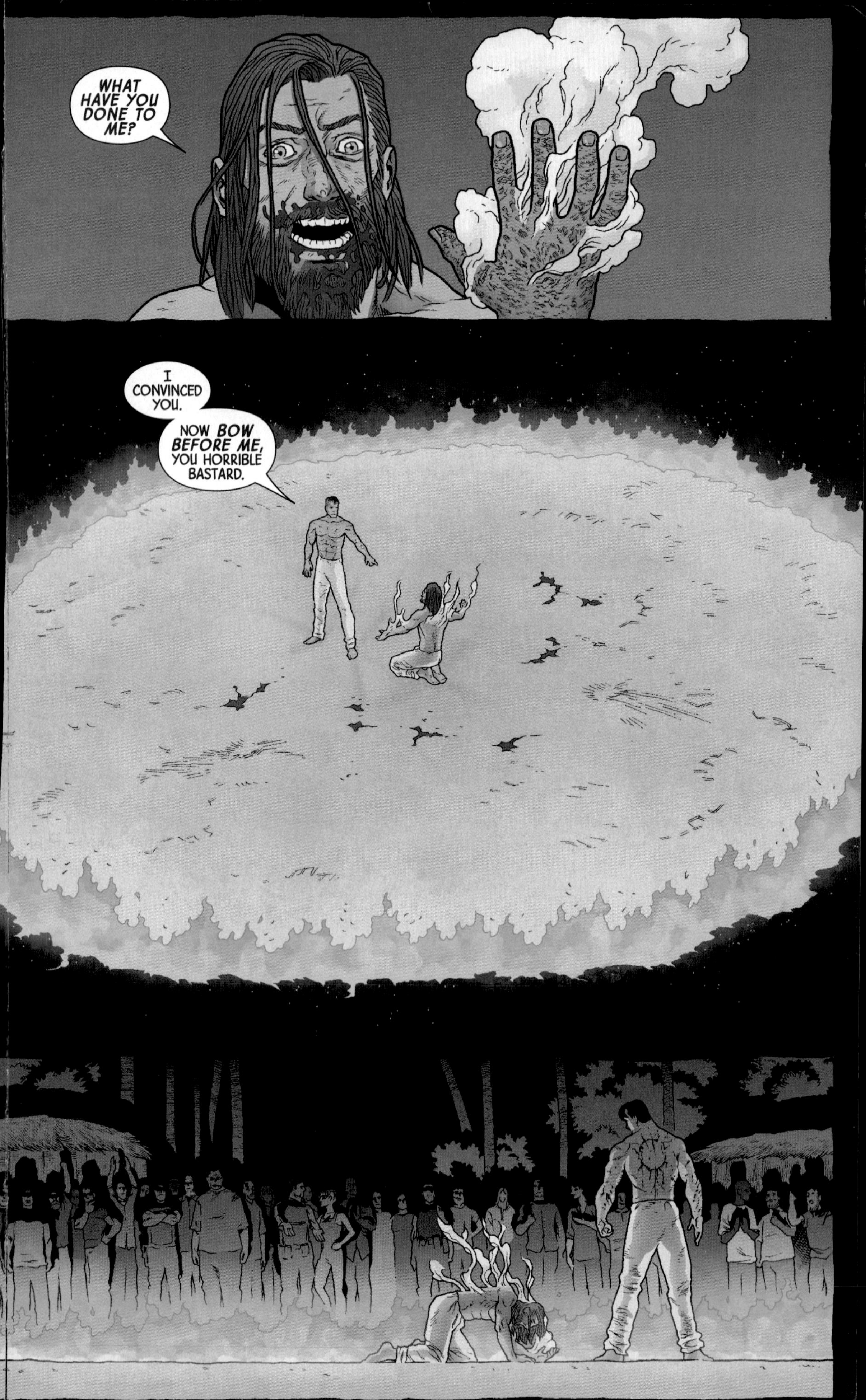
WHAT HAVE YOU DONE TO ME?
I CONVINCED YOU.
NOW BOW BEFORE ME, YOU HORRIBLE BASTARD.

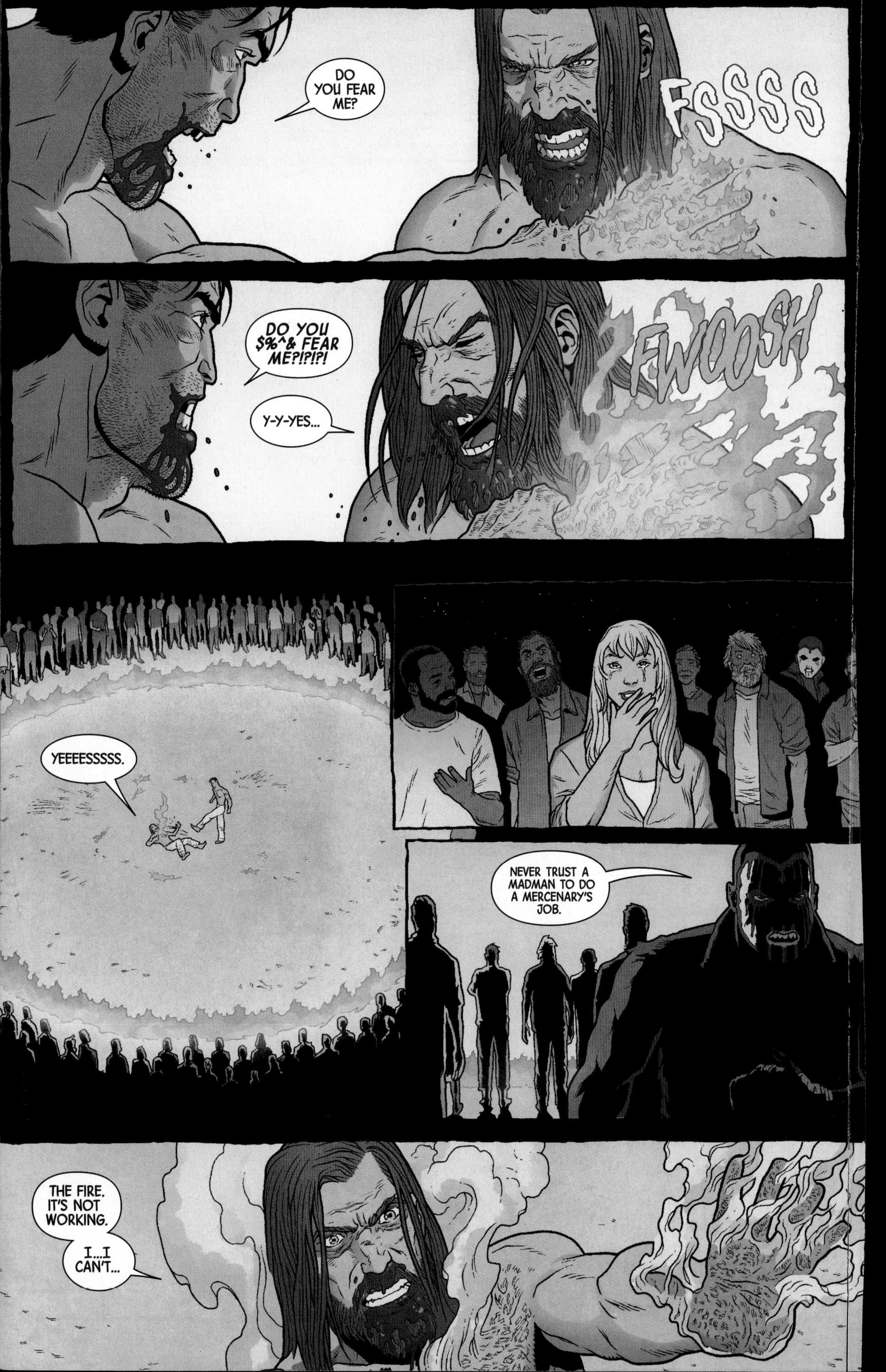
DO YOU FEAR ME?
FSSSS
DO YOU $%^& FEAR ME?!?!?!?!
Y-Y-YES...
FWOOSH
YEEEESSSSS.
NEVER TRUST A MADMAN TO DO A MERCENARY'S JOB.
THE FIRE. IT'S NOT WORKING.
I...I CAN'T...

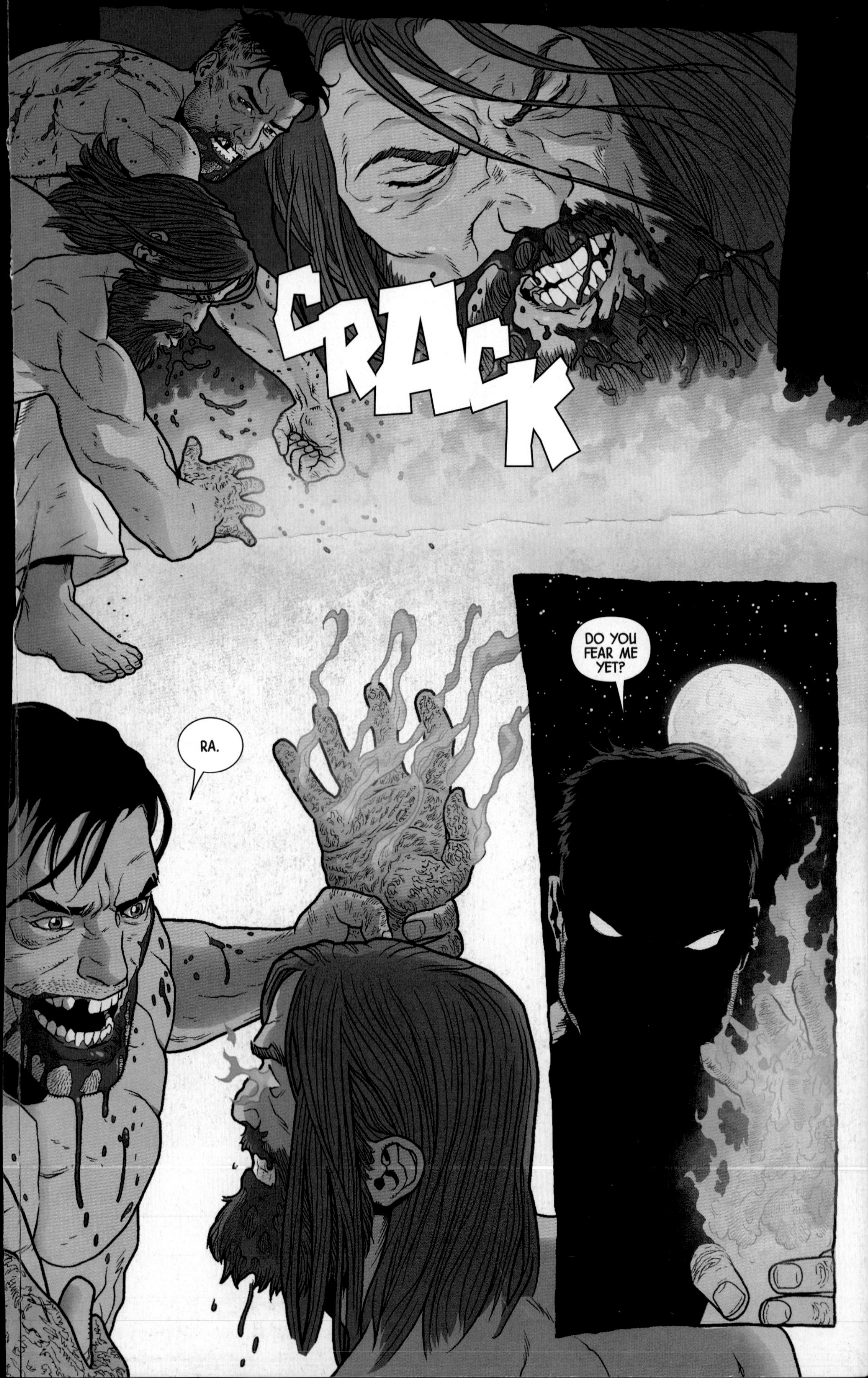
CRACK
RA.
DO YOU FEAR ME YET?

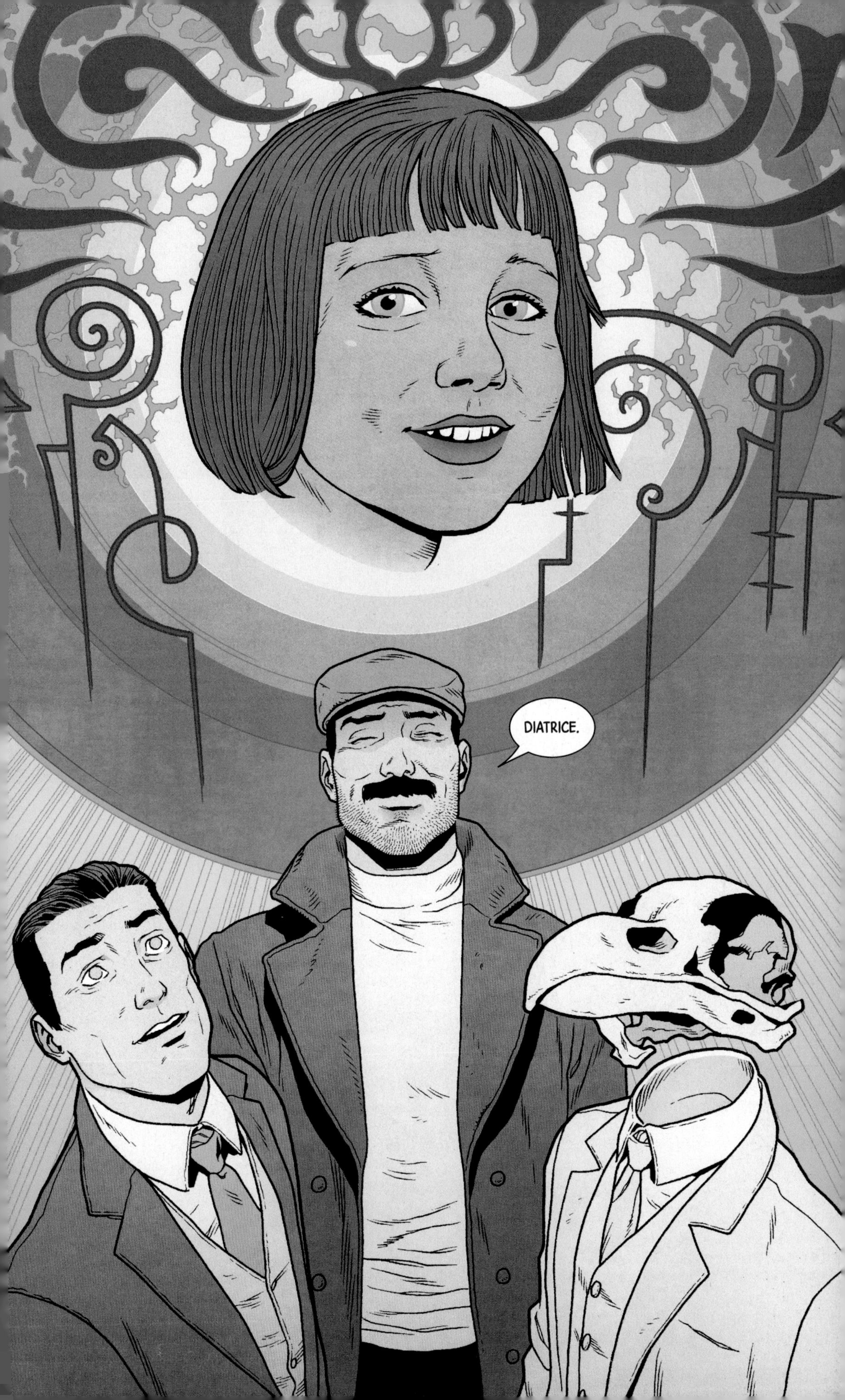
DIATRICE.

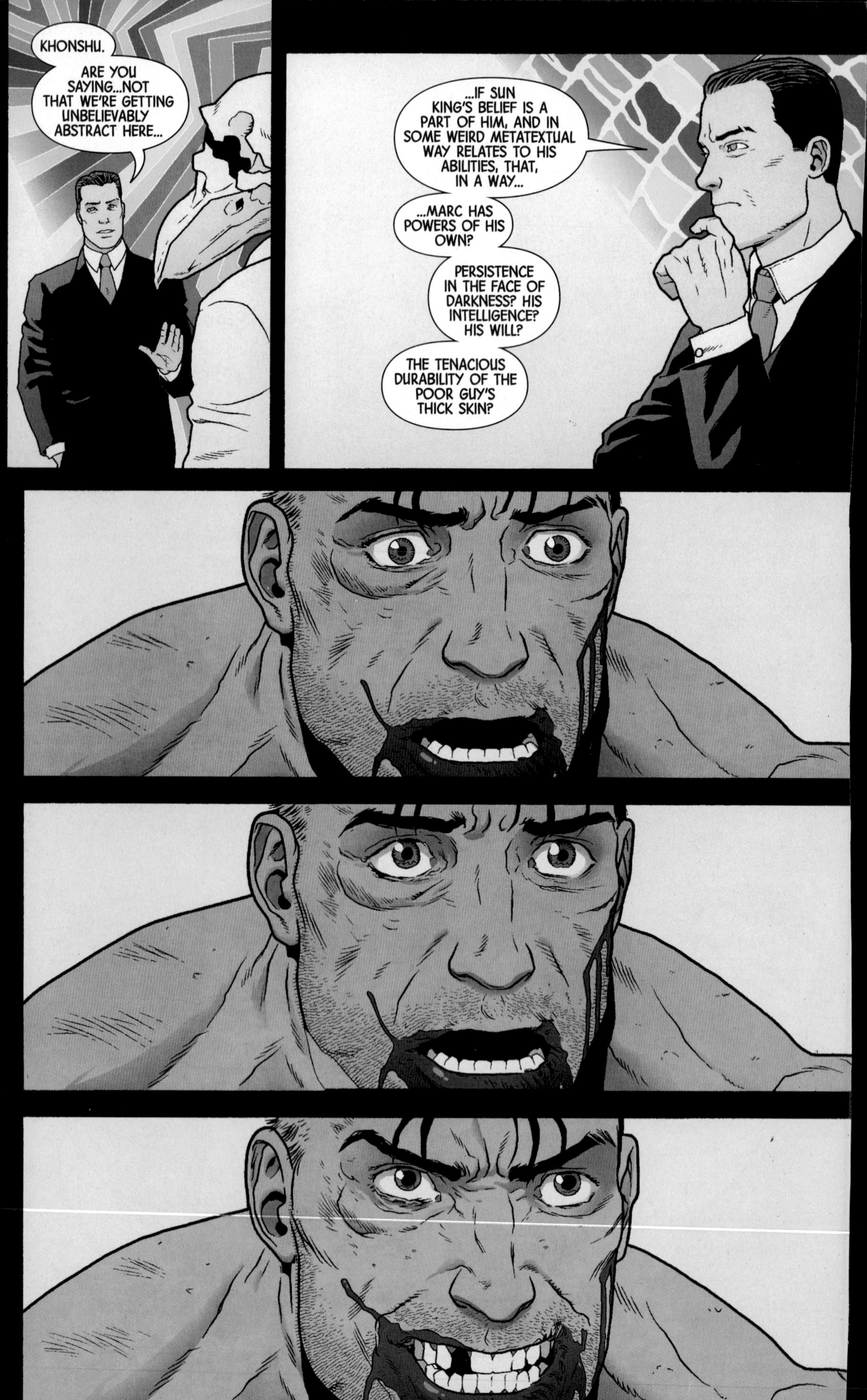
KHONSHU.
ARE YOU SAYING...NOT THAT WE'RE GETTING UNBELIEVABLY ABSTRACT HERE...
...IF SUN KING'S BELIEF IS A PART OF HIM, AND IN SOME WEIRD METATEXTUAL WAY RELATES TO HIS ABILITIES, THAT, IN A WAY...
...MARC HAS POWERS OF HIS OWN?
PERSISTENCE IN THE FACE OF DARKNESS? HIS INTELLIGENCE? HIS WILL?
THE TENACIOUS DURABILITY OF THE POOR GUY'S THICK SKIN?

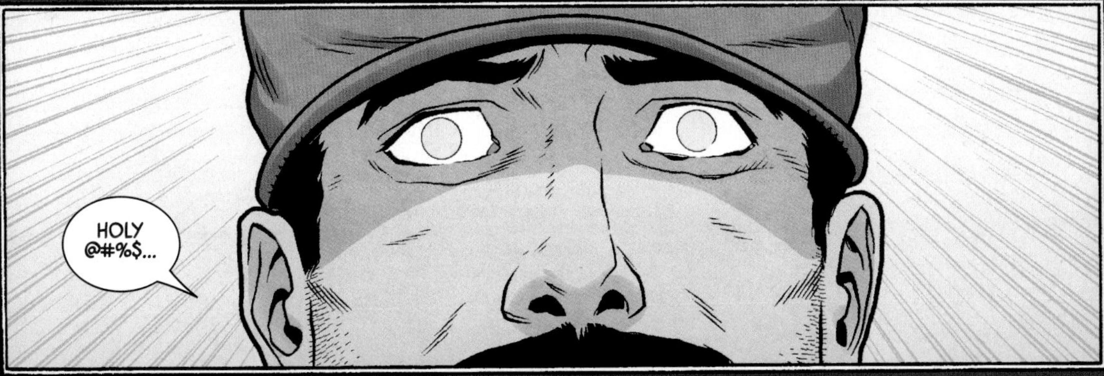
HOLY @#%$...

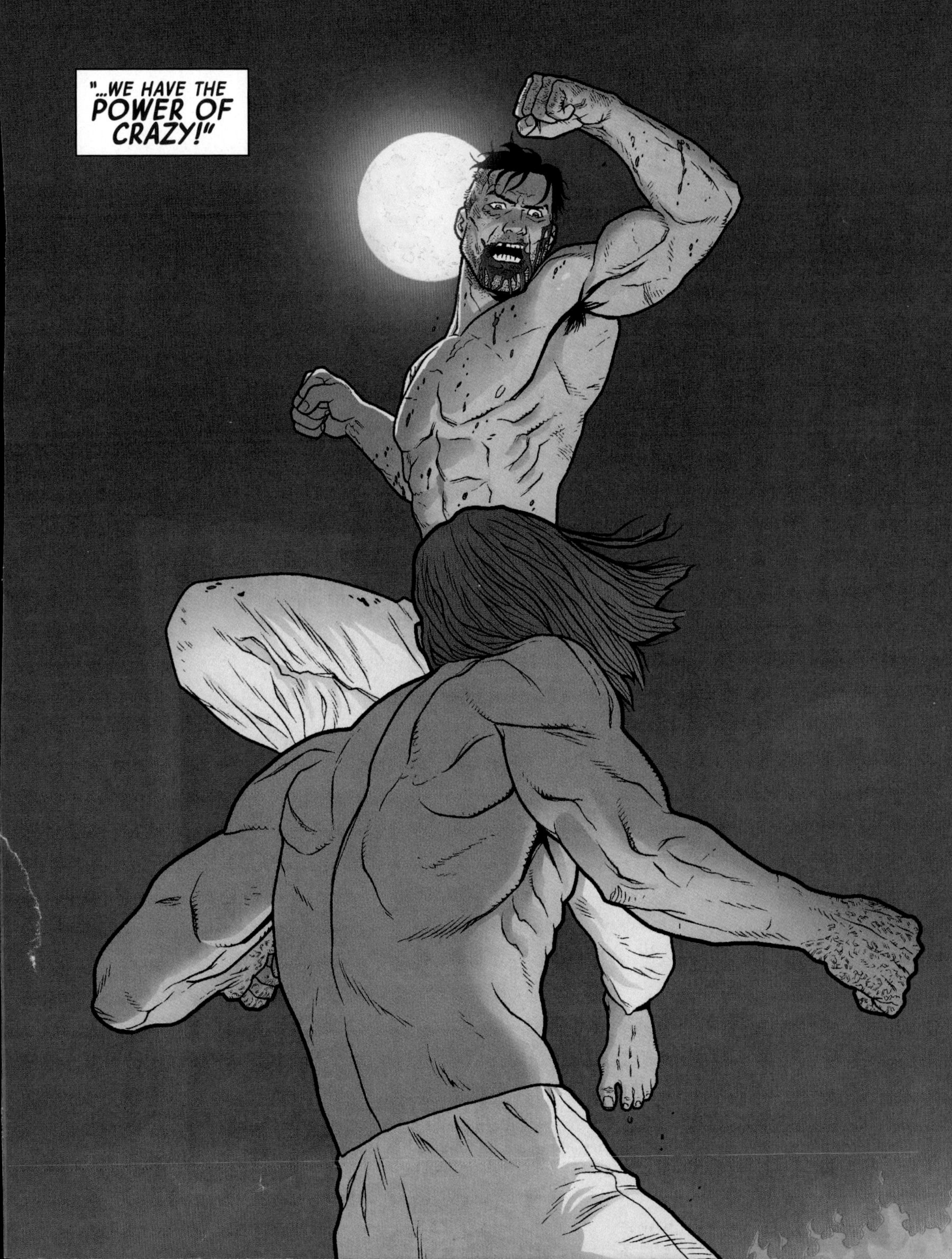
"...WE HAVE THE POWER OF CRAZY!"

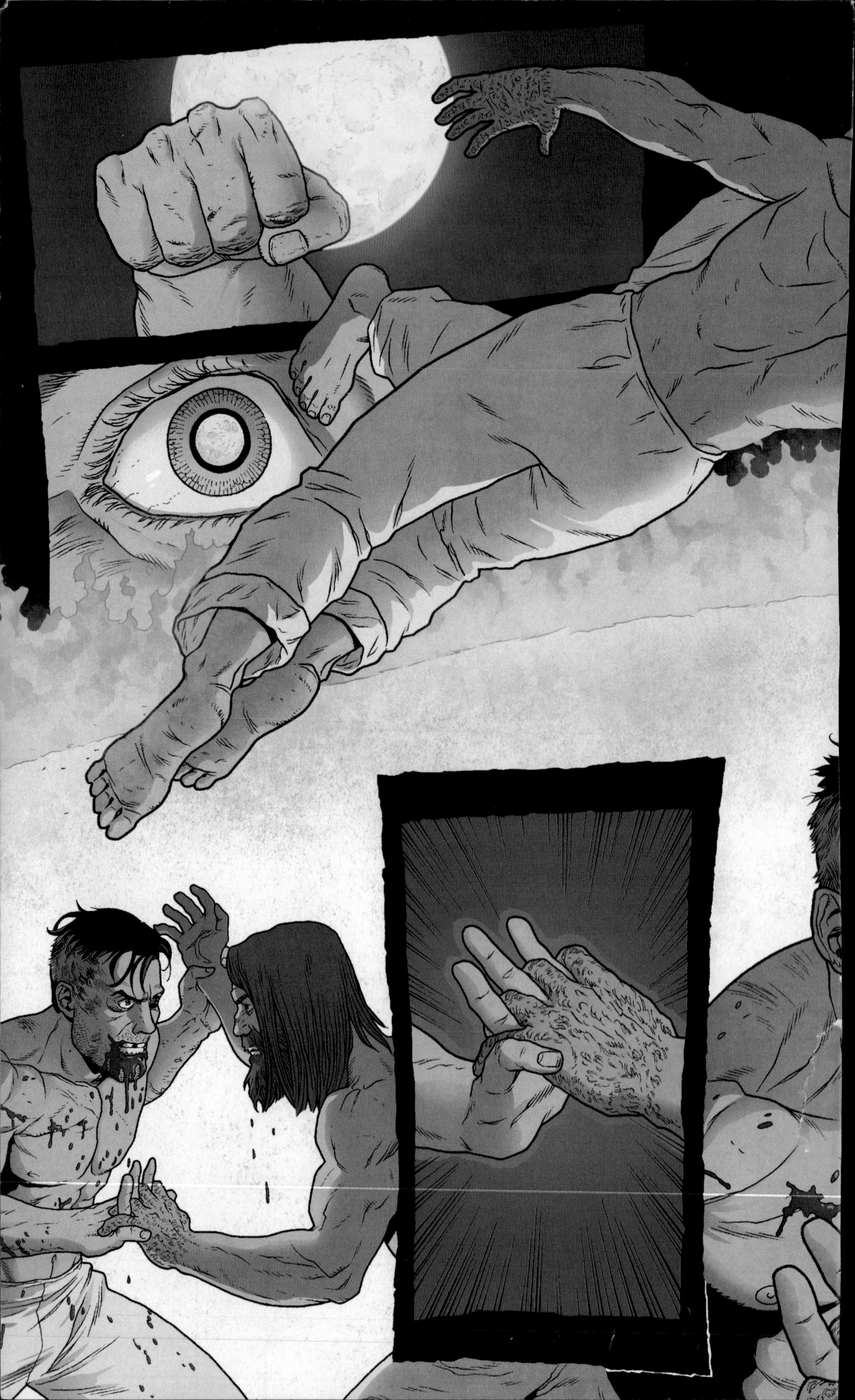